FOREIGN AID REEXAMINED

FOREIGN AID REEXAMINED

A Critical Appraisal

Edited by

JAMES W. WIGGINS AND HELMUT SCHOECK

Papers by

J. FRED RIPPY

ELGIN GROSECLOSE

GEORGE P. MURDOCK

WILLIAM S. STOKES

HELMUT SCHOECK

WILSON E. SCHMIDT

PETER T. BAUER

GOTTFRIED HABERLER

WARREN S. THOMPSON

ALFRED G. SMITH

H. G. BARNETT

JUSTUS M. VAN DER KROEF

DAVID NELSON ROWE

JAMES W. WIGGINS

Public Affairs Press   Washington, D. C.

Preface

This volume brings together papers originally prepared for a symposium on culture contact in undeveloped countries held last year on the campus of Emory University, Atlanta, Georgia.

All authors had the opportunity to benefit from criticism and comments, oral and written, during and after the symposium. Subsequent revisions of the original drafts ranged from minor to major.

Each paper in this volume should be regarded as the independent work of its author. The views expressed are always his own. He is responsible for facts and their interpretation. No collective responsibility of any kind was intended by the editors or the participants.

Each contributor selected his own level of abstractness or concreteness on which he chose to argue his analysis. Invitations to the symposium were extended to authors whose past work promised a fair amount of essential agreement on premises without which a fruitful symposium is hardly possible.

Several of the chapter headings differ from the titles of the original symposium papers. In these instances, the editors, in collaboration with the publisher, thought it advisable to simplify titles or to devise new ones in order to avoid repetition of key words and to allow for smoother transition from chapter to chapter.

The papers by Gottfried Haberler and Peter T. Bauer are given in a condensed version; these two authors chose not to revise their papers for publication.

The editors of this volume propose to discard the term "underdeveloped" country. It is a misleading concept whose originators knew the rhetorical reasons for the prefix "under" instead of "un." We called our conference a symposium on culture contact in *undeveloped* countries. Some of our contributors have followed suit in their terminology, others retained the popular expression. In some papers both terms are used interchangeably.

As was inevitable, some proponents of generous foreign aid have lately been referring to the United States as an "overdeveloped" country. Surely, it would seem, an "overdeveloped country," which might well include West Germany and Switzerland, owes the "underdeveloped countries" a living at some median level of "international equality." The editors of this volume, and several of the contributors, consider this an untenable and self-defeating proposition.

For this reason, the term "underdeveloped" country ought to be dropped from responsible discourse. It is a rhetorical device. Interestingly enough, in the German scholarly literature on this subject, after a period of experimentation with the term "*unter*entwickelte Länder," a new term seems to have gained acceptance: "Entwicklungsländer—meaning "Developable countries." This term, or "undeveloped," as long as the core population of an area is actually capable and willing to develop further, might be preferable.

JAMES W. WIGGINS AND HELMUT SCHOECK

Department of Sociology
  and Anthropology
Emory University

The Contributors

H. G. BARNETT, Professor of Anthropology, University of Oregon. His publications include *Innovation* (1953), *Anthropology in Administration* (1956), and *Indian Shakers* (1957). From 1951 to 1953 he was Staff Anthropologist, Trust Territory, Pacific Islands; more recently has been an advisor to the Netherlands New Guinea Government.

PETER T. BAUER, Smuts Reader in Commonwealth Studies and Fellow of Gonville and Caius College, Cambridge University, England. His works include *The Rubber Industry* (1948), *West African Trade* (1954), and *The Economics of Under-developed Countries* (with B. S. Yamey, 1957).

ELGIN GROSECLOSE, economic consultant and international economist, Washington, D. C. Selected works include *Money: The Human Conflict* (1934), *Introduction to Iran* (1947), and *The Carmelite* (1955). He served as Treasurer General of Iran in 1943 and studied the Iranian economy in 1951 under a Fulbright fellowship.

GOTTFRIED HABERLER, Professor of Economics, Harvard University. His publications include *Prosperity and Depression* (1942), *Quantitative Trade Controls, Their Causes and Nature* (1943), and *Readings in Business Cycle Theory* (1944). He has been President of the International Economic Association and the National Bureau for Economic Research. He has also served with the Board of Governors, Federal Reserve System.

GEORGE P. MURDOCK, Professor of Anthropology, Yale University. His works include *Our Primitive Contemporaries* (1934), *Social Structure* (1949), and *The Evolution of Culture* (editor, 1931). He is a past President of the American Anthropological Association and founder of the Cross Cultural Survey, now known as Human Relations Area Files, Inc.

J. FRED RIPPY, Professor of American History, University of Chicago. His publications include *Latin America and the Industrial Age* (1947), *The Capitalists and Colombia* (1931), and *Historical Evolution of Hispanic America* (1945).

DAVID N. ROWE, Professor of Political Science, Yale University. Selected works include *American Constitutional History* (1933), *China Among the Powers* (1945), and *China: An Area Manual* (1954). He was born in China and has spent a major part of his life travelling, teaching, and writing in the Far East and in Southeast Asia. He has also served as a U.S. official on many assignments abroad.

WILSON EMERSON SCHMIDT, Professor of Economics, George Washington University. Published works include *International Economics* (1957) and *American Private Enterprise, Foreign Economic Development, and the Aid Programs* (co-author, 1957).

HELMUT SCHOECK, Professor of Sociology, Emory University. His larger works include *Nietzches Philosophie des Menschlich-Allzumenschlichen* (1948), *Soziologie, Geschichte ihrer Probleme* (1952), *U.S.A.: Motive und Strukturen* (1958). During a post-doctoral research fellowship at Yale University (1953-54), in part devoted to a comprehensive use of the Human Relations Area Files, he began work on a comparative sociological and anthropological theory of economic growth and innovation.

ALFRED G. SMITH, Professor of Anthropology, Emory University. His works include *Synthetics versus Singapore* (1948) and *Gamwoelhaelhi Ishilh Weleeya* (1951). He has served the Federal government as an expert on Southeast Asia, the Far East, the Pacific area,, and Oceanic languages.

WILLIAM S. STOKES, Professor of Political Science, University of Wisconsin. His major contributions include *Honduras* (1950), *Violence As a Power Factor in Latin American Politics* (1952), and a contribution to *The Caribbean: Its Political Problems* (1956). He was recently appointed to the Chair in Comparative Political Institutions at Claremont Men's College.

WARREN S. THOMPSON, Director Emeritus, Scripps Foundation for Research in Population Problems, Miami University. His larger works include *Population Problems* (1953), *Plenty of People* (1948), and *Population and Peace in the Pacific* (1946). He has studied recent cultural and demographic changes in the undeveloped countries of South and East Asia.

JUSTUS M. VAN DER KROEF, Professor of Sociology, University of Bridgeport. His major publications include *Dutch Colonial Policy in Indonesia* (1953), *Indonesian Social Evolution* (1957), and *Indonesia in the Modern World* (1954-56). He has lived and taught for many years in Indonesia.

JAMES W. WIGGINS, Professor of Sociology and Chairman of the Department of Sociology and Anthropology, Emory University. His publications include *Language and Society, The School in Modern Society,* and *Society's Interest in the Marital Status.* He lived for more than a year in the Central Philippines.

Contents

PART I

IDEOLOGICAL FACTORS

1: *Historical Perspective*

J. FRED RIPPY

The foreign-aid programs of the United States owe their existence to humanitarian, economic, and political motives. As World War II approached its end the humanitarian motive was mainly responsible for the Relief and Rehabilitation Administration set up by the United Nations, to which taxpayers of the United States made a contribution of some three billion dollars. At the same time the economic motive was already strong. It might have led to the adoption of a program of large grants and cheap loans to foreign countries even if the menace of Soviet aggression had not appeared. But this Soviet menace, when belatedly discovered, added a strong political motive to the other two.

COMPULSORY BENEVOLENCE

The humanitarian motive requires little illustration. What needs to be stressed however, is the fact that the people of the United States are being subjected to compulsory benevolence without reciprocity to a much greater extent and more constantly than ever before. The main advocates of this benevolence are several powerful religious organizations. Church and state therefore are in a sense linked together in violation of the principles of separation of these institutions. Making a plea for official foreign assistance, Reverend Eugene Carson Blake, president of the National Council of the Churches of Christ in the United States, declared on April 12, 1957: "It is my conviction that we must be willing to make sacrifices and revise our policies toward the rest of the world to bring them more in line with the Christian values . . . . Christian duty compels us to help others nations financially and technically."[1] This is typical of the attitude of religious groups, whether Protestant, Jewish or Roman Catholic. The Congregational Christian Churches resolved, June, 1956: "National wealth and power are . . . to be used in the ser-

1

vice of human welfare, both within and beyond the nation; it is the particular responsibility of the nations that are strong to help bear the burdens of those that are weak." [2] The American Friends Service Committee declared on April, 1957: "We believe that the . . . heritage and tradition of our Nation place upon us a compelling moral and spiritual obligation adequately to respond to the needs and aspiration of the peoples in the economically underdeveloped countries." [3] Similar quotations could be multiplied indefinitely. Clergymen have supported these programs from the outset with a zeal so constant that one wonders whether church leaders ever advocated separation of church and state with any other motive than that of religious toleration and whether their vigorous support of these programs will compel citizens to contribute to global charity from now until judgment day.

Speaking for a group acting in behalf of the separation of church and state, Stanley Lowell appeared before the Senate Special Committee to Study the Foreign Aid Program and offered a plea only for religious toleration throughout the world, seemingly unaware of any other aspect of the problem. [4] The so-called "voluntary" relief agencies of the United States, in which religious groups are dominant, are also busily engaged in the violation of this fundamental principle of our political system by substituting compulsory for voluntary benevolence.

Moreover, the public officials of the United States have adopted the views of the religious and humanitarian groups. In his inaugural address of January 20, 1949, Harry Truman stressed this humanitarian motive. "More than half of the people of the world are living in conditions approaching misery," he declared. "Their food is inadequate. They are victims of disease. Their economic life is primitive and stagnant . . . . Our aim should be to help the free peoples of the world . . . to produce more food, more clothing, more materials for housing, and more mechanical power to lighten their burdens." [5] And in his message of June 24, 1949, he emphasized the same motive, not merely calling upon "private enterprise and voluntary organization in the United States" to respond to "one of the greatest challenges of the world today" but requesting also that Congress vote appropriaions for the purpose of assisting the earth's impoverished peoples everywhere. [6] Secretary of State John Foster Dulles, long closely associated with church organizations, declared early in 1956: "The United States cannot live either happily or safely as an oasis of prosperity in a desert of misery. No wealthy individual can live happily in a community of poverty to which he is indifferent. It is the same with the society of nations. Always the wealthy and economically developed nations have in fact helped the less developed nations to develop."[7] But Dulles forgot to point out the difference between voluntary and enforced assistance; and a year later he stressed the same motive, referring to the same oasis and the same desert, and attempting to justify compulsory charity by an appeal to the "brotherhood of man."[8]

No protest is being raised here against voluntary benevolence and generosity. On the contrary, judicious voluntary benevolence is welcome. But we question the wisdom of global charity thrust upon the taxpayer by the state. This is an apparent violation of a fundamental principle of our system of government.

THE BANKER'S MOTIVE

The economic motive probably has been more influential than the humanitarian in the launching and extension of these programs. At any rate, the economic motive seems to require fuller discussion in order to disclose its continuous significance. The two global wars of the twentieth century resulted in an immense expansion in this country of production for export, and the export of capital in its various forms was adopted in large measure with two objectives in view: avoidance of contraction in production and consequent economic depression: and avoidance of drastic tinkering with the tariff and the domestic economy.

Immediately following World War I billions were invested overseas by private capitalists of the United States, not only in war-torn Europe but also in the new and retarded nations. Propaganda filled the newspapers and magazines. Executives of the rich private foundations jumped on the bandwagon.[9] The government of the United States fostered the movement. Salesmen of foreign securities sweated and swarmed.

But the billions invested abroad did not enable the United States to avoid the worst economic depression in its history. Something went wrong; perhaps it was the high tariff; perhaps it was the fault of the investment bankers. Men looked about for the culprits, and Congress decided to investigate the bankers. Both the Senate Committee on Finance and the Senate Committee on Banking and Currency held long hearings on the subject in the early 1930's.

The main justification offered by the bankers and bondsalesmen for promoting the foreign investment spree of the 1920's was the stimulation of foreign trade. Little was said about the profits accru-

ing to the investor. The returns from overseas had almost ceased
to come in.

Senator Robert La Follette: "In your judgment, is there a direct
connection between these large flotations of foreign securities in this
country and the tremendous expansion of the export trade during the
period preceding the depression?" Banker Thomas P. Lamont of
the J. P. Morgan firm: "Oh yes . . . . I have no doubt that it had a
strong bearing; otherwise where in the world would our foreign
buyers have gotten money with which to buy our cotton, wheat,
copper, meats, and all that sort of thing?" The last phrase probably
revealed the banker's reluctance to make specific mention of manufactured goods. [10]

Charles E. Mitchell, National City Bank: "Foreign investments
. . . very largely control the volume of the export business of the
United States. They should have, therefore, a sound basis of desirability to the most critically patriotic of Americans." The bankers
should be praised and not blamed. But did the bankers hold any of
the securities as an investment? Not if they could help it. Senator
Tom Connaly: "With reference to bonds, you are like the saloon
keeper who never drank." Banker Mitchell: "With respect to bonds
in general, we are merchants." [10A]

Clarence Dillon, of the firm of Dillon, Read and Company: Capital must be invested abroad in order to "get rid of our surplus production, agricultural, mineral, and manufacturing," and our surplus
savings. "The only credit that is available for foreign loans is the
surplus credit in this country." But Senator Pat Harrison asked
whether a good part of the capital sent overseas was not used to
build factories whose output would eventually reduce exports from
the United States. Banker Dillon, failing to come to grips with
this question, continued: "I think the lending of money abroad for
the developing of the resources of our potential customers . . . is very
good business, not only good business but essential business if we
are going to sell our surplus products."

Senator Reed Smoot scolded his colleague: "Senator Harrison, is
your theory as follows: that when they have these billions . . . more
than they could possibly have loaned in the United States, with no
demand . . . in the United States, the bankers should have kept all
that money in their vaults . . . ? Senator Harrison: "I think . . . if
we did not have so much money loaned in foreign countries at this
time we would have . . . more money to loan to American citizens."
Harrison could have added that the citizens who bought these bonds
might have done more buying in the domestic market if they had

not sent their money abroad. Perhaps Senator Thomas P. Gore interrupted too quickly with a question about interest rates. Banker Dillon responded: "If there is a demand for money in this country and you can get equally good security abroad at a higher rate, why, the demand in this country would probably have to meet that rate." Senator Gore: "So it is not always a question of surplus. It is somewhat a question of rate." And Gore might have made a similar comment regarding the export of so-called goods: it was a question of price. [11]

Senator John Thomas of Idaho: "Does the cutting off of the flotation of these loans affect the foreign situation?" Banker James Speyer: "There is no doubt about that." Speyer wanted an arrangement of the old foreign debts "in a big and comprehensive way" so that foreign investment could be resumed: otherwise "our exports will suffer just as surely as we are sitting here, because our best customers have no money with which to buy . . . ." Were our best customers overseas, or did the banker inadvertently omit the word foreign? [12]

Ray W. Morris of Brown Brothers, Harriman and Company emphasized the fact that foreign-loan operators did not "Take anything out of this country except American goods and American services" paid for by the proceeds of American loans. "It is no coincidence that our exports attained their peak on a wave of foreign borrowing and that since foreigners have been unable to borrow here our exports have rapidly declined." The loan made it possible for foreign consumers to "absorb some of this excess production . . . to the definite benefit of America." [13]

Otto H. Kahn, member of the firm of Kuhn, Loeb and Company, spoke warmly in defense of the bankers. The "granting of credits for the purpose of facilitating trade and thereby stimulating the economic life of all the world, a repercussion of which is bound to redound to the advantage of America, . . . is a legitimate, natural and old-established banking function." [14]

FROM ROOSEVELT TO TRUMAN

But the pendulum seemed to be on the verge of making an opposite swing in 1932-1933. Franklin D. Roosevelt spoke scornfully in 1932 of the effort to avoid surpluses by the export of capital: [15]

"What if we produce a surplus?"

"Oh, we can sell it to foreign consumers."

"How can the foreigners pay for it?"

"Why, we will lend them the money."

"I see," said little Alice, "they buy our surplus with our money. Of course, these foreigners will pay us back by selling us their goods?"

"Oh, not at all," said Humpty Dumpty. "We set up a high wall called the tariff."

"And," said Alice at last, "How will the foreigners pay off these loans?"

"That is easy," said Humpty Dumpty, "did you ever hear of a moratorium?"

And so, at last, my friends, we have reached the heart of the magic formula . . . . The absorption of the surplus was to be through . . . the "development of backward and crippled countries" by means of loans.

Referring again to the subject, Roosevelt said: [16] "As I pointed out in my speech at Columbus, one of the ways that they were going to stimulate foreign trade . . . was to lend money to backward nations, to crippled countries, so as to enable them to buy goods from us with our money . . . Another way would be just to give things away! I am not sure that . . . giving away is not better . . . because at least when we give things away we save the cost of keeping books. And, moreover, when we give things away we . . . have no disappointment in failing to receive payment from our debtors."

The Republicans, according to Raymond Moley, had assumed that the depression in the United States had been caused largely by the loss of export markets occasioned by a sharp decline in foreign purchasing power, thus accepting the view of international bankers, shipping companies, and exporters. "But we agreed," said Moley, "that the heart of the recovery program was domestic." And so the New Deal set out to reform the economic system rather than rely for prosperity "upon an unreal foreign purchasing power." [17]

But that was true only in part and not for long. The Roosevelt administration was soon attracted by the lure of foreign trade. If it had any other motive for the recognition of Soviet Russia in 1934 than the hope of gaining fuller access to markets and investment opportunities in Russia, that motive was never clearly stated. Moreover, the Roosevelt administration attempted to promote exports by devaluing the dollar; by direct subsidies to the exporters of wheat and cotton; by paying high prices for imports of gold and silver; by cheap loans to foreign purchasers through the Export-Import Bank, by subsidizing the merchant marine; and by the Trade-Agreements Program; and the Truman administration not only followed these policies but tried to foster exports in other ways. No group of politicians in the entire history of this nation ever showed greater solicitude for foreign markets than did the politicians of these two Democratic administrations.

Secretary Cordell Hull began to press for authority to negotiate international trade agreements early in 1934. "The primary object of this new proposal," he said, "is . . . to reopen the old and seek new outlets for our surplus production. Nearly 80 percent of the world's population . . . are today living below the poverty line," Hull declared. "Some enterprising nation or nations will and must produce and export the many different commodities necessary to supply these people thus in need." [18] Apparently the Secretary of State assumed that these billions of paupers would somehow be provided with the means of payment, but he did not dwell upon this point.

Appearing before Congress in behalf of the trade program, Secretary Henry Wallace urged that surplus farm products must be exported in order to avoid "retiring surplus acres;" and contended that high tariffs caused unemployment "even more certainly" than low tariffs. It was merely a question of where the unemployment should be, whether in the efficient industries producing goods in large measure for foreign markets or in the inefficient industries producing entirely for the domestic market. By reducing the volume of American imports and thus reducing foreign purchasing capacity, high tariffs were injuring the export industries. [19]

Now and then the opposition managed to inject a few comments. Congressman Roy O. Woodruff observed, for example, that the exporting industries were mainly mass-producers which utilized labor-saving machinery to the utmost. If these industries should be greatly expanded at the expense of the small consumer industries employing more labor in proportion to their output, how would this transformation promote full employment and prosperity? Moreover, if favored by government policy, the industries manufacturing machinery for mass-production would expand their exports of this machinery, and large exports of such machinery would eventually enable foreign countries to supply their own markets and thus close them to American mass-produced goods. [20]

But the star witness for the opposition was a journalist named Samuel Crowther, who urged that some government agency be set up to keep careful accounts in order to determine scientifically, if possible, whether exports financed by foreign investments or sent abroad at the expense of industries producing for the home market were beneficial to the nation. Crowther doubted this, and expressed the opinion that the day of vast exports in peacetime had passed. The old assumption that "half of the world should make and the

other half grow" was no longer valid, he contended.   All wished
to engage in manufacturing and all were trying to expand and diversify
their agriculture.   Anybody who sought to enrich this nation by expanding exports was "chasing a rainbow."   Great Britain chased that
rainbow for nearly a century and came to grief.   After inflicting
grave injury upon English farmers and heavy losses upon British investors overseas, English political leaders found their foreign markets
shrinking and their labor on the dole, and returned at last to the
protectionism of earlier years. [21]

The Hull trade program was approved repeatedly, but neither
this nor any other measures adopted by the Roosevelt administration
lifted the nation out of the depression and provided full employment.
It was World War II that furnished the solution for the surplus problem and the economic crisis associated with it.

But what would happen after the termination of hostilities?   This
question caused the New-Deal statecraft no little worry.   Secretary
Hull came back to Congress early in 1943 for another renewal of his
authority to negotiate trade bargains.   "Important as was the trade-
agreements program in the past," he argued, "it will be more significant than ever, from the viewpoint of our material interest, when
the fighting stops."   "When that happens," he continued, "almost
every metal-working plant in the United States, and many other
factories, and mines and farms, will be faced with the termination of
war orders, and will be looking urgently for markets for their peacetime products."   Francis B. Sayre, Hull's special assistant, was alarmed by what he thought he saw on the road ahead.   "When our soldiers
return from the battlefields we must find a way to give them jobs
and security," Sayre declared.   "Otherwise our free-enterprise system is doomed and we shall reap the whirlwind."   Trade barriers
must be removed.   William L. Clayton, wealthy cotton exporter and
Assistant Secretary of Commerce, talked of both foreign trade and
foreign investment as means of avoiding the crisis of peace.   "In
numerous agricultural and industrial products our capacity to produce has . . . exceeded domestic consumption," he asserted.   "When
peace comes, vast areas abroad must be reconstructed.   Others
should be developed in order to raise the standard of living, which
in itself, creates new markets.   There will be many opportunities
abroad for the investment of American capital."   He urged the nation to be willing to import and invest abroad as well as to export. [22]

Hull's authority to negotiate trade agreements was extended in
1943; and two years later, after the death of Roosevelt and the resignation of Hull, another extension was requested.   With the global

war drawing rapidly to a close, the members of the Truman administration were frightened by the prospect of peacetime surpluses and
unemployment.   Secretary of State Edward R. Stettinius remarked:
"In this country we shall have to reconvert our greatly expanded capacity. . . . We shall have to reconvert our greatly expanded productive capacity . . . We shall have to provide jobs and wages and material goods for as many people as possible. . . . The world has never
before been so eager to acquire the products of our fields and factories. The demand for our goods will rise just as fast as we permit foreign countries to earn the dollars to pay for them."

Assistant Secretary of State William Clayton declared: "At
the end of the war we will have what I call a lopsided industrial economy. We will have a great surplus capacity of production of certain
types of goods. . . . " He thought that an export surplus of four
billion dollars annually during the next few years would be required
in order to avoid depression and unemployment, and urged loans and
credits to foreign countries sufficient to take care of this huge excess
of exports over imports. Commerce Secretary Henry Wallace exhor-
ted: "In the critical days of reconversion and demobilization, the
maintenance of full productive employment will be a matter of primary national concern. If exports can be maintained at an annual
rate of $10,000,000,000 or more . . . they may well provide work for
5,000,000 American citizens. . . . We must be prepared to make productive foreign investments at moderate rates of interest."   Fred M.
Vinson, then in charge of reconversion, recommended both an increase
of imports and large foreign investments. Stacy May, economist and
favorite of the research foundations, was deeply disturbed about the
prospects of the fat "war babies," particularly the metal industries,
and was eager to keep them in operation at full capacity even if this
should require drastic reduction of tariffs and the shifting of millions
of workers away from plants manufacturing mainly for the domestic
market.[23]

The Truman administration was very busy in the spring of 1945
with measures designed to promote exports. At the same time when
the life of the trade-agreements program was lengthened, the Bretton
Woods Agreements, establishing an international bank and an international stabilization fund, were pushed through Congress; and the
battery of arguments was the same in both cases. Secretary of the
Treasury Henry Morganthau asserted that the purpose of the Bretton
Woods Agreements was the orderly "expansion of foreign trade upon
which the future prosperity of our agriculture and our industry depends." "Before the war we were the largest exporting nation in

the world," he said. "We needed exports to maintain jobs, to absorb part of the output of American factories and farms. . . . After the war we will have even more reason for exporting. . . . And that is what the Bretton Woods proposals are about." Harry D. White, Morganthau's assistant, also stressed the necessity of financing exports, declaring that this was the primary interest that impelled the United States to urge the establishment of the bank and the stabilization fund, for "unless these foreign countries are enabled to get on their feet financially, they will not be able to buy goods from us." Fred M. Vinson ably buttressed this contention with some statistics: "More than 50 per cent of our cotton and 30 per cent of our tobacco crops must be exported. A considerable part of the output of our important industries . . . [must be] sold abroad. Twenty-two per cent of our office equipment, 17 per cent of our agricultural machinery, 14 per cent of our industrial machinery and automobile production must be exported." Mr. Clayton repeated his statement regarding the "lopsided" condition of American industry and his recommendation regarding heavy exports of capital. [24]

If space permitted, a similar economic motivation could be disclosed with references to the origin of the social and economic provisions of the United Nations Charter. Alluding to half of Roosevelt's "four freedoms" proclaimed early in 1941, Secretary Stettinius wrote this statement into his report to Truman on the results of the San Francisco Conference which drafted the Charter: "The battle for peace must be fought on two fronts. The first is the security front where victory spells freedom from fear. The second is the economic and social front where victory means freedom from want." And Secretary Stettinius added: "We cannot provide jobs for the millions now in our armed forces and maintain prosperity for ourselves unless the economy of the rest of the world is restored to health." [25] Further light is thrown on this subject by the schemes of Roosevelt and Harry Hopkins in connection with the Teheran and Yalta conferences. As early as September, 1944, Patrick Hurley, then on a special mission for Roosevelt, was disturbed by the project of the president to develop the resources of the Near East. "The whole plan," wrote Hurley, "is predicated on your desire to raise the standard of living of other countries as a means of substaining our standard of living." Protesting against this plan, Hurley declared: "The standard of living in other nations cannot be substantially or permanently raised by lend-lease or doles. The American taxpayers would not be able to pay for a continuance of relief for the world on a lend-lease basis." [26] The record of the Yalta Conference contains this pertinent item (February 7,

1945): "The President . . . went on to say that . . . Persia did not have the purchasing power to buy foreign goods, and if expansion of world trade was to occur measures must be considered for helping those countries like Persia that did not have any purchasing power. Then Harry Hopkins passed a note to FDR suggesting a TVA for Europe, and the record continues: "The President added that . . . in Europe . . . certain countries had adequate supplies of . . . coal and water power, whereas other countries within fifty miles had neither. He felt that this was wrong." The United States had a TVA and Europe ought to have a TVA. The United Nations should provide purchasing capacity for nations which had little or none. [27]

The Point Four Program: An International TVA

As early as 1934 Senator David A. Reed of Pennsylvania had suggested in discussing the tariff that "to increase our export business without increasing our imports" would be "ideal;" and Roosevelt and his New Dealers did not require many years to find a formula that would tend to harmonize the conflicting interests that clustered around the tariff issue. In fact, before the end of 1942 Roosevelt and Wallace had suggested both the formula and the slogan that might lead to its adoption. Substitute philanthrophy for investment. Reconstruct the war-damaged countries. Uplift the retarded peoples. Mitigate the world's misery and thus avoid the risk of economic depressions. Wallace had remarked in the spring of 1942 that "everybody in the world" should have "the privilege of drinking a quart of milk a day"—a statement which his critics changed to "a bottle of milk for every Hottentot." [28] Before the year ended Roosevelt had said: "There will be rehabilitation abroad . . . not only for humanitarian reasons but from the standpoint of America's own interest, for it will mean better purchasing power abroad for American products." Just as the New Deal has stimulated business in the United States by increasing the purchasing capacity of the underprivileged here, so likewise would aid to foreign countries foster American business by adding to purchasing power in foreign lands and thus expanding American exports. [29]

During the months following his original statement Wallace frequently repeated his formula. "There must be an international bank and an international TVA," he declared in November, 1942, and near the end of December he said: "Our surplus will be far greater than ever a few years after this war comes to an end. We can be decently human and really hardheaded if we exchange our postwar surplus of goods for peace, and for improving the standard

of living of so-called backward peoples." Early the next year he announced: "If American missionaries of a new type . . . can work in
cooperation with a United Nations investment corporation to develop flood-control works, irrigation projects, soil conservation, rural
electrification, and the like, it will make possible an expansion in
half the area of the world reminiscent of that which was stirring
in our own land during its rapid growth." Appealing to a romantic attachment to the frontier tradition, Wallace predicted that the United
States would find its lost frontier beyond the seas.[30] He pointed to "new
horizons abroad" and called upon his countrymen to look east to
war-damaged Europe, west across the Pacific, and south toward
Latin America. Cheap financial and technical assistance to the
peoples of all these lands would mean the difference between prosperity and depression at home. [31]

Others were quick to take up the formula and the slogan. John
D. Black, Harvard professor and government consultant, averred in
1943: "Along the path from lend-lease for feeding the starving
people . . . of Europe, to lend-lease for reconstruction, and finally
lend-lease for keeping the peace . . . lies the safest approach to the
desired goals" of free enterprise and full employment. [32] In his
capacity as Assistant Secretary of State, Dean Acheson went before
the House Special Committee on Postwar Economic Policy and
Planning in 1944 to urge cheap foreign loans and official encouragement of private foreign investment as means of maintaining exports.
"So far as I know," he said, "no group which has studied this problem, and there have been many, as you know, has ever believed that
our domestic markets could absorb our entire production under our
present system." [33]

From all these and many other statements that might be quoted
it should be clear that capital exports have been considered in the
United States as an important remedy for the ills of the nation's
economic system, and that the emphasis was finally shifted from
the pecuniary to the philanthropic in the argument for such exports, but without abandoning the profit motive for all those engaged in the export business.

It is in this light that Harry Truman's Point Four must be viewed.
It was not a "bold new program;" its planning had been in progress
for nearly a decade. If his inaugural message made an appeal to
humanitarianism it also contained a familiar economic argument. "All
countries, including our own, will greatly benefit," he declared. Experience shows that our commerce with other countries expands as

they progress industrially and commercially. Greater production is the key to prosperity and peace."

And he continued to stress the economic motive after the Soviet danger was recognized as well as before. Addressing the Newspaper Guild Convention on June 28, 1950, Truman stated the economic motive more bluntly: "We want to have a prosperous world that will be interested in buying [able to buy] the immense amount of surplus things we are going to sell . . . I want to keep this factory organization of ours going full tilt." [34] Writing from Washington, D.C., on April 19, 1952, Felix Belair reported to the *New York Times*: "If the United States should succeed through the point 4 program in raising the living standards of these [underdeveloped] areas as much as 2 per cent, the President explained, the resulting demand for United States products of all kinds would be sufficient to keep the productive machinery going full tilt as far ahead as anyone could see." [35]

Until 1951, little emphasis was placed on the growing need for foreign raw materials occasioned by the depletion of domestic supplies. Attention was centered mainly on exports. But in the course of that year's hearings on the Mutual Security Program, both imports and exports were stressed. Note this statement by Nelson Rockefeller: [36] "Manufacturing capacity . . . is moving ahead of . . . raw material production . . . The question is from where do we get the raw materials we import. The answer is that 73 per cent of our needs for strategic and critical materials come from the underdeveloped areas . . . . There is another point also in our relations with the underdeveloped areas. If at some time in the next five or ten years we have a peace economy, and our military production goes down, in my mind there is a very real question of what we will do with this additional 20 per cent plant capacity . . . . The one . . . [segment] of the free world we can look to for markets is the underdeveloped areas . . . ."

Observe also the following argument by Henry G. Bennett, speaking for the Technical Cooperation Administration: [37] "The point 4 program is not just a program to do good. It is . . . in our own self-interest. We are increasingly economically dependent upon the underdeveloped countries . . . . An absolutely vital 73 per cent of raw material requirements come from the underdeveloped areas . . . . The underdeveloped areas [also] offer the greatest prospect for future markets for United States production. The problem of markets is very acute and if, as we hope, our . . . capacity for military production should become surplus, unless markets are found for the products of these industries the standard of living of our people would be seriously endangered ... However, we cannot commandeer these raw materials, nor can we force them to take our manufactured goods. The democratic way is to seek the cooperation of ... peoples and governments."

On April 8, 1952, during a session of the House Committee on Foreign Affairs, Congressman Walter H. Judd, once a medical missionary in China, indulged in a little confidential musing: [38] "During the last half of the thirties we got the appearance of a return to prosperity and got the people back to work even though it was not all productive. We did it by public works and relief. Then during the first half of the forties it was by war, production of military goods; and during the second half of the forties it was by European and world relief and recovery. The first half of the fifties it is by expenditures for a world rearmament program. Suppose we come to 1955 and we are secure. What are we going to do ... to keep so overexpanded an economy in full operation, if these extraordinary expenditures are cut off? Whether we have Republicans or Democrats in power, we will have a tailspin here ... But we do not need to discuss that on the floor [of the House] .... What we ought to have in the last half of the fifties is a secure world in which we can carry out enormous investments abroad."

After this summary of the economic motivation for the distribution of the wealth of the United States throughout the world, I shall add a final quotation from the Report of the Senate Special Committee to Study Foreign Aid dated May 13, 1957:" The future growth of this Nation ... requires an expanding world commerce as well as expanding sources of basic materials. This dual expansion depends to a considerable extent upon the economic development of other countries ... especially ... the so-called less developed nations whose economic techniques and organizations are far behind the economically advanced nations." [39]

THE ANATOMY OF FOREIGN AID LOBBIES

The political motive back of the foreign-aid programs does not require elaborate comment. It has been obvious and convincing since late 1947 or early 1948. Almost nobody in this country has disputed the menace of Soviet expansion or Soviet ambition to dominate the globe, or most of it. Many of our citizens believe that the United States has never confronted a graver peril, and high officials of this country have adopted the policy of promoting national security by searching for allies and obtaining their permission to establish military bases within their several domains as well as by inducing and helping them to arm themselves for defense. It is impossible, however, to measure the influence of this political motive in comparison with the other two and thus determine whether the amount of assistance to foreign countries is greater than the strict requirements of national security; and one may doubt whether the means are always well adapted to the ends.

The combination of these three motives in an inseparable mixture results in a powerful political force almost impossible to moderate and restrain. The champions of these programs are so well organized and have command of such effective means of achieving their objectives that successful resistance is almost impossible. Political careers can be promoted by responding to the appeals of organized pressure groups or marred by opposing them. No patriot wishes to take the risk of exposing his nation to the danger of conquest and no one can be certain of the magnitude of the peril. Those who believe that enforced benevolence and the favoring of special groups may injure the nation as a whole do not have the organization and the funds to make their viewpoint prevail or even to gain for it an adequate consideration. Both political parties are committed to the programs, and the majorities in both have such a firm control on the nation that opponents can do little more than hope that politicians will not weaken the power of the country while contending that they are adding to its strength. The methods they employ are as clever as can be devised; and at times they seem devious and dishonest.

Citizens of the United States are so unaccustomed to such crises in international relations that they are easily swayed by slogans. Their critical faculties are so underdeveloped that they suggest the failure of our educational systems. When told that world leadership has been "thrust upon" their nation they accept the slogan without question. They accept it in spite of the fact that the missionaries of their country have been in every land for more than a century, in spite of the fact that their political leaders have usually envisaged themselves as acting in a cosmic setting and as charged with the mission of converting the world to their point of view, and despite the further fact that their economic leaders have long been in search of markets and investment opportunities all over the globe. If this nation must now assume the role of an Atlas this is largely because of its past activities and interventions overseas.

When told that "national maturity" requires the assumption of most of the world's burdens the American people quickly accept the slogan that maturity and wisdom are synonymous. They never attempt to ascertain the exact meaning of "mutual" or "cooperation."

Nor do they stop to analyze the phrase "free world;" instead of discovering its limited meaning—free from Soviet domination—they are likely to think that all peoples outside of the iron and bamboo curtains are free from oppressions, even though the majority of those in the retarded countries are ruled by despots. When assured that these foreign-aid programs are promoting "free enterprise" or "private enterprise" they meekly accept the assurance in spite of the fact that such programs seem to be fostering state planning and State Socialism both at home and abroad. Their approval is easily won for any policy described as "realistic" or "imaginative," whether it is sound or not. They seem to approve all policies described as "calculated risks" without noticing that all the risks are calculated in favor of additional expenditures abroad. Repeatedly told that the nation is rich and steadily growing richer, they appear never to suspect that such a broad generalization may have little significance for themselves or for many millions of their fellow citizens. When informed that the distributors of their hard-earned tax money must be paid high salaries to induce them to engage in this enterprise it appears never to occur to them to ask whether such agents should share in the sacrifice, as might be expected of patriots in time of national peril.

Never has this nation had so many pressure groups so well organized and financed, and never have they been so successful in winning the favor of public officials. The following list of those insisting upon the expansion and perpetuation of the foreign-aid programs is incomplete:

(1) Manufacturers producing for export and requiring more and more raw materials from foreign countries together with the big labor bosses controlling the work in these industries; (2) shipping companies which have gained preference in handling cargoes sent abroad; (3) export and import agencies; (4) bankers and commission merchants; (5) "voluntary" relief agencies composed of organized clergymen and their lay associates; (6) individuals in pursuit of government employment at generous rates of pay; (7) rich foundations in search of new ways to justify their existence; (8) university administrations and staffs eager to expand their activities, to gain prestige, and to obtain additional incomes through increased prestige, through government contracts, and in return for giving advice, sound or foolish, on government policies and procedures; (9) farmer organizations and farm *blocs* in Congress seeking benefits for agriculture and avoidance of the peril to agrarian interests of large

accumulations of surpluses in the Commodity Credit Corporation; (10) diplomats eager to lighten their tasks by means of cheap loans and grants; (11) many organizations of women, compassionate and eager to serve; (12) unassimilated groups of immigrants and their sons urging that assistance be given to their national kinsmen overseas; (13) politicians seeking the votes loyal to all these pressure organizations, more easily obtained than the votes of others who are more dispersed; (14) the top ranking bureaucracy of the United Nations; (15) various foreign countries threatening to become unfriendly or to adopt Communism if they are not financially favored.

Who has the hardihood to contend that all of these groups are interested solely in the security and welfare of the United States? What politician has the courage to defy any large numbers of them or the wisdom to separate the sheep from the goats?

By multiplication of the channels through which this aid is distributed the people of the United States are confused and frustrated. The most important channels are these, some of them concealed from all except the most alert citizens: (1) direct aid through "voluntary" relief agencies; direct aid under a law providing for emergency relief, which resulted in the distribution of millions of Christmas packages, and according to a law authorizing the disposal of surplus agricultural commodities (surplus in part because of high and rigid price supports); overpayment for foreign exchange by government personnel abroad; and the regular annual appropriations under the title of "mutual" assistance and technical "cooperation;" (2) indirect contributions through the United Nations and its numerous affiliated agencies and through the Organization of the American States and its subsidiaries. Not even the "experts" can agree on the total annual outlay; perhaps the average has been from six to eight billion dollars per annum since 1946.

The word duplicity has been used to describe some of the methods employed to obtain appropriations; and the description does not seem unjust when applied to the activities of two congressional committees during the latter part of the year 1956 and the first half of 1957, both of which indulged in propaganda under the pretense of impartial appraisal. Nor does the executive department of the national government seem to have been free from guilt.

The Honorable James Richards, chairman of the House Committee on Foreign Affairs, after a vigorous stand with respect to the appropriation for "mutual" assistance which appeared to indicate that he was opposed to waste and extravagance, presided over hearings slanted in favor of larger and permanent expenditures abroad, and was rewarded by a special mission to the Near East. Of the nine-teen experts *invited* to present their views to this House Committee, all except two or three were well known to be enthusiastic supporters of the perpetuation and enlargement of foreign assistance. [40]

Voted $300,000 for a scientific appraisal of the foreign-aid pro-grams, Senator Theodore Francis Green hired eleven organizations of "experts" and ten individuals for the purpose of making "profound studies" and on-the-spot surveys; and of these twenty-one groups and individuals, nearly all were supporters, and known in advance to be supporters, of long-term and expanded foreign aid. The Senator did not need to learn the views of most of them; he merely used the $300,000 to reward them for their endorsement. [41]

The two reports authorized by the national executive were some-what better balanced. Although one of these was made by Eric Johnston of the Foreign Development Advisory Committee a man in warm sympathy with the programs, the other was under the chair-manship of Benjamin Fairless, a cautious and conservative big busi-nessman—cautious and conservative, but nevertheless the head of a mass-producing industry (big steel) inflated by war and defense armament and interested in stimulating exports in order to avoid in-flation. Better balance might have been had by substituting for Johnston some capable industrialist engaged in production mainly for the home market. Toward the end of the year 1956 Dwight Eisen-hower appears to have been captured by the spenders unlimited; any other conclusion would have to be based upon the assumption of equivocation during his campaign for his second term or a sudden change accounted for entirely by the crisis in the Arab world.

EFFECTS OF THE FOREIGN AID TREND

So much for the methods utilized to obtain funds. What of the re-sults? Appraisal of achievements abroad will be left largely to other members of this symposium. Only a few generalizations will be ventured on this subject here. Foreign aid may have prevented Soviet expansion in some important instances, although this "contain-ment" probably should be attributed more largely to the superior mili-tary equipment of the United States. It is likely that the truth of the matter will never be ascertained. Concentration on key targets from now on, along with greater efficiency, seem to be urgently re-quired. The assets of our people should not be wasted by overstaff-ing, extravagance in salaries, favoritism toward exporters, and senti-mental benevolence at the expense of coerced taxpayers. In com-parison with traditional diplomacy at the height of its achievement, the programs are likely to be of minor significance in world politics, even more likely in the future than in the past because of the vastly different circumstances encountered in Western Europe and in the retarded countries. New jealousies will arise among the beneficiaries or old jealousies will be accentuated. The programs are a form of intervention that is bound to antagonize opposition groups everywhere, for they are in effect the equivalent of a policy of supporting governments that happen to be in power, domestic or otherwise. Equally important is the fact that such aid cannot induce governments to refrain from policies deemed to be in their own or their national interest. A clash, or even an apparent clash, between the policies of the United States and those of recipient governments can instantly nullify the favorable effects of the program. There is also the danger that such programs will foster the drive, already too potent in these countries, toward overexpansion of government personnel, thus increasing the evil of bureaucratic exploitation, and danger that such countries will be encouraged to expect social benefits which they cannot afford until they are more fully developed. Finally, they are apt to be led to anticipate perpetual aid from the United States or to the firm belief that they can maneuver in such a fashion as to obtain it; and this is a problem which could involve serious consequences for the United States, a problem that has not received sufficient attention.

Within a decade or so the United States may be compelled to terminate these programs at the risk of offending recipients who have been accustomed to count upon this assistance, or to continue them at the peril of grave injury to our national economy and way of life. Senator Richard Russell of Georgia has already clearly foreseen this problem. On April 8, 1957, he queried Secretary Dulles with reference to it and commented as follows: [42] "Now what is the objective of this worldwide program . . . ? Is it to bring those countries up to our level . . . or . . . to England's level, or to the level of France or Italy? If the people who are receiving this aid know what our objective is, I think we could[eventually] cut it off; but with an open-end program . . . delivered on the general thesis of morality and our obligation to help those who are less fortunate than we are, I can see no place where you could ever end that program short of either bankrupting this country . . . [or] bringing us down to their level, or else . . . [having] us perform the Herculean feat, the Atlas feat, of lifting the whole world up to our level."

That the ending of these programs will prove more hazardous than their beginning seems very likely.

This discussion will now be concluded with some comments regarding impact of these programs upon the United States. I shall
begin by assuming that the programs will be continued for several
years to come, perhaps in substantially larger measure than the strict
demands of national security require. A combination of humanitarians,
profit-seekers, and citizens prompted by a sincere desire to promote
national security will be hard to resist because of the impossibility of
separating the various groups having different motivations. If continuance of the policy seems inevitable it is better to negotiate than to defy,
better not to confine one's efforts to persistent scolding and to point out
those who are likely to suffer economic injury.

The slogan that the United States is a very rich nation and steadily
growing richer is by no means a magnanimous slogan for millions of
its inhabitants. In view of the enormous public debt—some $278
billion, plus many billions more in contingent liabilities for trust funds
and mortgages—in view of the heavy burden of taxes, national, state,
and local, which take an average of nearly a third of the peoples'
earnings, and much more in many instances; in view of the rapid ex-
haustion of unrenewable natural resources and the danger that the
nation will soon be subjected to a mighty "squeeze" by those who
control the sources of supply, this optimistic generalization may not
be valid for the United States as a whole; and it certainly exaggerates
the prosperity of more than a fourth of its people, including most
of those who formulate and preserve our ideals and specialize in the
maintenance and improvement of our culture—in fact, all of those
who neither produce nor sell material goods and must depend upon
so-called fixed incomes, which already have been reduced to less
than half their former value by rising taxes and prices. Important
among these millions are artists, *literati*, teachers, philosophers, and
preachers. Continuance of these foreign-aid programs and other
extravagant spending could result in inverting the cultural apex of the
nation by pushing those engaged in promoting the higher culture
down to the bottom stratum of our social order. Millions of our
people pay doubly for these immense expenditures—heavy taxes and
inflated prices—and obtain no direct material benefits in return.
It is one of the ironies which ought to be explored elsewhere in this
symposium that so many ardent advocates of foreign aid programs
come from the very groups which are bound to suffer most.

Flattering figures presumed to indicate national wealth by pre-
senting estimates of average *per capita* income are a cruel deception.
For example, the national average for the year 1954 was $1,770; but
the figures for 32 of the 48 states with a population of some 72.6

millions were below the national average, and far below it in many cases, as the following figures show. [43] Average income *per capita* in Mississippi was $873, in Arkansas $979, in South Carolina $1,063, and in Alabama $1,091.

The costs of these programs are said to be insignificant, only 8 to 10 per cent of the expenditures of the national government and a much smaller percentage of the total national product. But these figures are also deceptive. The truth is that the cost of these foreign-aid programs cannot be accurately determined because of a number of imponderables. To what extent, for example, do they contribute to inflation at the expense of those who receive no material benefits from them? To what extent have they been successfully used and will they continue to be so utilized as arguments for larger government expenditures at home? By what yard stick can one measure the hampering effects of such expenditures on tax-loaded private enterprises which do not share in the material profits derived from the programs? Such are some of the costs that can never be accurately calculated. It cannot be doubted, however, that these programs expand the functions and the economic activities of the Federal state at the expense of private enterprise and that not a few who participate in the distribution of these funds have little regard for private enterprise so long as they are well paid for undertaking this distribution. Some of them, in fact, such as Gunnar Myrdal, are advocates of a "global welfare state." [44]

But the costs of these foreign-assistance programs, whatever they may be, represent only one of the just grievances of taxpayers and consumers who derive no direct economic benefit from them but suffer economic injury instead.

Salaries of top bureaucrats of the United States who distribute foreign aid all around the world are seldom as low as $11,000 a year, with more than half as much again in fringe benefits of various sorts; their pay is more likely to range from $13,750 to $22,500, plus allowances and differentials for hardship posts amounting to almost as much as their basic pay. [45] Encouraged by this type of sacrifice, the high officials of the United Nations were equally extravagant. The total compensation of the Secretary-General in 1956 was only $68,000, while 21 under secretaries and deputy secretaries were paid $18,000 each and were given allowances of $3,500 each. Excluding the Secretary-General, there were 1,262 positions out of a total of 4,006 paying from $7,330 to $18,000, plus various allowances and fringe benefits. Surely thousands of the distributors of this global aid are the most highly paid missionaries the world has even seen. If they

22 FOREIGN AID REEXAMINED

were eager to cling to their positions and provide still more, their attitude would seem very human indeed. [46]

1. Senate Special Committee to Study the Foreign Aid Program, 85 Cong., 1 sess., Hearings (1957): "The Foreign Aid Program," pp. 555-556.
2. *Ibid.*, p. 656.
3. Ibid., p. 710.
4. *Ibid.*, pp. 636-640.
5. The State Department, *Point Four* (Washington, 1950), p. 95.
6. *Ibid.*, p. 97.
7. Senate Committee on Foreign Relations, 84 Cong., 2 sess., *Hearings* (1956): "Mutual Security Act of 1956," p. 24.
8. Senate Special Committee to Study the Foreign Aid Program, 85 Cong., 1 sess., *Hearings* (1957): "The Foreign Aid Program," pp. 396-397.
9. The University of Chicago's Harris Foundation held a conference on the subject of foreign investment in 1927; it happened that all of the participants enthusiastically favored such investment. See Quincy Wright, ed., *Foreign Investments* (Chicago, 1928). I know of no conference sponsored by the private foundations which questions the prudence of this investment boom.
10. Senate Committee on Finance, 72, 1 sess., *Hearings* (1931-32): "Sale of foreign Bonds and Securities in the United States," pp. 50-51.
10a. *Ibid.*, pp. 64-67.
11. *Ibid.*, pp. 447-454.
12. *Ibid.*, pp. 619-620.
13. *Ibid.*, pp. 1575-1576.
14. *Ibid.*, p. 137.
15. Samuel I. Rosenman, ed., *Public Papers and Addresses of Franklin D. Roosevelt* (New York, 1938), I, 674-675.
16. *Ibid.*, I, 724.
17. Raymond Moley, *After Seven Years* (New York, 1939), pp. 70, 105, 184.
18. House of Representatives, Committee of Ways and Means, 73 Cong., 2 sess., *Hearings* (1934): "Reciprocal Trade Agreements," pp 4-6.
19. *Ibid.*, pp. 45-46.
20. *Ibid.*, p. 86.
21. *Ibid.*, pp. 448-453 et passim.
22. House Committee on Ways and Means, 78 Cong., 1 sess., *Hearings* (1943): "Extension of Reciprocal Trade Agreements Act," pp. 4, 145, 963-964.
23. House Committee on Ways and Means, 79 Cong., 1 sess., *Hearings* (1945): "Extension of the Trade Agreements Act," pp. 12, 23-24, 438, 443, 681-682, 1147.
24. Senate Committee on Banking and Currency, 79 Cong., 1 sess., *Hearings* 1945): "Bretton Woods Agreements," p. 6; House Committee on Banking and Currency, 79 Cong., 1 sess., *Hearings* (1945): "Bretton Woods Agreements," pp. 107, 159-160, 475-576.
25. Department of State, *Conference Series*, No. 71. pp. 109-110.

26. Don Lohbeck, *Patrick J. Hurley* (Chicago, Regnery Co.), p. 234.

27. State Department, *The Conferences at Malta and Yalta* (Washington, 1955), pp. 715-716, 724. See also pp. 315-318 for memoranda regarding a loan of ten billion dollars to Soviet Russia proposed by Henry Morganthau on January 10, 1945. It was to be a 35-year loan with interest at 2 percent, and Morganthau's main argument for it was that it would be "a major step" in Roosevelt's "program to provide 60 million jobs in the post-war period" within the United States. On January 20, 1945, W. L. Clayton drafted an opposition memorandum in which he wrote: "While we are naturally desirous to increase our trade to the Soviet Union to the maximum, and it is in our interest to do so, it would be tactically harmful to deepen the impression they already have that no matter what happens we are going to have to sell goods to the Soviet Union to keep our own economy going." Roosevelt's remarks on the subject of economic development and foreign trade must have caused Stalin to smile with satisfaction; for he must have thought that FDR was confirming the Marxist dogma that capitalist countries must send their goods and capital abroad or suffocate.

28. Henry Wallace, *The Price of Victory* (New York, 1942), p. 15.

29. *New York Times*, Nov. 25, 1942.

30. Henry Wallace, *The Century of the Common Man* (New York, 1943), pp. 40, 58-63.

31. Henry Wallace, *Sixty Million Jobs* (New York, 1945), pp. 132-147.

32. Quoted from Black's essay in Seymour E. Harris, ed., *Postwar Economic Problems* (New York, 1943), pp. 298-299.

33. House Special Committee on Postwar Policy and Planning, 78 Cong., 2 sess., *Hearings* (1944), pp. 1081-1082.

34. Printed in *Congressional Record* (daily), June 29, 1950, app., p. 5032.

35. *Ibid.*, April 22, 1952, App., p. 2531, quoting from *New York Times*.

36. House Committee on Foreign Affairs, 82 Cong., 1 sess., *Hearings* (1951): "The Mutual Security Program," p. 356.

37. *Ibid.*, p. 1434.

38. House Committee on Foreign Affairs, 82 Cong., 2 sess.,*Hearings* (1952): "Mutual Security Act Extension," pp. 545-546.

39. Senate Special Committee to Study the Foreign Aid Program, 85 Cong., 1 sess., *Report* (May 13, 1957), No. 300, p. 9.

40. House Committee on Foreign Affairs, 84 Cong., 2 sess., *Hearings* (1956): "Foreign Policy and Mutual Security."

41. The Document cited in note 39, above, contains a list of these studies and surveys. Consult also the following document which seems to have been filled deliberately by Senator Green with the pleas of the advocates of long-term and ever-expanding foreign assistance: Special Committee to Study the Foreign Aid Program, 85 Cong., 1 sess., *Hearings* (1957): "The Foreign Aid Program." Still another Congressional committee furnished an even more striking illustration of bias. The subcommittee on international organizations and movements of the House Committee on Foreign Affairs pretended to appraise national sentiment by holding *Hearings* in six urban centers: Laconia, N. H.; St. Louis and Kansas City, Mo.; Miami, Fla.; Boise, Idaho; and Gary, Indiana. Prior to the taking of the testimony, the sentiment among the groups who testified was appropriately slanted by the circulation of literature among discussion

panels and by speeches of Congressmen at banquets immediately preceding the *Hearings.* The *Hearings,* published under the hopeful title of "Building a World of Free Peoples," were cited as evidence before authorization and appropriation committees of favorable nation-wide "grass-roots opinion." A more unscientific assessment of popular sentiment would be difficult to imagine! It was a clear case of propaganda under the guise of appraisal. Representative A. S. J. Carnahan of Missouri was the chairman of the subcommittee and was lauded by its other members as a great statesman in both St. Louis and Kansas City. Naturally Harry Truman expressed his views at length.

42. Senate Special Committee to Study the Foreign Aid Program, 85 Cong., 1 sess., *Hearings* (1957): "The Foreign Aid Program," pp. 404-405.

43. This statement and the data presented are based upon the *Statistical Abstract of the United States* (Washington, 1956), pp. 10, 259, 290, 299 and pp. 308-309. Consult also the following document: U. S. Congress, Joint Committee on the Economic Report, 84 Cong., 1 sess., *Hearings* (1954): "Low Income Families," pp. 8-29.

44. See Myrdal's *An International Economy* (New York, 1956), pp. 21-29. A good part of this volume is a plea for an international redistribution of property and income.

45. The most convenient source of information on the salaries of the higher-rank bureaucrats of the United States is the *Official Register of the United States,* an annual publication for sale by the Superintendent of Documents, Washington, D. C. Statistics on salaries paid by the United States government cited here have been extracted from the *Register* for the year 1956.

46. The United Nations, *Budget Estimates for the Financial Year* 1956 (New York, 1955) pp. xiv-xv; and the same for the year 1957, pp. 13-14.

2: *Diplomacy of Altruism?*

ELGIN GROSECLOSE

The foreign aid program, as an instrument of United States foreign policy, is now ten years old. To it has been committed upwards of 70 billion dollars,[1] a sum representing around 25 percent of the national debt, and the annual appropriations have been a major factor in the recurring budgetary deficits of the federal government. Despite this massive effort, its success is questionable. During the decade, the area and population under Communist domination, and therefore hostile to the United States, has steadily extended to embrace the land mass from the Baltic to the China Seas, and upwards of 900 million population. In addition, other vast areas have been infected with Communism, turning their governments neutralist in the East-West political struggle and often friendly to Soviet policy. Among these are the Indonesian archipelago with its population of nearly 85 million, India with its nearly 400 millions, and less populated countries like Afghanistan, Burma, Egypt, and Syria. In consequence, the Administration's budget for foreign aid has met increasing criticism. Congressional support, at one time overwhelming, has steadily diminished. Disclosures by investigating committees of waste and extravagance in the administration of the program have added distrust, and it is not surprising that the whole concept of foreign aid has aroused anxiety among the electorate.

"When thine eye is single, thy whole body is full of light"[2] is useful Biblical counsel in examining the foreign aid program. The failures of this stupendous and unprecedented experiment in statecraft can be imputed to its lack of singleness of eye. The foreign aid program, in short, is a patchwork of conflicting ideologies, contradictory purposes, and confusing mechanisms. This paper will attempt to explore some of these contradictions.

THE CONFLICT OF BENEVOLENCE AND SELF-INTEREST

The motivations of the foreign aid program, as Professor Rippy so well points out in his contribution to this symposium, are a compound of benevolence, politics, and commercial self-interest—motives that pull in a dozen different directions and lead to conflicting results. The commercial self-interest intruded less as a positive effort on the part of big business to capture foreign markets and extend its industrial empire than as a pervasive fear, immediately following the end of the War, of widespread unemployment. Foreign aid, it was hoped, by creating purchasing power abroad with United States dollars, would provide a market for U. S. products and keep American factories humming. More recently, of course, under Public Law 480, the foreign aid program has been a major instrument for the disposal of United States agricultural surpluses in the interest of the American farmer, but this seems to have been a case of riding on the coat-tails of the program rather than propelling it. Generally, however, economic motives have been muted. During the 1957 hearings on the authorization bill before the House Foreign Affairs Committee, not a single business man appeared to advocate foreign aid, but the testimony of a score or more of government officials filled five volumes of record. What is more to the point, the only segment of the public to appear before the Committee was the religious and philanthropic interest, represented by some eighteen spokesmen. These reflected the varied religious coloration of the community: Greek Orthodox through Roman Catholic, Protestant Episcopal, Methodist, Lutheran, Presbyterian, Unitarian, Jewish.

Here is the ground of conflict. Government officials, sworn to uphold the Constitution, are properly concerned with the security of the United States. Foreign aid, within constitutional limits, must be an instrument of foreign policy and devoted exclusively to the advancement or defense of American political interest in the world at large. As President Eisenhower emphasized, in his radio address to the country on the foreign aid program, in May 1957, "This purpose—I repeat—serves our national interest."

At the other end of the spectrum stand the representatives of Church and Synagogue, who advocate the foreign aid program as an expression of moral concern and a discharge of a moral obligation to the world. As Father James L. Vizzard, S.J., vice president of the National Catholic Rural Life Conference, stated before the House Foreign Affairs Committee, "In the mutual security program, we have the opportunity of providing the world with one thing it desperately needs: a shining example of pure, undefiled and disinterested service."[3] Or as the Right Reverend Angus Dun, Episcopal Bishop of Washington, declared to the same Committee, "It can be said of those of us who are responsible leaders in the major churches—and I speak particularly of the Christian churches—that our faith, our responsibilities and our experience all combine to give us a profound concern for the foreign aid policies of our Nation, especially in the nonmilitary aspects . . . we are bound to the conviction that men and nations with an abundance of technical skills and wealth hold them under stewardship and will be judged by the exercise of that stewardship; and that foreign aid programs which aim convincingly at mutual welfare are constructive contributions to freedom, justice and peace." [4]

To these endorsements, Rabbi Abraham J. Feldman, President of the Synagogue Council of America, added the following: "We of the Synagogue Council of America devoutly hope that the Congress of the United States will enact this legislation to help, in the words of the psalm, 'rescue the poor and needy; deliver them out of the hand of the wicked.' This, we believe, is the great moral and historic obligation which confronts our country in its role as the leader of the free world." [5]

The economic and technical assistance phases of the foreign aid program, responding to this pressure from churchmen and philanthropists, may therefore be described in charity as a well-intentioned experiment in magnanimous diplomacy. It is an attempt to employ disinterested service as an instrument of foreign policy. It represents an effort to identify Church and State, that is, to convert the government into an instrument of the moral conscience. It conforms to various totalitarian ideologies, both Fascist and Communist, in that it represents an effort to identify the State with the totality of the social life, and to use the mechanisms of the State, rather than those of Church or philanthropic societies, as instruments of foreign benevolence.

How did this view of the function of government acquire such hold on the morally alert element of the population? What are the historical roots of this tendency so contrary to the main stream of American tradition?

Historical United States Benevolence

Benevolence has always been an incident of American foreign policy, but not until the inauguration of the foreign aid program was it ever thought of as a continuing function of government on behalf of the altruistic impulses of the people. Thus, as early as 1794, within five years after the Constitution came into effect, Congress voted an appropriation for the relief of refugees in Santo Domingo, and again in 1812 to citizens of Venezuela suffering from the calamity of an

earthquake. In 1921, Congress authorized a relief mission to Soviet
Russia, then suffering from famine, despite the fact that relations between the two governments were strained, if not hostile.[6] A little
later funds were voted for earthquake relief in Japan, although again
relations between the two governments were not cordial.

A characteristic of these appropriations was that they were considered as expressions of the national good will, but not of continuing
responsibility. While the constitutionality of such appropriations for
the benefit of alien peoples in distant lands has never been brought
into court, the question has been argued. Charles A. Beard, discussing the limitations to the general welfare clause of the Constitution,
quotes Justice Joseph Story as saying that a tax would be unconstitutional if laid for objects "wholly extraneous (as, for instance, for
propagating Mahometanism among the Turks, or giving aids and subsidies to a foreign nation, to build palaces for its kings, or erect mon-
uments to its heroes."[7])

It was in this spirit that in joining in the agreement for the United
Nations Relief and Rehabilitation on November 9, 1943, public policy was declared to be: "that immediately upon the liberation of any
area by the armed forces of the United Nations or as a consequence
of retreat of the enemy, the population thereof shall receive aid and
relief of their sufferings, food, clothing and shelter, aid in the prevention of pestilence and in the recovery of the health of the people."

Motivated generally by a humanitarian interest and in a mood of
hope the United States in 1945-46 dedicated some $8 billion in various
forms of effort to restore a disrupted world economy.[8]

Aid as Continuing Responsibility

In 1949 the idea was first advanced officially that the United
States government should assume a continuing responsibility of aid
toward areas of the world not under the American flag, and toward
peoples of the world who neither were citizens of the United States,
nor subscribed to American doctrines, nor paid taxes to the United
States treasury, nor were in alliance with the United States, nor were
in any way bound to the United States by ties of race, religion, culture, or affection. This extraordinary proposal was presented by
President Truman as the fourth point in his inaugural address, and
so became known as "Point Four." It stated: "Fourth. We must embark on a bold new program for making the benefits of our scientific
advances and industrial progress available for the improvement and
growth of underdeveloped areas."

There is nothing explicit in this statement about the national interest. It is pure altruism. The newly elected President went on to deny expressly any ulterior interest or national motive: "Such new economic developments must be devised and controlled to benefit the peoples of the areas in which they are established . . . The old imperialism—exploitation for foreign profit—has no place in our plans."

Dedication to human welfare, as distinct from the national interest, has been the appeal by which the staff of the foreign aid program has been largely recruited. In fact, a major criticism of the administration of this vast enterprise is that the men who handle these billions distribute them as though they were provided by the ravens. Thus, a Point Four Administrator refers to the ideal field man as "almost a missionary," and speaks of the program as "an attempt to pay back to the countries of the world some of the things we in the past have gained from other countries." [9] A Secretary of State speaks of the foreign aid technicians as "shirt sleeve diplomats," and as "modern Johnny Appleseeds" who "ride horseback or walk among the farmers of other countries," and who "sift the soil in their gnarled and expert hands." [10] And a State Department leaflet on employment opportunities abroad offers, as one of the compensations of foreign aid work, "the satisfaction of helping people who are eager to make progress along the road to economic betterment."

Strings of National Interest

But the foreign aid program never was pure altruism. Indeed, as noted, the constitutional validity of any program of pure altruism is questionable. While the citizen has the right, in his personal capacity or through his church or benevolent society, to engage in foreign benevolence, there is nothing in the structure or theory of our system of politics that permits such activity by the federal government either in its own name or on behalf of the citizenry. Foreign benevolence is in fact incompatible with the function of government, which, as presently conceived, is an instrument created to defend and promote the interests of the citizens over which it is sovereign.

Thus, the Act for International Development of 1950, which initiated the technical assistance program, tacitly acknowledged the necessity of a look to the national interest by declaring that "technical assistance and capital investment can make maximum contribution to economic development only where there is understanding of the *mutual* advantages of such assistance and investment . . ." [11]

As the war-time partnership with Soviet Russia broke up and gave way to mutual hostility, the professed altruism in foreign aid has increasingly mingled with military objectives and the national political interest. By 1956, national interest was explicit in the appropriation acts for the foreign aid program. Public Law passed by the 84th Congress declared: "It is the sense of Congress that, in the preparation of the mutual security program, the President shall take fully into account the desirability of affirmatively promoting the economic development of underdeveloped countries, both as a means of effectively counteracting the increased political and economic emphasis of Soviet foreign-policy objectives and as a means of promoting fundamental American foreign-policy objectives of political self-determination and independence."

Actually, appropriations for military assistance have been an integral part of the overall foreign aid program since 1947. In that year, under the "Truman Doctrine," a program of military and economic aid to Greece and Turkey started in order to strengthen the resistance of these two countries to Communist aggression. Then followed the Marshall Plan, or European Recovery Program. This was primarily a program of economic assistance with the implicit objective of allaying political unrest and of curbing revolutionary tendencies; but with the formation of the North Atlantic Treaty Organization in 1949 military aid became an increasingly important element of total expenditures. Some $12 billion in grants and loans were given to the European Recovery Program through 1950; meanwhile, some $5 billion were spent in Asia prior to the outbreak of the Korean war, mostly in the form of military aid to the Chinese Nationalist government.

The Korean conflict that began in June, 1950, gave new emphasis to the military and national interest aspect of foreign aid, and thereafter the military aid portion of the total program steadily expanded. In 1951, military assistance represented only 24 percent of the total foreign aid budget; it was 38 percent in 1952, and since then has remained about two-thirds the total.

Confusion as to "Defense Support"

The dilemma of mingled benevolence and self-interest is most apparent in the way "defense support" funds have been applied. "Defense support" funds have been a category of the military aid budget. The theory behind them was that where an ally was spending more on its military establishment than its economy can support, the United States would make up the difference in the form of economic aid. Funds are consequently spent on a variety of economic projects that can be justified either on the grounds of military necessity or American benevolence. Former Ambassador Norman Armour, commissioned by the Senate Foreign Relations Committee to examine and report on the aid programs in Greece, Turkey, and Iran, had the following to say:

"One of the least understood categories of United States aid under the Mutual Security Act and the one capable of creating the most confusion is 'defense support.' In fact, one wonders whether this was not perhaps one motive in coining the phrase and establishing the category.

"The very vagueness of the classification enables it to cover a multitude of things, some quite completely unconcerned with defense. There is probably no single activity in the United States aid program, in one or more of the countries visited, which does not directly or indirectly receive assistance from defense support. In some countries, defense support is almost military; in others, almost entirely non-military. In some instances, the identical item is being shipped to a country under defense support and under military assistance." [12]

As a result of this and other criticism, "defense support" has been eliminated in the appropriations for foreign aid, but the evil remains. Confusion will continue to exist, whatever the title, for the fundamental cleavage in purpose exists.

FOREIGN AID AND DIALECTICAL MATERIALISM

A second ground of confusion and contradiction in the foreign aid program is its effort to combat the spread of Marxian Communism by the application of Marxian principles and Marxian techniques. The effect of this is to promote that which it seeks to destroy, to plough the ground and resow with the same seed.

A fundamental tenet of Marxism is dialectical materialism, the conviction that economics is the controlling force in history. Frederick Engels, disciple of Karl Marx and co-founder of militant Communism, spelled it out as follows: "The ultimate causes of all social changes and political revolutions are to be sought," he writes in *Anti-Duehring*, "not in the heads of men, not in their better insight into eternal truth and justice, but in the changes in the methods of production and exchange; they are to be sought not in the *philosophy*, but in the *economics* of the particular epoch."

The ideas of dialectical materialism, or economic determinism, have not been absent from the American scene. Their influence may be traced in various branches of the humanities, notably in the historical school of Charles A. Beard, and in much American social legislation and correctional administration. They have even entered judicial practice with appeals to hold society to blame for specific acts of violence committed by individuals, rather than the individuals themselves. [13]

The foreign aid program represents, however, the first mass effort to condition whole societies, the policies of governments, and the affections and loyalties of peoples, *by the administration of "environmental conditioning"*, through the mechanism of grants, loans, and other forms of material assistance.

That the proponents of foreign aid have a profound conviction of the efficacy of the Marxian dialectic is patent from a reading of the official literature, beginning with the classic statement of President Truman: "Greater production is the key to prosperity and peace. And the key to greater production is a wider and more vigorous application of modern scientific and technical knowledge." [14]

Other statements of this philosophy have been offered by Nelson A. Rockefeller, speaking as a high administration official, and by Mike J. Mansfield, United States delegate to the United Nations General Assembly. Writing in *Foreign Affairs Quarterly*, Mr. Rockefeller argued that the "hunger, misery, and despair" of the peoples of the underdeveloped countries were due to "economic systems which provide less than minimum needs of food, clothing, and shelter" [15] and Senator Mansfield (although he now seems to have had a second look at his philosophy) declared to the Economic and Financial Committee of the United Nations that the American people are convinced that the only solid foundation upon which we can build is worldwide economic advancement." [16]

A more formal statement of the theory is that found in the study prepared for the Senate Foreign Relations Committee by the Center for International Studies of the Massachusetts Institute of Technology. Entitled "The Objectives of United States Economic Assistance Programs," this report states:

"The proposition is that a comprehensive and sustained program of American economic assistance aimed at helping the free underdeveloped countries to create the conditions for self-sustaining economic growth can, in the short run, materially reduce the danger of conflict triggered by aggressive minor powers, and can, in say 2 to 3 decades, result in an overwhelming preponderance of societies with a successful record of solving their problems without recourse to coercion or violence."

"The proposition presumes," the study adds, "that a feasible and properly designed program of American economic assistance could within two decades catalyze self-sustaining economic growth in most of the underdeveloped free world." [17]

The study concludes: "An effectively designed program of aid for economic development is the best instrument available to the United States for encouraging the growth of politically mature, democratic societies." [18]

Some foreign aid advocates and administrators have become so completely enamoured with this materialistic view that they asperse the value of purely human contributions to history. The virtues which generations of schoolboys have been taught to revere as the springs of human achievement, they discount. Thus, a technical assistance administrator declared: "Dignity and independence are fine words, but they are just words where people are hungry, ignorant, and afflicted with disease all their lives." [19] One wonders if such a viewpoint would have sustained Washington's troops at Valley Forge, or the Turkish people in their struggle for independence in 1923.

The Theory Examined

The theory of foreign aid, here tested, poses a fundamental contradiction. The results are stated to be "politically mature, democratic societies." We do not know what the authors of the Study intended by the phrase, but we may assume it to mean a society in which all the members participated in political decisions, and in which they acted as mature citizens, that is, responsibly and without the caprice or sudden passion condoned in children. It would be a society, we may gather, that would not be carried away by whim, sudden passion, or private interest.

Since, however, societies are but aggregations of individuals, it is not possible to conceive of a politically mature, democratic society in which the vast majority of individuals were not politically mature in their behavior and democratic in their attitudes and convictions. This raises the question as to how any group of individuals can be changed in their personal attributes by a change in their material condition. Will a rise in the standard of living make a person less avaricious, say, or less subject to prejudice, hatred, jealousy, ambition, or other passions which have been the destruction of societies as well as individuals? If the proposition has any merit, then it could be argued that citizens should be classified according to their tax bracket, on the corollary that the higher the person's income, the less subject he would be to the passions of humankind, the more politically mature and democratic he would become, and hence the more desirable as a citizen.

Christian teaching, it may be remarked, has generally stood for the view that fundamental changes come from within, that no matter how much one whitewashes a sepulchre, it still contains dead men's bones. It is indeed a paradox, that with so many direct sayings on the subject from the Founder of Christianity, so many churchmen persist in the conviction that societies can be reformed, the world made peaceful, and universal freedom and justice assured by the mechanism of appropriating money and spending it for dams, cement mills, railways, seed wheat and new ploughs to increase the material abundance and raise the standard of wants.

THE SEED AND THE FRUIT

Much of the public confusion over the foreign aid program, and much of the misdirection and extravagance in the administration of the program, are traceable to the attempt to operate in contradiction to observed experience and in defiance of the lessons of history.

Thus, a prime objective of the program is to allay, in the recipient countries, the unrest and dissatisfactions which the Communist Party may exploit for internal revolution or which lead to foreign adventures that upset the international peace. But the program dismisses as inconsequential the causes of unrest that have kept the race in turmoil since history first was written, from the abduction of Helen to the ambitions of an Egyptian colonel. It has no balm to allay the fevers arising from territorial claims and the dynastic claims of princes, from boundary disputes, religious differences, racial jealousies, insults to nation or to national heroes, the ambitions of military commanders, and visions of national destiny. Of the causes of internal unrest that lead to rebellions and the overthrow of governments— such things as a sense of injustice over taxation and governmental impositions, official laxness and corruption, venal courts, police brutality, uncertain paydays, inflation of the money, impressments and conscriptions, expropriations and condemnations, official caprice, official impotence, and feeble leadership—the foreign aid program has nothing to say.

For over a hundred years Egypt has been the recipient of European capital and technical assistance in the development of the Nile Valley, and today exhibits modern railway systems, hydro-electric works, water impoundage and distribution systems, textile mills, banks and exchanges, and all the associated paraphernalia of modern economic civilization. But it cannot be demonstrated that in consequence Egypt has achieved a "politically mature, democratic society"; nor is there any evidence to suggest that the present political orientation of Egypt would be different had the capital and technical assistance been received from the United States. Indeed, it is hypocrisy to suggest that American capital and technical assistance are going to do better in Asia than European capital and technical assistance because the American variety is not "tainted" with a colonial motive.

Here is a diagnosis of the malaise of the East by one of its own people which illustrates how foreign aid is hamstrung by its dedication to the Marxian dialectic: "The young Indian or Chinese, Iranian or Arab who wreaks havoc in the streets of Asia is basically directing his defiance and hostility against the restraints of cultural and religious traditions, the sickly mysticism, the sacred superstitions, the autocracy of well meaning but unenlightened parents and teachers—all the forces that robbed him of dignity, self-confidence and freedom to grow; the forces that, earlier in his life, strangled his helpless, defenseless, unfinished self." [20]

The captivation of theorists and of large elements of the electorate with the possibilities of foreign aid is due in part to the apparent success of the European Recovery Program. Here is a case of assuming *post hoc, ergo propter hoc*. If it be admitted that American intervention in European affairs beginning in 1948 produced a stiffening of resistance to Communism, it has not been shown, nor can it be shown, that this was due to American economic assistance more than to the psychological effect of American concern and moral support. On the contrary, the great centers of Communist strength in Europe remained just where they were before Marshall Plan aid began, and in the very areas in which American aid was most liberally administered; that is to say, in the industrial districts. Communist strength in Italy, contrary to the "economic well-being" thesis, has been greater in prosperous northern Italy than in impoverished southern Italy, and foreign aid officials discovered, to their consternation, that Communist Party enrollment was frequently greater in the factories providing the highest wage rates, the most liberal employee benefits, the most congenial working conditions.

TEARING DOWN BY BUILDING UP

The paradox of the foreign aid program, in the area in which it proposes to operate with authority, namely, the economic sphere, is that the effect of pouring in funds and technical assistance to build up the economic structures of various foreign countries has most generally been only that of introducing confusion and instability into the economies. The reason for this is implicit in the theory of foreign aid. The theory premises a homogeneity of culture which is not prov-

en by observation. It assumes that what is good for the United
States of America is good for everybody, from the British Isles to the
islands of Micronesia. If steel mills, say, are significant in the American economy, they should be good also for the Indonesian. American
agricultural techniques should be of interest to the melon growers of
Iran and the yam farmers of Africa. This view overlooks the fact
that American techniques are themselves in a state of flux, and that
what was considered the last word in a science only a decade ago
is now antiquated. We may cite the agricultural practices of the
nineteen twenties, that of deep plowing for one, that nearly ruined
vast areas of the Great Plains by erosion and wind blowing of pre-
cious top soil. Margaret Mead, the anthropologist, has pointed out
that even so simple an innovation as an iron plough may have catastrophic consequences for agricultural communities in India. It throws
the carpenter out of work and upsets age-old community patterns.
It requires heavier draft animals which in turn need more fodder than
may be available. The wodden plough is light and can be carried
from plot to plot, and as a farmer may have several widely scattered
plots or strips, the iron plough makes necessary a general rearrange-
ment and consolidation of holdings. [21]

The result is that unless the United States government is prepared
to take over the management of the economy bodily, and reconstruct
it from top to bottom—a task for which it commands neither the
wealth nor the political fiat necessary to accomplish—it had better
leave reform for the people themselves to achieve through ways with
which they are familiar and which are fitted to their traditions.

The Turkish Case

Two instances out of many may be cited. In Turkey, under the
stimulus of the American aid program a large tractor import program
was instituted in an effort to modernize farming. As the tractors
were supplied to the Turkish government out of foreign aid funds,
and by the government to the farmers on easy purchase terms, the
momentary result was a glow of prosperity. But a tractor farm economy requires a completely different environment in which to operate
from the ox and wooden plough economy it supplanted. If the
tractors were to be kept fueled with gasoline and in repair, the farmers had to produce a surplus for the market. This required in turn
roads by which to move the crops to market. Involved also was the
development of foreign markets. This meant competition with other
exporting countries—notably the United States. The result is that
after ten years of foreign aid, Turkey is no nearer a self-sufficient

economy than ever. Turkey, which in 1945 had an export surplus of $33 million and in 1946 of $74 million has had trade deficits ever since, ranging to as high as $193 million in 1952 and $184 million in 1955. [22] Here is the conclusion reached by former Ambassador Norman Armour following his survey of the aid program in that country: "Basically, Turkey is suffering today from too much economic development, too fast, with too little . . . The United States must share some of the blame for Turkey's overambitious economic development." [23]

The Afghan Example

In 1950 the government of Afghanistan, actuated by the economic development theories of the foreign aid program, and aided by an Export-Import Bank loan, embarked on an ambitious scheme of water control and land reclamation in the Helmand Valley. This became eventually one of the largest American financed and constructed developments in Asia. The project, while it has its defenders, has not proven a success, partly because of lack of trained administrators, partly because of engineering defects, but largely, it appears, because it failed to take into account the reluctance of the tribes to leave their traditional nomadic life for the sedentary life of tillage. The failure of this attempt at environmental conditioning has not only put grave strains on the Afghan economy but has threatened the political stability of the country and thrown it in the orbit of Soviet Russia. This is the opinion of qualified observers, and the following from the report in the *New York Times Magazine* by Peggy and Pierre Streit who visited the country in early 1956 is illustrative: "The Helmand Valley Project, which was to have been a boon to Afghanistan, has today placed a dangerous strain both on the Afghan economy and on the nation's morale. Some Western observers in Kabul reason that recent Afghan-Russian trade agreements and the Afghan acceptance of a $100,000,000 Soviet credit represent a partial attempt to mitigate this plight. If this is so, the United States may have unwittingly and indirectly contributed to driving Afghanistan into Russian arms." [24]

Taxing Private Enterprise to Support Socialism

A further contradiction in the foreign aid program is the paradox of a government attached to the principles and system of private enterprise officially encouraging the development of statism and monopoly abroad. The United States is in fact doing concretely what Soviet Russia has been doing only through propaganda: it is pouring out vast sums to promote totalitarian and communistic economic and political systems. It fosters five-year plans, seven-year plans, state

planning boards, imitation TVA's; it has put governments into the
electric power business, into cement manufacture, into slaughter and
meat processing, textile manufacture, tanning, sugar refining, milk
processing, and other commercial undertakings. The list, drawn from
official releases and press reports, could be expanded. Clement
Johnson, chairman of the board of the U. S. Chamber of Commerce,
reporting to the Senate Foreign Relations Committee on the foreign
aid programs in Southeast Asia, states: "There is little or no encouragement for private enterprise. It is politically more popular to create state-owned, publicly administered monopolies which also afford
opportunities for patronage and special favors." [25]

Fortunately, some heed has now been given to this warning, for
the final act of ICA Director John B. Hollister, prior to his resignation in September, 1957, was to issue a directive that would prevent
foreign aid funds being used to put governments into business. The
State Department, however, does not seem to have given its approval
to this directive, and at this writing the policy is still in issue among
the administrative echelons. Probably no clear-cut decision will be
made until the electorate speaks.

The Effects of Over-Militarizing

A not unexpected consequence of the foreign aid program is that
in several countries the efforts to create stability have laid a train of
explosives that can be kept dampened only by the further expenditure
of American funds. This has been the effect of building up military
establishments beyond the capacities of the countries to support. Soldiers released from military service in which they have enjoyed a
livelihood and perquisites which they do not find in civil life become
a Praetorian element in the countryside ready to follow adventure
and revolution. How far such military establishments are an actual
necessity to our foreign policy, or how much they are actually a support to our foreign policy, are questions beyond the scope of this
paper; the fact is brought out as one of the inconsistencies of the program of foreign aid. The two major instances are Turkey and the
Republic of Korea. Turkey, with a population of 21 million, maintains an army of 400,000 men, one of the largest in the N.A.T.O.,
while the Republic of Korea, with a population of 22,000,000, maintains an army of 700,000, the largest in Asia, except for the Chinese,
and the second largest army in the Free World.

What is the opinion of official observers on this policy? Regarding
Turkey and Korea they are silent, but here is Mr. Armour's comment
on Greece: *"Do military and nonmilitary aid objectives conflict?—*

The point was made earlier in this report that some question exists whether the size of Greece's military establishment and of the military spending required to support it—the maintenance of which are among United States military aid objectives—is entirely in line with United States nonmilitary efforts to assist Greece in building a stable and prosperous economy . . . The United States mission felt, I think, that Greece's military expenses were not a seriously negative factor in Greece's economy, so long as United States assistance is available. But I am inclined to feel that this particular question needs further study. For in the end, United States military aid objectives for Greece and NATO force goals and requirements will not be realized or will be self-defeating if, at the same time, the Greek economy is weakened or its development deterred as a result." [26]

Clement Johnson, reporting on the aid program in Southeast Asia, comments as follows on the effect in Laos: "It doesn't take a graduate economist to reach the inescapable conclusion that, if the present massive United States expenditure is continued for 2 or 3 years and then is either discontinued or is materially reduced, a condition of near chaos would almost certainly ensue. The disbanded soldiery would probably resort to banditry. The hill folk who once led a marginal but reasonably contented existence, unaware of manufactured goods . . . would suddenly be made unhappy by finding all these desirable things again beyond their reach." [27]

Bribing Peter and Paying Paul—Or the Economy of Blackmail

A curious effect—a *reductio ad absurdum*—of the process herein discussed is offered in the case of India-Pakistan relations. The United States has been providing foreign aid to Pakistan, as a member of the Baghdad Pact, to assist that country in building up its military establishment as a thwart to Soviet ambitions in Middle Asia. Its neighbor India, with which Pakistan relations are just short of war over the disputed region of Kashmir, is engaged on ambitious Five-Year Plans for economic development. Indian economy is quasi-totalitarian, with about half its industry State-owned, and its political orientation is friendly toward Soviet Russia. India has, nevertheless, been a major recipient of foreign aid, much of which has gone into various State-owned industries. Foreign capital has been reluctant to enter India, and in consequence of these and other factors, the Indian fiscal position has badly deteriorated. India has therefore sent a delegation to the United States to seek a loan in the range of 1 billion 400 million dollars. A main argument being advanced why the United States should come to the rescue is that United States aid to Pakistan has compelled the government of India to divert funds from economic development to the military department in order to counter Pakistan's military strength.

Writing in the *New York Times* of September 22, 1957, C. Rajagopalachari, a former governor-general of India and a caustic critic of United States policies, states: "Nobody in India believes—and nobody in Pakistan believes, either—that there is any intention or likelihood of Russian aggression against Pakistan. It is, therefore, felt in India that American aid serves only to increase Pakistan's power for mischief against her neighbor. This belief has brought about a minor arms race in this part of the world . . . That it is necessary to execute the (Five Year) plan and that it is, therefore, necessary to borrow money from America are beyond controversy."

The Inflationary Effect

Another paradoxical effect of the foreign aid program, not understood by theoretical economists, is the inflationary effect of foreign aid. According to theory, foreign aid funds should be deflationary in effect in the recipient countries, since they increase the supply of goods available within the economy without increase of the money supply (since the goods are provided as U.S. gifts). This theoretical result does not follow in practice. The reasons are simple. The effect is somewhat like that upon a high school boy's allowance from the gift of an automobile. The young man has more possessions but less money, for even though the automobile may save him carfare, he becomes involved in the expense of gasoline, tires and repairs, not to say a whole scale of expenditure which the status of an owner of an automobile seems to impose. Foreign aid funds are usually given under conditions of counterpart contributions by the recipient government. Thus, if the United States donates a steel mill, the local government has to pay for its erection and operation. Often a whole web of new expenditure is involved, for such items as roads and housing facilities, the development of ore supplies, the construction of railways to handle the ore, communication facilities, and all the various items of so-called "social overhead." Stimulated by this activity, prices begin to rise, beginning with wages in the environment of the undertaking, followed by the prices of things which the workers buy. Finally, the government, to finance its share of the development, increases its borrowings, which add to the inflationary pressure, and finally resorts to the printing press.

The bare fact is that in every country that has been recipient of United States foreign aid, with the exception of one or two countries

of Europe (Germany in particular) currencies are notably weaker
than they were ten years ago.

Is a Foreign Aid Program Needed?

This discussion would not be complete without giving recognition
to the vocal demand of a large element of the electorate for some national expression of the moral conscience. The question to be considered is whether there is an alternative to the foreign aid program
as such an expression. The viewpoint expressed in this paper is not
that the moral conscience should be ignored, or that it should be denied expression; the view here taken is that the federal government
is not the proper instrument for the expression of the charitable and
benevolent impulses of the citizens. This is a government of dele-
gated powers, and the attempt to use it as a charitable agency abroad
is not only unconstitutional, but is self-defeating of such purpose.

The greatest contribution this country can offer to the rest of the
world, this paper submits, contrary to the Marxian thesis, is not the
material products of the American livelihood system, but the American idea. By the American idea is meant the complex of ideas imbedded in American political, economic, social, and moral practice,
that are the ultimate dynamic of American culture.

What is the American idea? Some think it is a Cadillac complex
and chrome plated plumbing, the right to throw bottles at the um-
pire, and to be noisy in foreign lands. It may be these things, and
worse, but it is also a group of ideas drawn from the parent cultures
of Europe and the Middle East—ideas which, developed, matured,
or simply re-furbished, are the proper coin with which "to pay back
to the countries of the world some of the things we in the past have
gained from other countries." Here are some of them, drawn from
Judeo-Christian Scriptures, that have made possible the economic
strength and industrial power of this country: dignity of labor; right
of the workman to his hire; equal justice before the law; personal
responsibility; confidence that for every problem there is an answer,
for every need a response; a just weight and a just balance; a respect
for exact truth.

If these components of the American idea are understood, then the
task is simplified: the American idea becomes one of a community
of ideas having a common purpose in the illuminated moral conscience of mankind. It will diffuse of its own accord, as irresistibly
as a fragrance on a breeze—from the activities of American overseas
commerce and communications; from overseas missionary and philanthropic enterprise; from the arts of the motion picture, radio, and

written word; and most importantly, from a foreign policy of confidence and courage and respect for the Idea.

1. The exact amount of foreign assistance is in dispute, because of the various ways in which aid is granted or committed, and the various concepts of what constitutes foreign aid. A compilation by Hermann Ficker, analyst in international finance and trade in the Library of Congress, printed in the *Congressional Record* for April 1, 1957, indicates that total foreign assistance made available since July 1, 1940 through June 30, 1957, is in excess of 130 billion dollars, or equivalent to nearly one half the national debt. These differences are an added illustration of the confusion into which the whole subject of foreign aid has sunk.
2. Luke XI, 34.
3. Mutual Security Act of 1957. Hearings before the Committee on Foreign Affairs, House of Representatives, May 28, 1957. Part II, p. 138.
4. *Ibid.*, p. 147.   5. *Ibid.*, p. 126.
6. It is of interest, however, that of the $60 million provided, $36 million came from the Red Cross and other private relief agencies, and the $24 million provided from the United States did not come directly from the Treasury.
7. *The Republic.* New York. 1943. p. 111.
8. *The Objectives of United States Economic Assistance Programs.* Senate Foreign Relations Committee Print. January, 1957. p. 4f.
9. Stanley Andrews to the press. May 25, 1952.
10. Dean Acheson at the Roosevelt Day Dinner of A.D.A., January 25, 1952.
11. Public Law 535, 81st Congress. Title IV. Sec. 402(c). Underscoring supplied.
12. Senate Foreign Relations Committee Print. Study No. 1. January, 1957.
13. See, for instance, *New York Times* account (August 19, 1954) of Brooklyn Felony Court hearings on murder charges against three youths.
14. Inaugural address, 1949.   15. July, 1951.
16. Department of State Bulletin, December 17, 1951.
17. *Op. cit.*, p. 20.   18. *Ibid.*, p. 25.
19. Jonathan B. Bingham to the *New York Herald-Tribune* Forum, March 22, 1952.
20. Fereidoun Esfandiary, "Is It the Mysterious—or Neurotic—East?" in *The New York Times Magazine.* March 24, 1957.
21. *Cultural Patterns and Social Change,* ed. by Margaret Mead. pp. 192 ff. (Mentor Books. New York. 1955).
22. Turkish Monthly Statistics, 194555.
23. Senate Foreign Relations Committee Print. Survey No. 1, February, 1957, p. 26.
24. *New York Times Magazine,* March 18, 1956, p. 56.
25. Committee Print. Survey No. 7. March, 1957, p. 3.
26. *Op. cit.*, p. 21.
27. Senate Foreign Relations Committee Print. Survey No. 7. March, 1957, p. 28.

3: *Byzantine Conquest of the United States*

George Peter Murdock

The Spanish-American War first demonstrated the military and naval might of the United States in an armed conflict with a major European nation. It brought us colonies in the Philippines, Guam, and Puerto Rico, and made us for the first time a world power. Americans were jubilant. Enthusiasm ran high over our glorious victories, and people of both political parties, with near unanimity, rejoiced at the nation's opportunity to play a new role in international affairs and to carry out a civilizing mission abroad where others had failed. This was, everyone agreed, our "manifest destiny."

The smoke of battle had hardly cleared, however, when one calm voice was raised against this popular hysteria. The voice was that of William Graham Sumner, eminent economist and sociologist and, by common consent of most experts, the greatest social scientist America has yet produced. On January 16, 1899, before the Yale chapter of Phi Beta Kappa, Sumner stunned his audience with a powerful address entitled "The Conquest of the United States by Spain." [1]

"We have beaten Spain in a military conflict," said Sumner, "but we are submitting to be conquered by her on the field of ideas and policies. Expansionism and imperialism are nothing but the old philosophies . . . which have brought Spain to where she now is. These philosophies . . . are seductive, especially upon the first view and the most superficial judgment, and therefore it cannot be denied that they are very strong for popular effect. They are delusions, and they will lead us to ruin unless we are hard-headed enough to resist them."

We know today, more than half a century later, that Sumner was right and that the new foreign policy which he decried was wrong, despite its enormous popularity. Our adoption of colonial imperialism from Spain, even though with time its acceptance fortunately grew half-hearted and we came ultimately to repudiate it in part in

43

the case of the Philippines, has done us irreparable harm in our international relations. It has left a permanent residuum of suspicion in Latin America which even the most vigorous "good neighbor policy" cannot wholy allay. It has created an enduring ambivalence in our natural policy regarding our remaining colonial possessions. We cannot decide, for example, whether to treat the Puerto Ricans as colonial dependents or as full-fledged Americans, and have followed a mixed course which satisfied no one. The same ambivalence has pervaded our foreign policy respecting the nations of southern Asia and northern Africa which have recently been sloughing off their colonial shackles, and has prevented our assumption of leadership in those parts of the world, leaving their inhabitants vulnerable to the seductive blandishments of the vastly harsher imperialists of Asia's heartland.

Recently our country has adopted another new philosophy of international relations—as "seductive, especially upon the first view and the most superficial judgment" as that which Sumner inveighed against, and no less ominous in its potential consequences. Again we have as our "manifest destiny" a great "civilizing mission"—that of assisting all the less fortunate peoples of the world to achieve a level of economic productivity and a standard of living comparable to our own. So laudable are our motives that few take the trouble to assess realistically the possibilities of success or to weigh the grim incidental consequences of the effort. Those who do are hounded from the public forum and subjected to unrestrained contumely. As in Sumner's day, both major political parties have embraced with equal fervor the new philosophy of international relations, which may thus be appropriately named the "Truman-Eisenhower policy," although, of course, it had its roots in Lend-Lease under the Roosevelt administration.

The present writer dares to emulate Sumner's role as a Cassandra because of his conviction that the new philosophy is as fundamentally unsound, as inherently self-defeating, and as potentially dangerous as that which Sumner attacked. He has even adopted the title of the latter's essay with the change of a single word. Medieval Byzantium provides as apt a model for our present ideological conquerors as did Spain in 1899. The great historian of Byzantium, Charles Diehl,[2] has pointed out how the foreign policy of the Eastern Roman Empire sought always to impress less fortunate peoples with the wealth and prosperity of Constantinople, and used lavish foreign aid as its principal diplomatic instrument. To the Byzantine rulers, says Diehl: "The crudest, simplest, and most direct way of influencing foreign nations was by means of money. Money was always regarded by Byzantine diplomats as being an irresistible argument, and was used indiscriminately and sometimes unwisely, in and out of season . . . This squandering of resources and neglect of vital interests was more than once a matter of concern to observant and thoughtful men," but, notes Diehl, it was never abandoned as the cardinal principle in international relations.

Since the ostentatious flaunting of our own material prosperity, the Pharisaical assumption of the superiority of our own "American way of life," and the wholesale distribution of foreign aid are equally central in the Truman-Eisenhower foreign policy, it is sobering to note their results in Byzantium. Lulled by a false sense of security, the Byzantines failed to maintain their own military and economic strength. Then, when the Turks threatened, friends purchased by money proved false friends, and the once resplendent Eastern Empire shrank to a hollow shell and ultimately collapsed without a struggle. Somehow, as a model for contemporary national policy, Byzantium seems scarcely preferable to Spain.

The express aim of our foreign aid program is directed cultural change. No one knows better than the experienced applied anthropologist how resistant cultures are to change, and how disappointingly limited and partial have been the successes in even the most intelligently planned and executed programs for conscious adaptive improvement. Even the enthusiast, unless he is impervious to the evidence of actual experience, can scarcely escape being sobered by the record of a series of such projects in the field of public health recently assembled by Benjamin Paul.[3] Here he will learn, for example, of the attempt by a rural hygiene worker, in a Peruvian town with a dangerously contaminated water supply, to induce housewives to boil their water before consumption. After two years of conscientious effort, with government, foundation, and local medical support, she was able to persuade only 11 out of 200 housewives to adopt so seemingly obvious a precaution.

In another reported case, a team of eight trained people, with generous funds and complete support from the local press and such organizations as the Parent-Teacher Association, spent six months in a Canadian rural town in a concerted effort to develop a more rational public attitude toward problems of mental health. With exceptional candor, the leaders report not only the complete failure of their program but also its unanticipated negative consequences. "The people . . ., initially friendly and cooperative, had become increasingly aloof as the months went by, despite every effort on our part to be tactful and friendly. From apathy they resorted to withdrawal; and when our interviewers returned . . . at the end of six months . . ., they were dismayed at the outright antagonism they encountered."

Directed culture change is, of course, by no means impossible, however difficult. But it requires a very high degree of professional competence in the fields of anthropology, economics, psychology, and sociology, a deep insight into the nature of the culture undergoing change, and administrative planning of exceptionally high quality. Since these requisites are rarely fulfilled in the execution of our foreign aid programs, the few examples of striking success, however publicized, can scarcely conceal the dismal general record of partial and complete failures.

Foreign aid seeks to transform the subsistence economies of the so-called "underdeveloped areas" into complex modern economies of modern type in which the accumulation of effective productive capital will ultimately proceed at a pace sufficient to ensure a permanently rising standard of living. Some of the most serious obstacles to such an achievement have been realistically presented by Marion Levy,⁴ and are well worth summarizing:

1. Underdeveloped countries, attempting to bypass all the intermediate stages of industrial evolution, largely lack both the skills and the materials necessary for converting existing resources into effective productive capital.

2. The extraordinary economic self-sufficiency of underdeveloped areas must be converted to a high level of interdependency in the allocation of goods and services through the development of extremely complex specialization involving enormous changes not only in industrial and administrative organization but also in non-economic systems of traditional values. During the transition, moreover, such countries become exceedingly vulnerable to fluctuations in world tastes.

3. The achievement of industrial modernization on a scale sufficient to meet international competition requires the accumulation of vast amounts of investment capital by masses of people who have been habituated to hoarding their savings or employing them for conspicuous consumption rather than putting them to use to form effective productive capital.

4. Late-comers cannot afford to wait for the gradual development of individual capitalistic enterprise by which alone all modern industrial systems have been created, and hence feel constrained to hasten the change through government enterprise. Not being subject to automatic correction through individual trial and error, such

efforts require a miracle of planning and coordination. Failures consequently tend to be numerous and starkly tragic in their scale. One thinks, for example, of the East African "groundnut scheme" and of the attempts of Iron Curtain countries to collectivize agriculture.

Since no program for the economic transformation of underdeveloped areas can succeed unless it is brought into close alignment with automatic social and economic forces trending in the same direction, planners should study carefully the factors which have, in particular cases, either favored or prevented the independent development of a modern industrial system. Levy[5] has, for example, analyzed with care and insight the contrasting factors in Japan and China which in the one case brought about a rapid and peaceful conversion from an unspecialized subsistence economy to a highly industrial modern economy and, in the other, effectively inhibited such a transformation. If vast sums are to be expended in foreign aid, common sense suggests that at least they not be squandered recklessly but be allocated to regions and projects where there is at least a gambler's chance that they may be employed effectively.

Devotees of foreign aid are singularly oblivious to demographic realities. It is an indisputable fact, however obscure the reasons, that every society which has independently developed an industrial economy has been characterized by a falling birth rate, which has enabled it to convert economic gains into an enhanced general standard of living. It is likewise beyond argument that the underdeveloped countries of the world, practically without exception, have dense populations with very high birth rates which reveal not even an incipient tendency to decline. Every innovation in medicine or public health, every improvement in diet or nutrition, every gift of money or surplus agricultural products, serves only to keep alive great numbers who would otherwise have perished from disease, malnutrition, or famine. The resulting population increments divide and absorb both the increments in production and the largesse from abroad, with the inevitable consequences of increasing dependency and pauperization and a constantly falling rather than a rising standard of living. Foreign aid, whatever its nature, has thus tragically injured the very ones whom it has sought to assist, and it has no reasonable prospect of ever genuinely helping any society which has not come realistically to grips with its own population problem.

Experience and theory unite in demonstrating that foreign aid has not accomplished, and cannot accomplish, more than a minuscule proportion of what it aims to achieve. Everything else goes irretrievably "down the drain." But why should not a prosperous society indulge its vanities, even at the cost of heavy economic waste? Other people waste their economic substance recklessly in the consumption of alcohol, in conspicuous display, in lavish mortuary expenditures, and in other non-productive ways which presumably satisfy derivative human needs. We ourselves indulge our ethical sensibilities by prolonging the lives of the senile aged and incurably ill, by maintaining hopeless defectives and delinquents at public expense, by costly welfare programs for the unfortunate of many categories. Why should we not also, if we wish, pay "conscience money" to the unfortunate of other lands, even if it is totally wasted? We are rich, aren't we? Why shouldn't we spend what we have in any way that makes us feel better?

While this argument is honest, and perhaps unanswerable, it is never heard. Instead, the defenders of the Byzantine policy of Truman and Eisenhower delude themselves into believing that it achieves at least some of its ostensible purposes, and blind themselves to its unintended incidental consequences. It is these consequences, acutely damaging both to our own society and to those whom we would help, that provide genuine cause for alarm. The waste, excessive as it may seem to some, we might conceivably bear. But not the insidious corrupting effects on our own culture and society, and on the present and future welfare of the world at large.

Internal corrosion already manifests itself in the slackening of military preparedness. Like Byzantium, we are beginning to reduce our armed forces and to rely on those of allies whose support we have bought with gold. Her purchased friends deserted Byzantium in her hour of need. Can we reasonably expect that ours will do otherwise?

Our foreign aid program conceals from the public the effects of economically unsound fiscal policies, thus preventing their correction and assuring their perpetuation. Accumulated "surpluses" of cotton, grain, and dairy products resulting from our farm price support program, for example, are inconspicuously dumped abroad in the guise of "aid" or "loans." Often, as in the case of Poland, such transactions serve as a cloak for economic follies in both contracting countries.

Of all the untoward consequences, perhaps the most serious has been the creation of a powerful bureaucracy with a vested interest in the perpetuation of foreign aid. This constitutes the organized spearhead of a powerful pressure group of self-styled "liberals," many of whom exhibit a profound lack of confidence in the economic, social, and political institutions of the United States.

In the early decades of the present century, genuine liberals tended to be thoughtful and studious men and women. Refusing to accept shibboleths of their day, they carefully examined the best available literature on economic theory and on social and cultural evolution in order to reach fact-minded decisions on current issues such as the protective tariff, the income tax, social welfare legislation, and the claims of socialism. With the coming of the Depression, some of their views became popular, and they were joined and ultimately swamped by masses of emotional, credulous, and unstudious people who styled themselves "liberals."

These uncritical, herd-minded "liberals" dominate our intellectual circles today, and exert a powerful influence in Washington. They have been persuaded by propaganda—in the teeth of factual evidence which has convinced the genuine liberal—that private economic enterprise is selfish and sordid, and that public enterprise is, by contrast, both ethically pure and more democratic. They are puzzled by our country's prosperity, and ashamed of it, and are determined that its results be shared with other peoples, who are morally at least as deserving. They crucified a small opposing group who incautiously adopted the slogan "America First," but have lacked the honesty to label their own philosophy appropriately as "America Last."

This claque applauds loudly all proposals for foreign aid—the more vociferously the more the policies of the country in question diverge from our own in the direction of "neutralism." But they respond with reluctance and notably restrained generosity to appeals for aid from victims of floods in the northeastern states, of droughts in the southwestern states, or of hurricanes in the Gulf states. This niggardliness becomes especially striking in respect to foreign areas for which the United States has an unquestioned legal and moral responsibility, e.g., the Ryukyu Islands and the Trust Territory of the Pacific.

The writer can qualify as an expert on both these areas. He knows them at first hand both during World War II and since, he is fully familiar with literature, and he maintains relations with the personnel in both areas. He must report with sorrow that the Micronesians and Okinawans alike are incomparably worse off under their present American administrations than under earlier Japanese rule. In the Trust Territory the present civilian administration struggles along bravely with funds insufficient to maintain even an adequate communications system, much less other necessary facilities and services. Koror, the former Japanese capital, once a thriving town with good streets, electric lights, shops, and motion picture theaters, has degenerated to a straggling primitive village without modern facilities.

Okinawa, a literate country with an ancient Oriental civilization, has fared even worse. We shall confine our comments to the land situation, crucial in this overpopulated agricultural island. Prior to the war, the average farm household held only 1.6 acres of land, from which its members had to derive not only their subsistence but also a surplus in cash crops with which to purchase clothing, tools, and other necessities. After the war, our government repatriated nearly 100,000 Okinawans who had settled in Manchuria, the Philippines, and Micronesia, and at the same time withdrew permanently from cultivation a substantial proportion of the best agricultural land for military installations. For this we paid an arbitrary rental absurdly below real values. In addition, we have used land wastefully. On the author's last visit, for example, a large block of exceptionally fertile fields was in the process of being condemned to build a golf course for American personnel. Our land policy has reduced the Okinawans to stark economic dependency. It should evoke no surprise that Naha, the largest city on the island, in its last two municipal elections has chosen a Communist as mayor.

With but an infinitesimal proportion of the funds which we have distributed in aid to foreign and even hostile nations, we could have made our administration of the Ryukyus and of the Trust Territory a model to be proud of. Moreover, we could thereby have bettered appreciably our diplomatic position in the Far East. A member of the Japanese Diet told the writer several years ago that, in his opinion, the future policy of Japan toward the United States would be governed more by our actions in Okinawa than by any other single factor. Yet, with everything to gain, we have lost everything. We here see the quintessential expression of the policy of America Last. As areas where the United States has a special legal and moral responsibility, Micronesia and the Ryukyus must yield priority in aid to foreign countries, including "neutralist" and even Communist ones.

The corrosion engendered at home by our foreign aid program can be matched only by its deleterious effects abroad. Some years ago the writer, in testifying before the Foreign Relations Committee of the U. S. Senate on the Marshall Plan, predicted that unless foreign aid were substantially curtailed the name of the United States would become "a hissing and a byword among the nations." Subsequent events have yielded spectacular confirmation. The intensity and universality of anti-Americanism throughout the world today receives floods of comment, interpretation, and suggestions for correction in the press and popular periodicals—but never a denial. Few have noted, however, that its primary cause lies in our foreign aid program.

Scarcely a nation has escaped having our greater wealth and prosperity flaunted before their eyes, demanding notice. As human beings, they cannot but react with envy. The far-reaching political implications of this motive, hitherto hardly suspected, have recently been subjected to thoughtful analysis by Helmut Schoeck.[6] The mass cry, "Break up the Yankees," can arise as easily in the international scene as in professional baseball, and for similar invidious reasons.

Another effect should have been predicted from the behavior of the British after World War I. When we suggested that they might pay a token portion of their war debts to us, their rage found expression in the epithet "Uncle Shylock," which today resounds throughout the world. The principle expressed in the folk saying, "Lend to a friend and lose a friend," applies in international as in inter-personal relations.

Since no yardstick exists for the equitable distribution of foreign aid, some nations inevitably feel that they are being discriminated against in the amounts they receive. Whenever we give to one country, we are likely to anger two or three. The small or unlucky hog at the trough finds it easy to displace his displeasure toward him who has brought the pail of swill.

Since the receipt of aid creates the expectation of continuation, and produces adjustments which make continuation seem imperative, any reduction in amount causes frustration and arouses anger. Disappointed hopes have the same effect. When Nasser failed to receive the anticipated funds to build the Aswan Dam, his rage found expression in the seizure of the Suez Canal. His reaction precisely paralleled that of the Cairo beggar who, receiving a smaller coin than he has hoped for, spits in the face of the donor.

The giver of foreign aid can never win. To expect to be appreciated or liked is incredibly naive. The only rewards to be realistically anticipated are envy and dislike, or, if the benefactions are generous enough, full-fledged hatred.

A particularly insidious danger in foreign aid arises from the fact that it must be delivered into the hands of those who hold the reins of power in the country in question. These may and sometimes do convert it corruptly to their own personal gain.[7] In the best case they filter it through the existing power hierarchy, whose members or supporters derive all or most of the benefits. There is no practicable means whereby we can channel any substantial portion to those disadvantaged but powerless groups whose plight has aroused our sympathy. A gift or loan made to Spain or Yugoslavia, for example, does not benefit the Spanish or Yugoslav people. It merely strengthens Franco or Tito and the ruling cliques who support them.

Recent American history has seen one other folly as egregious as that of foreign aid embraced with comparable unanimity by both political parties and the people at large. In the case of Prohibition, however, a popular revulsion set in after about a decade and brought it to an inglorious end. Perhaps mass common sense will once again assert itself, and prevent our final conquest by Byzantium.

In conclusion we may inquire whether there is not available some alternative national policy which avoids the dangerous pitfalls of the present one and offers superior prospects of success. The outlines of such a policy emerge from a recognition of the essential nature of political organization and of the contrasting characteristics of different types of states. A recent work of major importance by Karl Wittfogel[8] has enormously clarified the basic issues both theoretically and factually, and provides, at least by implication, the blueprints for an adaptive program of political action in both the domestic and the international spheres.

Wittfogel clearly distinguishes two major types of complex political systems. One, the "Oriental despotism," usually originates in agricultural societies depending upon large-scale irrigation works and is characterized by political absolutism, a massive, centralized, controlling bureaucracy, the suppression or fractionation of private property, the absorption or rigid subordination of the ecclesiastical, military, and educational organizations, conspicuous consumption or display by the wielders of power, unrestricted exploitation of the masses of the population, terroristic techniques of social control, and creeping corruption culminating in ultimate stagnation after a brief initial period of creativity. Political systems of this type, in which the state is stronger than society and men outside the ruling apparatus are essentially slaves of the state, have developed independently in ancient Egypt, in pre-Columbian Mexico and Peru, and in eastern, southern, and southwestern Asia.

Contrasting sharply with Oriental despotisms is the "multi-centered state," typified by the feudal societies of medieval Europe and Japan. In political systems of this type the state is only one of a number of strong social institutions, and its power is effectively checked and restrained by vigorous competing organizations such as the church, craft and merchant guilds, and the private owners of land and industrial capital. The individual is offered vastly superior protection and a much wider range of opportunities. As a consequence, political systems of this type, instead of undergoing gradual stagnation, reveal great flexibility and the capacity to react adaptively through progressive social change.

The international situation in the world today exhibits an alignment extraordinarily close to that between the two major types of political systems differentiated by Wittfogel. With a few notable exceptions like Spain, the "free world" consists of states of the "multi-centered" type, while the "Iron Curtain" countries fall without exception into the pattern of bureaucratic Oriental despotisms. Far from representing the emergence of new postcapitalistic configurations, as their propaganda claims, the latter are obvious reversions to a widespread pre-capitalistic typology and differ from earlier Oriental despotisms chiefly in their more complete bureaucratic regimentation of agriculture, commerce, and industry, in their even more ruthless subjection of the individual, in their even more refined techniques of terror, and in the even more cynical hypocrisy of their rulers. The "neutralist" countries, such as Egypt, India, and Indonesia, lie in regions habituated for millennia to despotic rule, and their current policies reveal the basic predilection of their leaders for this type of political organization.

The dichotomy, it must be emphasized, has nothing to do with the distinction between socialism and laissez-faire capitalism. Conservative theorists and apologists have rendered a definite disservice in their diatribes against "creeping socialism." They have detracted attention from the crux of the issue, which is not whether the state is strong or weak and not whether it does or does not perform essential social services, but simply whether it is all-powerful or must bend to the will of, and reconcile, the conflicting interests of genuinely influential independent organizations. What we too often decry as "pressure groups," e.g., our larger religious sects, our labor unions, our farmers' and veterans' organizations, and our associations of industrialists and of business and professional men, provide our chief bulwark against the corruption of total power. So long as these remain vigorous and influential, we may safely assign the performance of social services to either private or public enterprise in terms of their relative efficiency in the individual case.

In regard to the international situation, the comparative analysis by Wittfogel provides a basis for a restrained long-range optimism. The greater inherent resiliency and adaptability of the "multi-centered" type of state bodes well for the survival of the free world. The expansion of the Communist form of Oriental despotism seems to have slowed practically to a halt. Moreover, there are grounds for believ-

ing that its initial period of creativity has come to an end, and that
the inevitable next step of spreading corruption leading to ultimate
stagnation is already under way. Recent events in East Germany,
Poland, and especially Hungary bear witness to deep-seated internal
unrest, and suggest that it is now too late for Soviet Russia to risk
unleashing the dogs of war on a global scale lest her satellites and
even her own subjects seize the opportunity to cast off their oppres-
sive shackles.

The foreign policy of the United States may thus be geared to the
inevitable processes of history, which now march on her side. The
time for exclusively defensive rearguard action may well be past, and
we can in the future perhaps follow a more positive course than we
dared to take in Korea or Hungary. Military assistance to fundamentally "multi-centered" allies is doubtless still justified, provided
we do not slacken our own preparedness. Aid of any kind, however,
should be given to despotic regimes like those of Spain and Nationalist China only as strictly emergency measures. It should be withheld entirely from "neutralist" countries except under the most rig-
orously imposed conditions designed to prevent its strengthening the
hands of despotic at the expense of democratic elements.

Economic aid on any continuing basis should be abandoned entirely, for the antagonism it arouses threatens to destroy our fundamental solidarity with the rest of the free world. On occasion, of
course, we may extend generosity to a dependable friend in a temporary emergency. Japan has never ceased to be grateful for the
help we rendered at the time of her last catastrophic earthquake,
but in no case has continuing foreign aid engendered anything but
negative reactions.

We must be especially alert to preserve our own "multi-centered"
institutions, such as our democratic electoral process, our civil liberties and academic freedom, our independent judiciary, our freedom
of speech and of the press, and our private property in land and in
business and industrial enterprises. We must likewise guard carefully our economic wellbeing, devising effective measures to control
both inflation and recession, and above all avoid oppressing our population with an expanding bureaucracy and a mounting burden of
taxation. For unless we succeed in these matters, we shall concede
victory without a struggle to Byzantium, the very archetype of Oriental despotism.

1. Sumner, W. G. *The Conquest of the United States by Spain.* Boston: Dana Estes and Company, 1899. [Republished in *War and Other Essays,* ed. A. G. Keller, pp. 297-334, New Haven: Yale University Press, 1919].

2. Diehl, C. *Byzantium: Greatness and Decline.* pp. 30 ff., 55ff. New Brunswick: Rutgers University Press, 1957.

3. Paul, B. D., ed. *Health, Culture and Community.* New York: Russell Sage Foundation, 1955.

4. Levy, M. J., Jr. "Some Social Obstacles to 'Capital Formation' in 'Underdeveloped Areas.'" *Capital Formation and Economic Growth,* pp. 441-520. Princeton: Princeton University Press, 1956.

5. Levy, M. J., Jr. "Contrasting Factors in the Modernization of China and Japan." *Economic Growth: Brazil, India, Japan,* ed. S. Kuznets, W. E. Moore, and J. J. Spengler, pp. 496-536. Durham: Duke University Press, 1955.

6. Schoeck, H. "Das Problem des Neides in der Massendemokratie." *Masse und Demokratie,* ed. A. Hunold, pp. 239-272. Erlenbach-Zürich and Stuttgart: Eugen Rentsch Verlag, 1957.

7. See the Associated Press dispatch of March 27, 1957, reporting the charges made against certain Southeast Asian governments by Clement D. Johnson, chairman of the board of the U. S. Chamber of Commerce, after an investigatory trip made to that area for a Senate committee.

8. Wittfogel, K. A. *Oriental Despotism: A Comparative Study of Total Power.* New Haven: Yale University Press, 1957.

PART II

THE POLITICS OF ECONOMIC STAGNATION

4: *The Drag of the Pensadores*

WILLIAM S. STOKES

The wealthy, talented, educated, cultured, traveled upper-middle classes which govern everywhere in Latin America have never been denied the knowledge of technology. The libraries, book stores, and repositories of the United States Government Printing Office are packed with millions of items on health, sanitation, education, agriculture, industry, commerce, manufacturing, banking, accounting, statistics, business management, public administration and the like. Latin Americans are free to visit the United States any time to observe how we farm or manufacture or carry on administration. Institutions of higher learning are ready to accept graduate students. Professors are ready to impart knowledge of their specialties to the best of their ability. In fact, it is fair to say that the United States has always been willing to share ideas and experiences for the asking.

However, the evidence indicates that the leaders of Latin America never have done much asking. Probably no people on earth live more graciously and serenely than the elites which govern in Latin America. On the other hand, even in the most advanced countries such as Argentina, Chile, Uruguay, Brazil, Cuba and Costa Rica, it is evident even to the casual observer that the masses of the people live poorly. This derives in part from the fact that although the population of the United States and Latin America are roughly the same, the United States produces about six times as much as Latin America.[1]

If those people with maximum status, dignity, power and influence in Latin American society have not seen fit to spend their time and money in studying science, technology, and administration for adaptation to their own cultures, what are the reasons for their failure to do so? The hypothesis of this paper is that they have chosen not to do so because the values of Hispanic culture are in conflict with the values of modern-day technology. Consciously or unconsciously they prefer the values of their own culture and hence resist change. If the hypothesis of this paper is only partially valid, it follows that the present program of public economic aid will inevitably fall short of the stated expectations of its supporters. To accomplish what the supporters of economic aid say should be accomplished and which they claim can be accomplished would involve changing fundamental aspects of an entire way of life in Latin America. No state, such as the United States, has enough money to finance such changes. No combination of states such as the United Nations or the Organization of American States has enough money or power to accomplish such results in the foreseeable future. Cultural values develop slowly. People cling to them tenaciously. Some sharing of ideas and practices about how men should live can be furthered by programs of public and private economic aid. However, public economic aid programs are endangered by overselling and private, voluntary programs, which are more effective, have not received the favorable publicity they deserve.

Our experience with internationalism in general should be instructive. The position of the intellectuals as seen in the literature of the social sciences is clear. The great majority argued that logic dictated that if local problems should be solved by local organization and national problems by national organization, so international problems should be solved by international organization. International organization would discover the causes of war and provide means for their solution along with the solution of many lesser problems that plague states and create international tensions. Intellectuals in the social sciences oversold the advantages of internationalism. All can see that internationalism has made little or no progress in changing the pattern of international behavior. We still have tensions. States still employ violence in conducting their affairs. We still have localized wars. The possibility of world war remains. And the cost of internationalism is more than many people were led to believe would be the case. In the period from July 1, 1940 to June 30, 1945 the United States expended in net grants to foreign countries (lend-lease and grants-in-aid less reverse grants) a total of $40,255,660,000. From July 1, 1945 to June 30, 1956 the United States gave in net grants to foreign countries a total of $47,448,997,000. In addition, the United States made available in net loans and credits for the war and postwar period a sum of $11,755,110,000. This makes a total of $99,459,-767,000 for the period from July 1, 1940 to June 30, 1956 [2] This amount represents a substantial part of the public debt of the United States, which was for May 1, 1957, $274,374,220,802, or about $1,700 for every man, woman, and child in the United States. This surely must be the largest per capita debt of any medium-sized or large country in the entire world. Figures released by the Office of Building Economics of the Department of Commerce in May 1957 show the cost of lend-lease, Greek-Turkish aid, United Nations relief and rehabilitation, and military and economic aid (of which $46,815,000-000 was in outright grants) to be about $62,000,000,000 for the period since July 1, 1945.[3] Recently published volumes on international organization spend more time on the structure and procedure of international organization and less time on exaggerated and unsupported claims.[4] They are more cautious than the books of the 1930's and 1940's, but the job of over-selling has already been done.

The Latin American countries have shared in the economic aid programs of the United States. They have received lend-lease aid, military aid, grants-in-aid, and technical assistance aid. And, of course, practically all of the countries can be expected to be in debt to the United States through the Export-Import Bank at any given time. However, the amount of economic aid Latin America has received has been relatively small. Senator Byrd of Virginia produced figures in April, 1957 to show that in ten years since the end of World War II, the Latin American countries received about $357,000,000 in technical assistance and grants and about $316,000,000 in military aid.[5] The ICA (International Cooperation Administration) reported in August, 1956 that the United States contributed $72,600,000 for technical cooperation and emergency programs in Latin America for the fiscal year 1956. This was described as the largest amount of non-military aid for Latin America in any year since the aid program began in 1942.[6] These figures demonstrate that in comparative terms Latin America has not received much of the economic aid the United States has given to foreign countries. There is much evidence that most of the Latin American countries (probably all but Venezuela) would accept more technical assistance, grants, loans, and other economic aid. Although no Latin American country has formally asked for a Marshall Plan for Latin America, responsible Latin Americans have appealed individually for economic assistance paralleling the European aid program.[7]

The Latin American countries have officially urged the United States to consider an expansion of the aid program for Latin America at the Tenth Inter-American Conference at Caracas early in 1954 and at the Inter-American Economic Conferences in Rio de Janeiro and Buenos Aires of 1954 and 1957. One of the principal interests of the Latin Americans in the Organization of American States is in the technical assistance program.[8] Latin Americans have consistently supported economic aid programs for underdeveloped countries in the United Nations. On January 9, 1957 eighteen Latin American countries joined in circulating a resolution in the General Assembly calling for the drafting of a statute to create a United Nations fund for economic development, although it was known that all the major countries, except France, opposed such a fund at the present time.

All the official reports of committees and commissions studying foreign economic aid speak approvingly of the present program. All urge that the program be continued. Some reports advocate an expanded program, and some recommend that foreign aid be made a permanent part of United States foreign policy. The President's Citizen Advisers on the Mutual Security Program was commissioned on September 27, 1956 to draft a report. The Coordinator of the seven-man group was Benjamin F. Fairless. His staff interrogated appropriate officials in Washington and visited eighteen countries in Europe and in the Near and Far East, spending two to three days in each country.

The Fairless group met with United States officials from eight other countries. General Walter Bedell Smith visited two Central American countries. General J. Lawton Collins traveled to four Latin American countries. Mr. Fairless released the report of his group on March 6, 1957. The purpose of the study was to examine the present program of economic aid. The committee agreed unanimously that the present program was worthwhile and should be continued. The Report read: "We are convinced that the best security for Americans is collective security, and that the best hope for diminishing the burden is economic development."[10]

The International Development Advisory Board, established by law in 1950, was created to advise the Government on technical assistance and economic aid. The thirteen-man board, headed by Eric Johnston, issued its report on March 7, 1957. The most important part of the seven-point program was concerned with whether the United States should open up a new program to aid underdeveloped countries. The Board agreed unanimously that the United States should take such action through the creation of an International Development Fund to operate through the ICA of the Department of State on a flexible and long-term basis. "The fund should be established through permanent legislation and should have two areas of responsibility: providing technical assistance and providing capital for development in Latin America, Asia and Africa, including the Middle East."[11]

On April 8, 1957 Secretary John Foster Dulles appeared before the Special Senate Committee to Study Foreign Aid Programs. The Committee was made up of the full membership of the Senate Foreign Relations Committee plus the chairman and ranking minority members of the Appropriations and Armed Services committees. It was created in July, 1956 for the purpose of making a detailed and intensive study of the foreign aid programs. The Chairman of the Committee is Senator Theodore Francis Green of Rhode Island. Secretary Dulles took this opportunity to summarize the rationale for foreign aid and also to present the Administration's recommendations to the Committee. He said the essential reasons for foreign programs were that, "The security and prosperity of the United States are bound up with the continued security and prosperity of other free nations." Unless the United States takes account of this fact, ". . . we shall face a peril, the like of which we have never known." The Secretary also defended foreign aid on moral grounds— the brotherhood of man and the belief in the dignity and worth of all individuals. He declared that military aid programs should be retained, but that they are not enough. The technical assistance and grants programs should be retained, but they are not enough. Therefore, the Secretary recommended that an economic development fund should be established "to provide assistance through loans on terms more favorable than are possible through existing institutions." [12]

The Senate Committee issued its final report on May 12, 1957. As was expected, it recommended continuance of military and assistance programs. In addition, however, the Committee supported Secretary Dulles' proposal for the creation of a new fund to provide loans for development purposes. However, in order to avoid a situation in which "soft loans" would be made which in effect would turn out to be grants, the Committee specified that a Government corporation should control the fund, with representatives from the State and Commerce Departments, the Export-Import Bank and the United States directorate on the International Bank for Reconstruction and Development to be on the board of directors. The Committee attempted to work out provisions which would guarantee that all development assistance should be on a repayable loan basis. The proposal for a development fund appears to be seriously supported by the Administration. When President Eisenhower reduced his budget requests for foreign aid on May 9 by $520,000,000, bringing it to a total of $3,880,000,000, he earmarked $500,000,000 for the first year's installment for the development fund. [13]

All of this evidence leads me to believe that the politicians in both parties are convinced that the continuation and even expansion of foreign economic aid is necessary to defeat Communism in the Cold War and is also desirable for economic, humanitarian, and moral reasons. It is therefore fitting that attention be devoted to the objectives and expectations of the economic aid program in Latin America. There is a vast literature on various aspects of economic aid and technical assistance in Latin America. The Ford Foundation sponsored the publication of an 83-page bibliography on the subject.[14] There is also an uncritical historical account of public and private efforts to provide aid prior to the Point Four Program.[15] However, the most serious effort made to evaluate economic aid programs in Latin America was carried out by the National Planning Association. In 1953 the Ford Foundation gave the NPA $440,000 to finance the project. Some 50 individuals participated directly in the 3-year project. In 1955 and 1956 a series of reports were published, including the comprehensive report and recommendations of 1956.[16]

The things that need to be done in Latin America, according to the NPA, which by direct statement and repeated inference can be done through the help of technical assistance and economic aid, are illustrated by the following phrases taken from the Comprehensive Report of 1956: "persisting poverty of large masses of the people;" "most farms are small and primitive;" on manufacturing and retail trade: "firms using old-fashioned methods;" "illiteracy;" "poorly educated citizens;" "great need for improvement" in combatting disease and malnutrition; governmental centralization "discourages initiative by states, municipalities and local governments;" Latin America needs "rapid development on many related fronts—agriculture, health and sanitation, education, transportation, power, and industry, among others;" improvement in "public administration procedures;" programs in "mining, industry, transportation, labor and community development;" "Latin America needs capital, and no amount of technical cooperation can ever substitute for such capital;" "There has been a growing emphasis on technical cooperation in such fields as industry, mining, power development, transportation, labor, housing, and community development;" "Further industrial development is needed in every country. But it is important to increase greatly the number of children in school; to expand health facilities; to educate farmers out of traditional subsistence patterns into commercial, choice-making agriculture; to improve the administrative efficiency of government itself; and to increase the number of Latin Americans who are trained to carry forward social and economic development programs," ". . . in most countries, the fields of health, agriculture, education, and public administration should receive major attention in the public and private technical cooperation programs;" "In industry, programs in most countries should give attention to increasing productivity in both large and small plants, to establishing research and testing laboratories, and to modernizing the methods of small firms. In labor, programs should help to improve labor governmental services, such as labor recruiting, apprentice training, and industrial safety; and to develop better labor-management relations," etc. [17]

These few phrases and statements are abstracted from a report of 192 pages. However, I think they represent the position of the NPA. It is fair to report that the NPA states that private, voluntary groups are a part of the technical assistance and economic aid program they have in mind. Some awareness of the resistance of Hispanic values to change can be found. There is one statement in the Report which recognizes that not all Latin Americans support technical assistance and economic aid from the United States: "Some in influential positions in Latin America still feel that it is primarily an effort of the government and people of a foreign country to impose a strange way of life upon them." [18]

However, from the series of reports of the NPA and in particular from the Comprehensive Report, it is clear that the NPA assumes that the Latin American countries want to effect important changes in many of the social, economic. and political institutions of their society. It is clear that the NPA believes that technical assistance and economic aid can and should play an important role in the changes that should be made. If such changes were to take place in the foreseeable future, they would represent a revolution in Latin American culture. I do not have the advantage of the working papers of the NPA, nor indeed of any of the other committees, commissions, or groups which have studied foreign aid, to guide my thinking. However, I have read carefully the reports, findings, and conclusions of these groups. In my opinion, none of them, including the NPA, give proper weight to the obstacle of cultural values to the achievement of the objectives they put forth for technical assistance and economic aid. I wish now to turn to an examination of some of the relevant values in Hispanic culture, the importance of which I believe has largely been overlooked.

THE PENSADORES AND TECHNOLOGY AND TECHNOLOGICAL CHANGE

The unavailability of education for the masses, lack of equality of economic opportunity, authoritarianism in various of the social institutions, and tradition help to explain the existence and perpetuation of a rigid class system in most of the Latin American countries.[19] Among those with status, dignity and influence in the community, few rank higher in the continuum than the *pensadores* or intellectuals —the poets, novelists, essayists, artists, and professional people. They are an important element, frequently the most important, in the upper-middle classes which govern everywhere in Latin America. It is therefore useful to understand the position of the intellectuals in Latin America. They have almost unanimously expressed the conviction that the values of Hispanic and Anglo-American culture are in conflict. More than that, the central theme in the thinking of the great majority of the intellectuals is the belief in the superiority of the values of Hispanic culture and the inferiority of the values of United States culture. Hispanic values must be defended and protected at all costs from the encroachment of United States culture. I have elsewhere explored in detail the evidence of cultural anti-Americanism of the nineteenth and twentieth centuries in Latin America.[20] Because technology and technological change are central to the objectives advocated by the supporters of foreign aid, permit me now to examine briefly the position of the *pensadores* in Latin America with respect to this point.

There is no school of literature in Latin America which argues that technology and technological change represent values which should be adopted, cherished, and used as a means to a more meaningful life. Indeed, Professor Eduardo Neale-Silva, distinguished professor of romance languages at the University of Wisconsin and authority on Josè E. Rivera, has informed me that he does not know of a single novel by any recognized author which treats technology as a legitimate, valuable part of Hispanic culture. Although I have not made a quantitative analysis of the content of the novels of Latin America of the nineteenth and twentieth centuries, I have made sample studies from time to time which would lead me to believe that almost without doubt a majority of the novelists of Latin America are indifferent to technology. They do not deal with the subject in any way whatever. An examination of the works of one of the greatest novelists of Chile, Eduardo Barrios, is in point. Most of the time he is completely indifferent to technology. When he does deal with the subject, it is with obvious hostility.[21] There are many novels which deal with technological coexistence. Usually the theme is culture contact of Indian and Hispanic groups, and usually the Indian is shown to have suffered from the effect of technological change. This is seen in the widely-known novel by Ciro Alegría, *El mundo es ancho y ajeno.*[22] José E. Rivera's classic, *La vorágine,* suggests that technological change produces a loss.[23] The Chilean novelist, Benjamín Subercaseaux, in telling the story of four Indians who were taken from Tierra del Fuego to England and later returned argues that what they learned was harmful to them.[24] The Brazilian novelist José Lins do Rego is one of the few writers in Latin America who consistently deals with technology and technological change. Lins do Rego emphasizes the problems created rather than the benefits to be derived.[25] The entire modernistic school of literature in Latin America, which is usually dated 1888-1916, is openly hostile to technology and to the values it represents.[26]

SIGNIFICANT INTERPRETATION

The Mexican Revolution, which began in 1910-11 and is still continuing, at least in the sense of controlling government, is generally regarded as the most important social, political and economic movement in Latin America since independence. The object of the Revolution was to effect a fundamental breaking with the past. More specifically, the Revolution sought to solve the problems of poverty, disease, and hunger which caused widespread distress among the masses. The Revolution therefore offered the *pensadores* an unexcelled opportunity to recommend that science and technology be made central values in the new social order. The evidence demonstrates that the revolutionary novelists did nothing of the kind. Indeed, there is not a single novel by any recognized revolutionary novelist in which technology or the desirablity of technological change is the central theme. The subject is simply ignored.

The most important two novelists of the Revolution are Mariano Azuela and Martín Luis Guzmán. Azuela's pre-revolutionary novel, *Los fracasados,* written in 1906, deals with a young man from the university who fights for his ideals in an atmosphere of evil, small-town politics. His *Mala yerba,* written in 1908, deals with the violence of the *hacendados* in exploiting the *pelados.* (The *mala yerba* is the grass of the landowner which chokes the *yerbas peonadas*). It is a novel which describes Mexican semi-feudalism and analyzes the psychological effect of the system on the *peón.*[27] In 1911 Azuela published his novel, *Andrés Pérez, Maderista,* in which he describes the disillusionment of a liberal newspaperman with the Revolution. The *porfiristas* changed their political colors, joined the *maderistas* and thus denied the Revolution the true leaders it needed. In 1930 Azuela published his classic, *Los de abajo.* This novel is written from the experiences of the author as a Lieut. Colonel in charge of a medical corps in the Revolution. It is written from the point of view of the meaning of the Revolution to the *campesinos* it was designed to help. Its pessimistic conclusions are that the masses did not understand the ideals of the cause. As a result of their failures and those of the leaders of the Revolution, the end effect was that the masses merely changed masters. In his *Los caciques,* written in 1931, Azuela still reflects pessimism. He describes how the reactionary rulers of a small town casually change their political affiliations when the Revolution comes into being and go right on reflecting the values of a feudal society. [28] Azuela has written other works. Some have been published posthumously. However, the books here reviewed fairly represent his interpretation of the Revolution.

Martín Luis Guzmán served under Carranza and Villa from 1913-16. His novel, *El águila y la serpiente,* which has been translated into English, ignores technology. His greatest novel of the Revolution is *La sombra del caudillo.* Guzmán was in Paris when President Calles ordered the execution of General Serrano and his supporters. The assassinations or executions deeply shocked Guzmán. *La sombra del caudillo* is a bitterly critical attack on the Revolution's rôle in the affair. In addition, Guzmán has written a remarkable four-volume study of Pancho Villa, in which he has used some material from Villa's archives. Guzmán is extremely critical of this leader of the Revolution. [29]

Some of the lesser novelists of the Mexican Revolution are more optimistic than Azuela and Guzmán, but in no case do they study Mexico's problems in terms of a lack of scientific, technological, or administrative development, nor do they insist on the need for values in these areas. Gregorio López y Fuentes' novel, *El indio,* is the story of the exploitation of Indians in a small village by white men and their emancipation through the Revolution. [30] Roque Estrada's *Liberaciòn* is the story of Manuel Haro, a liberal landowner who joined the Revolution and remained loyal to Carranza and Obregón. Although he found corruption and betrayal at the upper levels of the Revolution, he returns to the rural area and devotes his life to helping the natives. [31] Roque Estrada's *La Revolución y Francisco I. Madero* should be mentioned. Roque Estrada was one of Madero's political advisers, and this is a story of Madero's campaign. [32] Mauricio Magdaleno expresses some optimism in his novel, *La tierra grande,* [33] because of the defeats of the *hacendados.* It is probably accurate to say that there were no precursors of the Revolution among the novelists in Mexico. The nearest probably was Emilio Rabasa who published a four-volume novel in 1887-1888. His work is designed

mainly to show corruption in all levels of government in Mexico—
local, state, and national. [34]

This brief review of the works of the novelists in general and those
of the Mexican Revolution in particular demonstrates a lack of interest in the values of science and technology. This generalization is
likely to be supported in the literary production for any given year.
For example, Angel Flores, in reviewing Latin American literature,
both fiction and nonfiction, for the year 1956, makes clear that of all
themes used, technology and technological change are conspicuous
by their absence. [35] However, there are many illustrations of novels
which criticize passionately all aspects of technology when it is introduced into a Latin American country by United States private interests. For example, Miguel Angel Asturias and Joaquín Gutiérrez
dramatize alleged "exploitation" by the United Fruit Company in
Central America, [36] Baltazar Castro blames United States mining interests in Chile for the frustrations of Chilean workers, [37] and Rómulo
Gallegos never deals kindly with the men in his novels who represent
the values of United States culture— Mr. Builder in *La trepadora*,
Mr. Danger in *Doña Bárbara*, Mr. Davenport in *Canaíma*, and Mrs.
Hardman in *Sobre la misma tierra*. [38]

Of course, novelists, essayists, historians and other *pensadores* have
not been able to ignore technology in recent decades. The masses
everywhere in Latin America have been demanding higher material
standards of living. All political movements which gained power
succeeded in part because their leaders promised the masses to increase standards of living. In so doing, all have recognized the need,
at least theoretically, to effect changes in the methods of production
and distribution. "Industrialization" is one of the most-repeated
words in the Spanish and Portuguese languages at the present time.
Since about the 1920's, therefore, many novelists and even more
essayists have given grudging recognition of technology in life and
some have expressed a kind of doleful acceptance of the necessity
for changes. However, when the *pensadores* write about industrialization or technological change they almost always do so in theoretical or abstract or doctrinal terms— "las cuestiones primeras," as they
put it. They are infinitely more interested in speculation as to the
theoretical rôle of technology within the broad context of culture
than they are in empirical investigation into the meaning and practical
operation of technology in any of the fields in which they desperately
need improvements. They have appropriated terms to describe
mechanism in life which have overtones of distaste and disapproval.
Two such terms are *maquinismo* and *cosificación*. *Maquinismo*, ac-

cording to Pierre Maxime Schuhl in an essay published in 1955, is a two-edged axe. It can be used to advance some of man's interests, but the other edge is always there to destroy the traditional values of Hispanic culture.[39] Alberto Wagner de Reyna, Peruvian diplomat, warns that both the Marxist "comrade" and the "self-made man" of the United States culture tend to dehumanize.[40] In what is regarded as one of the most important books written on nationalism in Latin America in recent decades, Gustavo Adolfo Otero does not see in technology one of the factors that will help to develop the kind of constructive nationalism he wants and advocates.[41] Examination of essays and volumes on economic history and theory are useful in understanding the attitudes of Latin Americans in respect to technology and technological change of the kind envisaged by our foreign economic aid programs.[42]

There is, of course, a voluminous literature critical of United States investments and the operation of United States companies in Latin America. I have hundreds of such references in my files, and I have described and documented anti-American attitudes elsewhere.[43] Some of the flavor of present-day hostility to United States private economic operations is seen in the argument of Vicente Saenz, perhaps the most prolific of the anti-American writers in Latin American today. He describes private foreign companies as "las sociedades anònimas internacionalmente succionadoras." He likens such companies to the pirates and slavers of the sixteenth and seventeenth centuries and asserts that they have contributed to Latin America none of the benefits of their civilization, no culture, not even hygiene. The "economic imperialism" of the "great North American plutocracy"—the "monopolies" of "foreign capital'—have left Latin American mines empty of their riches and soils exhausted of their fertility. The resources of Latin America are going down the "financial gullet" of the "insatiable monopolistic octopus," more fearful than the alligator or the crocodile. Those governments in Latin America which permit United States companies to operate are guilty, according to Saenz, of "entreguismo" (giveaways).[44]

In recent years even foreign economic aid has begun to come in for similar attacks by some Latin American writers. Javier Márquez, writing in 1946, says: "In Latin America, the fear is always present that the economic aid which the United States would lend her may have that political significance; moreover, there is a very widespread thesis to the effect that no economic advantage exists great enough to compensate for the threat of some political influence. It is an opinion very generally held among all those who do not benefit directly from that aid, and among those who do not consider that they benefit enough from it; that is to say among the great majority of the people." [45]   Professor Clovis Kernisan, writing in 1955, urges Haitians to put their cultural and political values ahead of any foreign economic aid or assistance they might receive. [46]   González Casanova, also writing in 1955, sees dangerous political implications in the Point Four Program. [47]

It is clear that the *pensadores* do not accept and advance the values of technology and technological change represented by the kind of technical assistance and economic aid the United States has made available in the past and apparently will make available in larger amounts in the future.   The fact that the *pensadores* either ignore technology, accept it grudgingly and with many misgivings, or outright oppose it means that they are an obstacle to the development of a successful foreign aid program in Latin America.

I should like now to turn to another method of testing Hispanic values with relationship to the foreign aid program of the United States.

The Value of Non-Utilitarian Education— The Cult of the Doctor

One of the best ways to test the status of the value which technical assistance and economic aid represent is to see what kinds of education educators and the state see fit to establish and what kinds of courses university students see fit to select when they have a choice. An understanding of higher education in historical perspective is relevant to the modern-day position of the university in Latin America.

The Portuguese monarchy did not establish a single university in Brazil during the colonial period.   As a result, the sons of the Brazilian elite went to the University of Coimbra in Portugal to complete their studies.   The University of Coimbra was founded in Lisbon on March 1, 1290.   It was moved back and forth from Lisbon to Coimbra several times until it was finally located in Coimbra in 1537.   Down to 1772 Coimbra had only the faculties of theology, canon law, and medicine.   The period 1557-1772 is regarded as one of open decay for the university.   When the university was reformed in 1772 the faculties of mathematics and philosophy were added to the program.   Although several universities have been established in Brazil in the twentieth century, the University of Coimbra is still the only one in Portugal.

The universities which were established in Spanish America were modeled largely on Spain's leading institution, the University of Salamanca. The University of Salamanca was headed by a rector elected each year from among the doctors of the community. University positions were valued for their great social prestige in the community. Professors were paid such small stipends for their services, however, that they had to teach on a part-time basis only. Indeed, teaching was more an avocation than a profession. A candidate for admission to one of the three professional schools—theology, law and medicine—had to present a bachelor's degree which was based on study of Latin grammar, rhetoric, philosophy (the ethics, metaphysics, and logic of Aristotle), and mathematics.

The most important universities in the New World were the Royal and Pontifical University of Mexico, founded by royal edict on September 21, 1551 and opened in 1553, and the University of San Marcos in Lima, which was opened 1551-1576. The universities were primarily schools of theology for the training of priests. Although not all the professors were clerics, the great majority were Dominicans, Franciscans, and Jesuits. The faculties were law, theology, and medicine. Specific branches of study at Mexico included theology, canons, decretals of the popes, Roman law, scripture, and rhetoric. Occasionally other work was offered in the universities such as Indian languages, scholastic methodology, mineralogy and botany (Mexico), anatomy (Lima), and elementary chemistry and astronomy. The courses were delivered in Latin. Both professors and students were required under oath to accept the theory of the divine right of the Spanish King and such doctrines of the Catholic Church as the Immaculate Conception. [48]

Other colonial universities were modeled on Mexico, San Marcos, and Salamanca. For example, in Chile the Royal University of San Felipe was inaugurated in 1747 and opened its doors in 1756. Like the other universities, it was predominantly ecclesiastical, medieval in spirit, and poorly equipped. Although San Felipe included mathematics in its curriculum, it never graduated a student in that field. Indeed, it did not have many students in any field. By the end of the colonial period, there were ten major and fifteen minor universities in Spanish America.

Every work on higher education in the colonial period I have seen has emphasized the excessively literary, abstract, and dogmatic nature of the courses and instruction. Students studied grammar, rhetoric, Latin, and religious dogma (apologetics, theology, ethics) to the virtual exclusion of natural science, modern languages or literature. The discoveries of Newton, Bacon, Descartes, Copernicus and others led to some changes toward the end of the colonial period. There was at least some recognition of experimental science and the inductive method. The methodology and content of the instruction created cultural values which still persist, according to Fernando de Azevedo: "This tendency to put quantity above quality, erudition above culture, the value of eloquence above the passion of ideas, the 'more or less' instead of exactitude, if it did not have its origin in it, certainly was strengthened by the traditional type of teaching . . . in which it was not so much a question of appreciation as of sheer accumulation, and in which the spirit of exactitude, profundity, penetration, critical and aesthetic maturity was (as it still is today) sacrificed to the acquisition of an encyclopedic learning." [49]

The university was one of the institutions in the colonial period with maximum status. Professors were willing to offer their services practically without compensation in order to enjoy the prestige which their position brought to them. The courses which they taught were largely non-utilitarian, certainly non-mechanical or technical, but this enhanced the prestige of education. Learning was valued for its own sake. The sons of the elite therefore sought education. The evidence indicates strongly that they sought education for the prestige it brought to them rather than for the training it might provide. Titles were the proof of education, and they were avidly sought. Marcondes calls this *bacharelismo* in Brazil. Each university student took pride in his enormous ruby ring, the symbol of prestige he was permitted to wear by reason of his position. [50]

Change occurs at varying rates of speed in all cultures. Certainly higher education in Latin America has changed since the colonial period. However, it is also true that the colonial institutions have directly influenced the Latin American universities of today: (1) higher education still has maximum status in the community; (2) learning is still regarded as a value in itself, and therefore the courses offered still tend to be theoretical, non-empirical, and non-utilitarian; (3) the symbols of education are still passionately sought and service to the community which titles should guarantee is largely avoided. Almost everyone wants to be a medical doctor who does not practice, a doctor of pharmacy who does not mix prescriptions, a doctor of engineering who does not build, even a doctor of veterinary science who does not personally inject the diseased animal with the medicine it needs. The high status of titles such as *doctor*, *Lic.*, *Ing.*, and *Arq.* is seen in the excessive use of the symbols. Everyone has his calling card with whatever symbol of status he can claim ostentatiously displayed. Letters are signed with the title added. Name plates for homes and apartments display the information. Men are careful to address each other in the ceremonial fashion. In politics the *doctor* and *general* compete with each other for control of government. The Pan American Union publishes periodically a directory of the chiefs of state and cabinet ministers of the American republics. Almost any issue demonstrates the point I am making. I have in front of me the directory as revised to August 7, 1953. Starting with Argentina one finds a government made up of four generals, one captain, one admiral, twelve doctors, and only seven men who do not list titles. In Cuba the government was composed of one general, thirteen doctors, and four ministers who did not list a title (not counting the ministers without portfolio). [51]

The figures on enrollment in institutions of higher learning in Latin America show that relatively few students study to be scientists, technicians, inventors, businessmen, administrators, agronomists, or research specialists. Practically none of the graduate students conduct scientific research in the human and physical resources of their own countries with a view to discovering ways in which the general interest and welfare might specifically be advanced. I shall review the evidence mainly for the period immediately following World War II and then for the most recent period for which I have been able to obtain figures.

Germani shows that university enrollment figures for Argentina by percentages were as follows for 1917 and 1944: [52]

	1917	1944
MEDICINE	44	34
SCIENCE, ENGINEERING	22	26
LAW	20	20
ECONOMIC SCIENCES	4	12
HUMANITIES	5	8

Apstein and Crevenna found that in 1942 the University of the Republic (Uruguay) had 1,541 students enrolled in law and notarial practice and 1,159 students in medicine out of a total of 4,679. There were only 61 students enrolled in agriculture and 348 in engineering. [53] Pendle reported in 1952 that students in the University in Uruguay were enrolled as follows: [54]

LAW AND THE SOCIAL SCIENCES	3,100
MEDICINE	1,300
CHEMISTRY AND PHARMACY	1,000
HUMANITIES AND SCIENCES	900
ECONOMICS	700

ENGINEERING	500
ARCHITECTURE	410
DENTISTRY	250
AGRICULTURE	240
VETERINARY SCIENCE	140

In Colombia there are 35 public and 17 private institutions of higher education. Some of these universities have only one faculty, that of law. Others have only two faculties, law and medicine. Of the some 600 degrees granted each year, law and medicine have the largest number in the early years since World War II.[55] During the years 1937 to 1942 inclusive, the four universities of Ecuador granted 524 degrees, 400 of which were in law and medicine.[56] An official report of 1949 stated that in Ecuador law and medicine had equal registration with 28 per cent each. Engineering was third with 12 per cent.[57] The enrollment figures for the National University in Mexico for 1944 show medicine to be first with 5,031 students and jurisprudence second wtih 2,220.[58] At the University of Havana for 1942-43 the faculties with the greatest enrollments were: law, 2,813; education, 1,988, and medicine 1,645.[59] In 1945 at the University of Santo Domingo law and medicine had 732 students out of the total of 1,241 for the entire university. At the University of Haiti, medicine and law were one and two in enrollment.[60] In 1946 at the University of El Salvador law and medicine together had 662 students out of a total of 935. Law and medicine had 654 students out of 1,620 at the University of San Carlos in Guatemala in 1945. There were 232 students in law and medicine at the Central University of Nicaragua in 1945-46 [61]

In order to bring enrollment figures down to date, I wrote to what I considered to be the 80 most important institutions of higher learning in Latin America.[62] In order to be sure that the letter was worded properly, I consulted with colleagues as well as Latin American friends. I asked for total enrollment by fields for the most recent year for which such figures were available. Out of the 80 letters, I have so far received 33 replies. Of the 33 replies, 21 contained enough of the information I sought to warrant use in this sample. Sometimes such inquiries are not answered for a year or more. Some of the reasons I did not receive immediately a larger number of replies are: (1) some of the universities were closed down for political reasons; (2) some were in a state of reorganization; (3) some were not in session; and (4) some no doubt were not interested in my project.

These more recent figures, mainly for 1956 and 1957, substantiate the generalizations I made earlier about the nature of student choices in Latin American institutions of higher learning. A large percentage of the students enter the traditional fields of law, medicine, and engineering. For example, I devised a sample which included 13 universities from 8 countries which all had law, medicine, and engineering schools plus the figures for all the colleges and universities of Brazil for the years 1950-52. The total number of students in all of these universities was 82,135, out of which 54,540 or almost 66½ percent were in law, medicine, and engineering. Law, medicine, and engineering were the top three choices in Brazil (composite figures for 115 colleges and universities) and in 9 out of the other 13 universities in the sample.

It should be reiterated that the traditional fields of law, medicine, and engineering do not provide the kind of training which encourages the technological changes the foreign aid program contemplates. Empirical evidence based on the past experience and performance of the Latin American countries demonstrates this point. Law is perhaps the least related of these subjects to technology. Although medicine can contribute indirectly to technological change by improving the health of the people of a country, in fact many Latin Americans with the medical degree do not practice. The same is true with engineering. Both medicine and engineering are frequently taught more at theoretical than practical levels in Latin American countries. There are notable exceptions, of course. The Universidad Téchnica Federico Santa María at Valparaiso, Chile is a high level engineering school where the training is designed to produce working engineers. However, the enrollment at the Universidad Téchnica Santa María is small. For 1956 it was: Mechanical, Electrical and Chemical Engineering, a 6-year course, with a mathematics major required for entrance, 169 students; Constructores Civiles, a 4-year course, with a mathematics major required for entrance, 23 students; in addition, there were 287 students enrolled in an institute and in a school in which the training is in part professional and technical and in part preparatory for entrance to the two advanced schools above.

In contrast, the figures indicate that training to become farmers, veterinaries, specialists in animal husbandry, miners, or businessmen is almost always far down on the list of preferences. In Brazil, for example, there were 30 schools of law with 11,455 students and only 12 schools of agriculture with 1,188 students, a ratio of almost 10 law students to each student in agriculture. There were only 539 students studying veterinary science in all of Brazil. Argentina depends on agriculture and stock raising for a large part of its national income, yet at the Universidad Nacional de La Plata, there were in 1956 2,169 students in Juridical and Social Science and only 62 students in Agronomy and 42 students in Veterinary Science. Although I found 6,642 students in Medicine and 2,519 in Law and Social Science at the Universidad Nacional de Córdoba in Argentina, neither Agriculture nor Animal Husbandry was included in the 7 other *facultades* or colleges. At the Universidad de Nuevo León in México, there were 1,009, 682, and 585 students in Medicine, Engineering, and Law respectively, but only 55 students in Agronomy. At the Universidad de San Carlos de Guatemala, Agronomy with 92 students had by far the smallest enrollment of any of the colleges. Engineering had 865 students, Juridical and Social Science 862 and Medicine 652. The figures were similar at the Universidad Nacional de Asunción, Paraguay: Agronomy and Veterinary Science were least, each with 24 students, whereas Medicine, Economics, and Law had 503, 422, and 352 students respectively. At the Universidad Central del Ecuador (Quito, Ecuador) Agronomy had 111 students and Veterinary Medicine 63 students, but Medicine, Engineering, and Law had 559, 337, and 336 students respectively. Eleven universities in the total sample had no schools of Agriculture, Agronomy, Animal Husbandry, or Veterinary Science listed at all. In this critique I have focused on agriculture and related fields. I could just have easily demonstrated the abhorrence for technical, mechanical, business, or practical fields by reviewing other segments of the statistics from the sample.

Some Mexican institutions of higher learning show somewhat of a trend away from the heavy emphasis on non-technological fields, but the most interesting single deviation from the general impression is found in the Universidad de Panamá which for 1955-56 had the following enrollment:

PHILOSOPHY, LETTERS AND EDUCATION	810
PUBLIC ADMINISTRATION AND COMMERCE	553
NATURAL SCIENCES AND PHARMACY	436
ENGINEERING AND ARCHITECTURE	231
LAW AND POLITICAL SCIENCE	120
MEDICINE	70

No attempt has been made to judge the level or type of instruction in the institutions reviewed. However, in two separate studies published in 1950, Beals and Gillin are critical. Beals wrote, "South American social science, until recently, was almost wholly in the nineteenth century European tradition." Beals also stated: "The scientific approach in any field is of relatively recent development in

South America and in many countries still enjoys rather low esteem." In respect to curricula and teaching methodology Beals reported: "In the newer social science curricula the professional viewpoint persists. Specialization begins in the first year and there is little broad interdisciplinary training. On the other hand, the approach is often traditional, abstract, and highly theoretical. Teaching of research methods is almost unknown and even where a thesis is required for a doctorate, usually granted after the fifth year, there is rarely any original research involved as this is customarily understood in the United States."[64]

In July of 1950, the Department of Social Sciences of UNESCO sent Professor John Gillin to Argentina, Chile, Peru, Bolivia, Ecuador and Columbia for a period of four months to study the status of the social sciences in those countries. He spent about three weeks in each country. In all he interviewed more than 300 teachers and students and visited about 40 institutions. Some of his findings which are relevant to this study are: (1) measured by North American and European standards the social sciences in Latin America are inadequately organized and defective in research methodology; (2) no modern course in statistics is required in any of the countries; (3) French and Spanish speculative and philosophical methodology are preferred to empirical research.[65]

Latin American governments and United States agencies aid graduates of Latin American universities to come to the United States for additional instruction. It is to be expected that most of such students will select courses of study in the scientific and technical fields, because the terms of their scholarships or grants frequently make such selection necessary. However, exact information has not been available. I therefore wrote to the graduate schools of all universities in the United States with about 2,000 graduate students or more enrolled in 1956. Out of the 42 graduate schools I contacted, I received 38 replies.

Cursory examination of the statistical data in this sample suggests that Latin Americans enrolled in graduate schools in the United States are more inclined to select utilitarian, practical, and technical courses of study than in the case with Latin American students in their own universities. However, closer examination of the figures reveals that even in the United States large numbers of Latin Americans prefer to work in fields that are more theoretical and cultural than scientific and practical. At least this can be said: Latin America has produced more doctors of law than their culture has required for hundreds of years. Specialization in law surely should not have high priority among Latin American graduate students in the United States if their desire is to contribute to rapid technological change and the raising of standards of living in their respective countries. At the other extreme, one of the things Latin America most desperately needs to alleviate widespread poverty is modern, efficient, scientific agriculture. Now, if we add together all the figures for agriculture, agricultural economics, soils, soils science, poultry husbandry, agronomy, agricultural extension, plant pathology, dairy husbandry, dairy industry, horticulture, and veterinary science, we get 49 graduate students in all out of a total of 466. At the same time, there were 45 Latin American graduate students enrolled in law. There were only 28 students enrolled in business administration and business and public administration. There were, on the other hand, 20 students doing their graduate work in languages, mainly Spanish and English! And out of the total of 466 graduate students enrolled in universities in the United States (in the sample for 1956-57), only 2 were in commerce.

The Value of Leisure and Noble Employment

Hispanic culture has long been characterized by the belief that leisure ennobles and labor, especially technical labor, degrades. Indeed, this psychological attitude toward production probably explains better than any other single factor why the Latin American countries are, in varying degrees, backward in the material sense. The values in Hispanic culture with respect to work and leisure have a direct and important relationship to technical assistance aid programs of the United States.

The value of leisure and the hostility to technical pursuits can be traced back hundreds of years in Hispanic culture. By the time of the discovery of the New World late in the fifteenth century, Spain was, in terms of political power at least, an oligarchy of military, clerical, and landowning interests. The great grandees protected the lesser nobility in return for military aid when needed. The nobility in general protected and defended the small class of landowners, skilled artisans, and free laborers in return for service, agricultural produce, or money. The rural masses were bound to the soil as serfs. The Saracen invasion of 711 ruptured the religious, cultural, and political unity which was achieved under Visigothic domination (about 476 A.D.—711 A.D.). For eight centuries Christian-Visigothic Spain attempted sporadically to reconquer territories seized by the Moors. The Moors were dominant in Portugal from 711-1244. The *reconquista* exaggerated the rôle and importance of the *caballero* or knight. It created the cult of the chivalrous man on horseback. In addition, the Church took on military functions. Religious leaders led troops into battle. Monasteries were fortresses and staging centers for forays against the Moors. Finally, the *reconquista* strengthened the large landholder who increased his properties as territory was retaken from the Moors. There were, then, centuries in which the rôles of the knight, the priest, and the soldier were glorified, and in which the rôles of the businessman, banker, and trader were debased. During the Middle Ages large numbers of Jews emigrated to the Iberian peninsula to take advantage of what was then a relatively tolerant environment. The Jews entered commerce, industry, banking, and the professions. The Moors distinguished themselves in the same general areas and were particularly noted as traders.

We know from studying the Siete Partidas, one of the greatest of all codes of law, that by the middle of the thirteenth century the social, political and economic relations of Jews, Moors, and Christians were regulated in detail. Certainly the policy of the Castilian monarchs was to isolate the Jews and Moors from the Christians. Jews were prohibited from consorting socially with Christians. They could not legally eat or drink or have sexual relations with Christians. The laws provided that both Jews and Moors should exhibit distinctive symbols of their status, so that Christians could easily recognize them and act accordingly. Catholic tolerance that existed dissipated in the fourteenth and fifteenth centuries. Galling restrictions to the Jews, such as the revocation of the usury laws, were characteristic of this period. Christian Spaniards accused Jews of responsibility for the black death and other catastrophes and massacred thousands of them. As the *reconquista* reached its climax in the fifteenth century, Jews and Moors came increasingly to be regarded as enemies, regardless of whether they were injuring Spaniards or not. Finally, a few months after the reconquest of Granada in 1492 the Jews were ordered by decree either to accept Christianity or leave Aragon and Castilla. Although some accepted Christianity (to be known as *conversos* or *marranos*), much larger numbers emigrated. Within a decade, persecution of the Moors began, and finally in 1609 they were expelled. The persecution of the Jews and the expulsion of the Moors were symbolic of the superiority of the values of the nobleman over the values of the bourgeoisie.

All scholarly evidence indicates that the *peninsulares* (Spanish born in Spain) dominated all aspects of social, economic, and political life of the Spanish-speaking colonies in the New World. A similar situation prevailed in Brazil. They were the religious and military officers, the viceroys, captains-general, governors, intendants, judges, heads of the universities, and great landowners. They demonstrated their social superiority through "conspicuous consumption." They tried to outdo each other in acquiring land; they took pride in their patriarchal "big house;" they wore expensive clothing and personal adornments, had many servants, and ostentatiously proclaimed their lack of association with manual, productive labor or any kind of vile employment. The manual, productive labor and all kinds and types of vile employment were performed first by the Indians through systems of forced labor and later by Negroes who were brought in as slaves and finally by the mixed races produced by *mestizaje* (miscegenation). [66]

The Industrial Revolution could have effected profound changes in the value system of the Hispanic countries. It is not the task of this paper to explore this economic phenomenon. Suffice to say that the Industrial Revolution in both its theoretical and practical aspects did not impress the ruling groups in Spain and in Latin America. All evidence indicates that its influence was much less in Hispanic culture than, for example, in Anglo-American culture. The generalization is largely accurate for almost all of Latin America since independence that manual labor and technical activity have low social status. Ostentatious use of leisure (travel, patronage of the arts, conspicuous consumption) has maximum social status. Everyone has contempt for the kind of labor described in the following terms: "manual, productive labor;" "menial labor;" "physical labor;" "labor with the hands;" "mechanical labor;" and "vile employment." These are terms used in works by Bunge, Ingenieros, Augustín García, González Prada and others who have written about Latin American psychology. These noted Latin American writers all agree that in Hispanic culture work degrades; leisure ennobles. [67] In practical terms the historical experiences of Spain and Portugal in the Iberian peninsula and in the New World help to explain such attitudes. In theoretical terms, usually the Greco-Latin philosophy of humanism which argues that man needs leisure in order to develop his spirit is put forth and supported. In 1955 in an important essay, Sérgio Buarque de Holanda attempts in part to explain why Spain and Portugal never accept work and production as values in themselves. He said: "Action on things, on the material universe, implies submission to an external object, acceptance of a law extraneous to the individual. Not being required by God, it does not add anything to His glory, nor does it increase our own dignity. On the contrary, one may say it impairs and vilifies it. Menial and mechanical labor searches a goal external to man, and intends to attain perfection of a work different from him." [68]

In referring to upper classes in Colombia, Smith writes: "Never under any circumstances short of almost absolute starvation will they permit themselves to engage in any activities involving manual labor, for that would stigmatize them as acknowledging a mean origin and position. This attitude toward work, the utter impossibility of viewing it as honorable and ennobling, . . ." [69] Fernando de Azevedo says that in Brazil there is a ". . . horror at manual labor, . . ." He quotes Pedro Calmon as saying, ". . . no one has ever seen a white man take an agricultural implement in his hands." [70] Zimmerman writes: "Being a good worker is not considered an admirable quality in Monte Serrat—or, for that matter, in Brazil generally. The Puritan notion of associating wealth with the sweat of one's brow is quite foreign to their thinking. The person who works least or, at any rate, is engaged in an occupation where he does not have to use his hands, is the one who is accorded most respect." [71] Pierson, in showing that manual labor lacks status in Brazil, says: "The common saying, Trabalho e para cachorro e negro (Work i.e., hard manual labor is for Negroes and dogs), reflects this fact. To work with one's hands has been in Brazil long considered debasing for a white man." Beals states: "The middle-class family with two cars and no servants, the banker who washes windows in preparation for his wife's tea party, the professor in overalls wielding a shovel in his garden—all are incomprehensible in Latin America." [72]

It follows logically from the general principle that work is debasing, leisure ennobling, that the highest status is accorded those who live in ostentation without labor of any kind. It is logical also that the professions which are obviously dissociated from manual, productive labor or mechanical employment should have high status. Some of such high status professions are: top level bureaucrat, lawyer, doctor, poet, priest, general. Government employment is sought most seriously. To be a high level bureaucrat is to enjoy high status. A sinecure is best of all lower-level positions. It is widely believed throughout Latin America that secondary education permits the individual to consider himself privileged never to work with his hands. The Brazilian scholar Oliveira Viana states the value of government employment in this way: "Among us politics is, above all, a means of life; one lives from the State, as one lives from Agriculture, Commerce, and Industry, and everyone finds it infinitely more sweet to live from the State than from anything else." [73]

At a somewhat lower level of status are professions which are as-

sociated with the management of mechanical labor. Examples of
these kinds of professions are: foremen, engineers, white collar employees, and managers of business and farm establishments. Those
who work, of course, have little or no status in society. However, it
should be noted that little honor is extended even among the upper
classes to the scientist, inventor, or entrepreneur.

The most important implications of the value of leisure and noble
employment are obvious. There is no incentive among the best educated and most cultured people in society to use their brains and
hands in production and distribution. They do enough to acquire
the leisure which they seek but no more. I was told by technicians
in Chile in 1955 that improvements in factory layout had the result
of encouraging the owners to make two trips to Paris each year instead of the customary one. The lower classes of people, of course,
have to work to live. However, they are affected by the value system of the inheritors of Hispanic culture. They do not work up to
their potentialities. Quite the contrary. They do everything possible
to obtain shorter hours, more vacations, more security from discipline
or loss of employment. Almost everywhere in Latin America one is
impressed with the large number of celebrations, fiestas, or holidays
which all classes enjoy. Redfield found in studying the Mexican
village of Tepoztlán that there were more than 60 annual fiestas of
2-7 days each. [74]

Both the theory and practice of capitalism suffer in Latin America
from the value system. Indeed, capitalism has low status as an
economic system. However, almost everywhere in Latin America
the ruling classes are alarmed by the increasing demands of the
lower classes for higher material standards of living. Almost everywhere they seek an easy way out. Whereas capitalism has low status,
collectivism has high status. However, even when a country has been
able to achieve socialism, the basic values with respect to work persist. For example, one has only to study the case of Uruguay, the
country which has achieved the maximum development toward socialism. The public servants are many, obviously many more than are
needed to operate the Government's enterprises. They have acquired
the 29-hour work week for themselves, and most of them do not work
the full 29 hours. Indeed, I have found in visiting one government
ministry or building after another groups of serenely idle government
workers in every one of them.

There are secondary effects of the value of leisure and the hostility
to mechanical labor. In my opinion it helps to explain two seeming
contradictions—the widespread habit of gambling, particularly with

lottery tickets, and the habit of investing in land in the country or apartment or office buildings in the city. All classes of people have a deep, almost hysterical impulse, to acquire the capital they need to live the kind of life the value system requires for maximum dignity and status in the community by means other than labor. To achieve one's objective instantly, with one turn of the cards, with one lucky drawing of a lottery ticket is a universal drive. Conversely, the value of leisure and the hostility to mechanical employment would lead to the implication that Latin American peoples are not encouraged to thrift and savings so that capital might be accumulated and used for the purposes of investment. Research seems to bear out this point, as Roger Caillois showed in an interesting short study in 1949.[75] If a person has money to invest, it is logical that he would choose to put the money in land or office or apartment buildings, because his *rentas* from such activities are eminently respectable. But if he invests in vile activities, such as manufacturing or commerce, it is logical that he should do so as speculation, hoping to get in and get out. Those who have invested their money permanently in manufacturing, industry, or commerce take the position that they should sell to as few people as possible at the highest profit per unit rather than to as many people as possible at lowest possible profit per unit.

Concluding Remarks

Anyone who bothers to read the reports of the committees, commissions, and study groups which have examined the technical assistance and economic aid programs in Latin America will observe instantly that virtually no attention has been given to cultural values. The fact that cultural values are never cited as important obstacles to the achievement of the ideals of the technical assistance and economic aid programs lead logically to the inference that those who drafted the reports recommending the continuance and expansion of such programs believe that the values of Hispanic culture and the values of American culture are sufficiently similar to excuse any detailed examination of the subject. Indeed, I have the strong feeling that the supporters of economic aid for Latin America assume that the values of American culture and the values of Hispanic culture are largely the same—that what motivates the American is what motivates the Latin American, that what we want is what he wants, that the procedures which we find meaningful are the procedures he finds meaningful and so on.

My own research and thinking have led me to quite different conclusions. This is disturbing. The National Planning Association had

$440,000, the services of about 50 individuals, and three years to prepare its findings and to present its recommendations. Aside from my own time, I have expended only about $10 on postage to write to Latin American and United States universities to acquire data I needed. The books and documents are in public libraries. Surely the NPA has considered all the materials I have examined and many times more and found them largely irrelevant and perhaps meaningless. On the other hand, I have found such materials both relevant and meaningful. It is my conviction that not only the values which I have selected for discussion in this paper but the entire value system of Hispanic culture should be studied most seriously by the most serious scholars and practioners in international relations as a guide to the policies the United States should follow with respect to Latin America.

Let us assume that the anthropologists are correct in asserting that there are no superior races. Let us assume that the moral principle of the brotherhood of man has validity. Let us assume that the scientists have so far not been able to measure accurately the full mental or even physical potentialities of human beings. From these assumptions, it follows that what men believe to be important and unimportant and the way these beliefs are combined in social, economic, and political institutions determine in large degree how men will live. There are a few areas in Latin America, of which Haiti is the major illustration, in which population pressure on land has produced economic problems which are difficult to solve. However, in most of Latin America there are good people, good land, and good resources. Why are they not used to produce higher material standards of living for all classes of people than is the case at the present time? The research in this short paper demonstrates to me that it is not because the theory and practices of technology have been hidden from the leaders of Hispanic society. Quite the contrary. It has always been easy to learn about technical matters in almost all fields. Frequently such information can be obtained for the price of a letter and a stamp. The evidence indicates that the *pensadores* have not in the past and do not in the present see in technology a value which should be grasped eagerly and made a central part of Hispanic culture. The evidence indicates that when people have an opportunity to obtain higher education and to make a choice as to what kind of education they want, they choose courses of study which are more in the humanistic tradition than in the industrial, scientific tradition. Finally, the evidence indicates that mechanical work and production have low status and leisure high status generally throughout Latin America.

Therefore, on the basis of only the selected case studies of this paper, I would conclude that if Latin America desires a Revolution, a fundamental breaking with the past, in at least the economic aspects of life, what Latin America needs more than anything else is ideas and values. There have been few such revolutions in the last 2,000 years of Western Civilization. One of the few began in the United States a relatively short time ago. This was in large part a revolution that was made possible by ideas and values. In making this statement, I am aware of the school of thought which argues that the United States is rich because the riches and resources were here for the taking. I have to reject this point of view if for no other reason than the fact that I have observed riches and resources in Latin America which seemed available for the taking. In my opinion, the greatest contribution the United States could make to Latin America would be to share our knowledge of the ideas and values which provided the motivation and incentive to all men to develop and express their talents. I am inclined to believe this could be accomplished best (1) at the intellectual level by serious analyses of the origin, nature, development, and accomplishments of the values of United States culture, beginning with economic matters; and (2) by demonstration programs, in which larger numbers of Latin Americans might live in the United States for at least a year working in and observing United States culture. From what I could see in South America in the summer of 1955, the activities of the United States Information Agency are ineffective in the realm of ideas. The program is oriented to a kind of low-level advertising campaign involving the use of slogans and pamphlets condemning communism and boasting about the United States rather than the serious, scholarly approach which would have more effect with the intellectuals who have status and influence in Latin America.

With specific reference to the economic problems of Latin America, it is relevant to call attention again and again to the fact that the great economic progress achieved by the United States was through voluntary, private procedures. Government aided through research, advice, adjudication, regulation, and rules of free, fair competition, but the initiative in production and distribution was almost entirely private. I am convinced that voluntary, private methods of making technical assistance and economic aid available are more practical and more theoretically defensible in the short run and in the long run in Latin America than public programs of the type used in the past and suggested for the future. This follows from the nature of American capitalism, which is based on the incentive to produce efficiently and to serve a large market. Men think long and hard before they invest capital that has been accumulated through work and sacrifice. Once they invest their capital, they have incentive to make the enterprise successful. United States citizens probably have about $7,000,000,000 in direct investments in Latin America at the present time.[76] This is far more important in a quantitative sense than operations of the United States Government in aid programs in Latin America. In a qualitative sense, I think it can be assumed that the private, voluntary enterprises are making more contributions to the sharing of technological skills than are all government programs put together. Other voluntary private groups, such as churches, foundations, universities, labor unions, and the like in most cases have a focus that like private enterprise is sharpened in a practical constructive direction.

[1] See National Bureau of Economic Research, *Studies in Income and Wealth* (New York, 1947, Volume X), pp. 160-244; Simon G. Hanson, *Economic Development in Latin America* (Washington, D. C.: Inter-American Affairs Press, 1951), p. 1.

[2] *Congressional Record*, April 18, 1957, p. A3106. The figures were prepared for Rep. Lawrence H. Smith, Wisconsin, by Hermann Ficker of the Legislative Reference Service of the Library of Congress.

[3] *New York Times*, May 6, 1957.

[4] See, for example: Inis L. Claude, Jr., *Swords Into Plowshares. The Problems and Progress of International Organization* (New York: Random House, 1956); Farrington Daniels and Thomas M. Smith (Editors), *The Challenge of Our Times* (Minneapolis: Burgess Publishing Company 1953); L. Larry Leonard, *International Organization* (New York: McGraw-Hill Book Co., 1951); Gerard J. Mangone, *A Short History of International Organization* (New York: McGraw Hill Book Co., 1954); Amry Vandenbosch and Willard N. Hogan, *The United Nations: Background, Organization, Functions, Activities* (New York: McGraw-Hill Book Co.. 1952). For the Inter-American system, see Arthur P. Whitaker, *The Western Hemisphere Idea: Its Rise and Decline* (Ithaca: Cornell University Press, 1954); Charles G. Fenwick, *The Inter-American Regional System* (New York: The Declan X. McMallen Co., 1949); Lawrence S. Eagleburger, *Organization of American States,* M. A. University of Wisconsin, 1957.

[5] *Congressional Record,* April 15, 1957, p. 5072.

[6] *New York Times,* August 6, 1956.

[7] See Acierto (pseud.), "A Marshall Plan for Latin America," *Inter-American Economic Affairs* (September, 1947), pp. 3-20. See also original papers of Latin Americans at Conference on Responsible Freedom in the Americas, Columbia University, October 25-30, 1954 and published version of the papers edited by Angel del Rio, *Responsible Freedom in The Americas* (Garden City, New York: Doubleday and Co., Inc., 1955), pp. 47, 52, 221-222.

[8] Eagleburger, *Organization of American States, op. cit.,* Chapter V.

[9] *New York Times*, January 10, 1957.

[10] *New York Times*, February 13, 1957; March 6, 1957.

[11] *New York Times*, March 8, 1957.

[12] *New York Times*, April 9, 1957.

[13] *New York Times*, May 10, 1957; May 13, 1957.

[14] Documentation Incorporated, *Technical Assistance in Latin America; a Bibliographical study* prepared for the Ford Foundation (Washington, D. C., 1952).

[15] Merle Curti and Kendall Birr, *Prelude To Point Four* (Madison: University of Wisconsin Press, 1954). *See* also, Edwin A. Book, *Fifty Years of Technical Assistance: Some Administration Experiences of U.S. Voluntary Agencies* (Chicago: Public Administration Clearing House, 1954).

[16] Published under the general title *Technical Cooperation in Latin America*, the reports of the National Planning Association were issued under the following subtitles: *The Role of Universities in Technical Cooperation* (1955); *Technical Cooperation-Sowing the Seeds of Progress* (1955); *Organization of United States Government for Technical Cooperation* (1955); Arthur T. Mosher, *Case Study of The Agriculture Program of Agar in Brazil* (1955); *Administration of Bilateral Technical Cooperation* (1956); *Recommendations For The Future* (1956). See also, James G. Maddox, *Technical Assistance By Religious Agencies In Latin America* (Chicago: University of Chicago Press, 1956).

[17] *NPA, Technical Cooperation In Latin America: Recommendations For The Future, op. cit.*, pp. 4, 5, 6, 27, 86, 87.

[18] *Ibid.*, p. 9.

[19] This is an unsupported generalization with respect to a subject on which little has been written in English. However, full description of the social classes in Latin America along with detailed annotation can be seen in two chapters in a forthcoming volume I am now preparing for publication for the Crowell Company, entitled: *The Nature of Power In Latin American Politics.*

[20] "The Ideological Bases of Anti-Americanism in Latin America," paper prepared for conference on Twentieth Century Diplomacy, University of Kansas, August, 1957.

[21] Eduardo Barrios, *El hermano asno* (Buenos Aires: Agencia general de librería y publicaciones, 1923, 2 ed.), pp. 235; *Un perdido* (Santiago: Editorial Chilena, 1918), pp. 516; *El niño que enloqueció de amor* (Santiago: C. J. Nascimento, 1920), pp. 201; *Páginas de un pobre diablo* (Santiago: Nascimento, 1923), pp. 228.

[22] Ciro Alegría, *El mundo es ancho y ajeno* (Santiago: Ediciones Ercilla, 1941), pp. 509. This novel has been translated into English by Harriet de Onís and published by Farrar & Rinehart in 1941.

[23] José Eustasio Rivera (1889-1928), *The Vortex* (translated from Spanish by Earle K. James. New York: G. P. Putnam Sons, 1935), pp. 320.

[24] Benjamín Subercaseaux, *Jimmy Button* (Santiago: Ediciones Ercilla, 1950), pp. 907.

[25] See José Lins do Rego, *Bangué* (Rio de Janeiro: J. Olympio, 1934), pp. 310; *Doidinho* (Rio de Janeiro: J. Olympio, 2 ed., 1935), pp. 278; *Historias da velha Totonia* (Rio de Janeiro: J. Olympio, 1935), pp. 114; *Menino de engenho* (Rio de Janeiro: Adersen, editores, 1932), pp. 183; *O moleque Ricardo* (Rio de Janeiro: J. Olympio, 1935), pp. 283; *Pedro Bonita* (Rio de Janiro: J. Olympio, 1938), pp. 373; *Pureza* (Rio de Janeiro: J. Olympio, 1935), pp. 347; *Riacho doce* (Rio

de Janeiro: J. Olympio, 1939), pp. 372; *Usina* (Rio de Janeiro: J. Olympio, 1936), pp. 392.

[26] *See* A. Torres Rioseco, *Ensayos sobre literatura latinoamericana* (Berkeley: University of California Press, 1953), pp. 207. There are specialized studies, such as Fernando Díez de Medina, *Literatura boliviana; introducción al estudio de las letras nacionales del tiempo mítico a la producción contempóranea La Paz:* Alfonso Tejerina, 1953), pp. 379.

[27] Mariano Azuela, *Los fracasados* (México, D. F.: Ediciones Botas, 4 ed. 1949) pp. 249; *mala yerba* (English translation by Anita Brenner, New York: Farrar & Rinehart, Inc., 1932), pp. 244.

[28] Mariano Azuela, *Andrés Pérez, Madeista* (México, D. F.: Blanco Y. Botas, 1911), pp. 122; *Los de abajo* (México, D. F.: Ediciones Botas, 3 ed., 1949), pp. 261; *Los caciques* (México, D. F. Ediciones de "La Razón," 1931), pp. 177. *See* also Lesley Byrd Simpson (translator), Mariano Azuela. *Two Novels of Mexico; The Flies, The Bosses* (Berkeley: University of California Press, 1956).

[29] Martín Luis Guzmán, *El águila y la serpiente* (English translation by Harriet de Onís; New York: Knopf 1930), pp. 360; *La sombra del caudillo* (México, D. F.: Ediciones Botas, 1938), pp. 342; *Memorias de Pancho Villa* (México, D. F.: Ediciones Botas, 4 volumes, 1938, 1939, 1939, 1940), pp. 328, 336, 362, 359.

[30] Gregorio López y Fuentes, *El indio* (English translation by Anita Brenner, Indianapolis, Bobbs-Merrill Co., 1937), pp. 256.

[31] Roque Estrada, *Liberación* (México, D. F.: Editorial Cultura, 1933), pp. 418.

[32] Roque Estrada, *La Revolución y Francisco I. Madero* (Guadalajara, 1912) pp. 502.

[33] Mauricio Magdaleno, *La tierra grande* (México, D. F.: Espasa-Calpe, 1949), pp. 224.

[34] Emilio Rabasa,*La bola; la gran ciencia; el cuarto poder; moneda falsa* (México, D. F.: Editorial Porrua, 1948, 2 volumes), pp. 360, 398.

[35] Angel Flores, "Latin American Literature," *The Americana Annual* (1957), pp. 445-446.

[36] Miguel Angel Asturias, *Viento fuerte* (Buenos Aires: Losada, 1950), pp. 205; *see* also Miguel Angel Asturias, *El señor presidente* (Buenos Aires: Losada, 1948), pp. 276; Joaquín Gutiérrez, *Puerto Limón* (Santiago: Nascimento, 1950), pp. 280.

[37] Baltazar Castro, *Un hombre por el camino* (Santiago: Cultura, 1950), pp. 240.

[38] See Anson C. Piper, "El yanqui en las novelas de Rómulo Gallegos," *Hispania* (noviembre de 1950), pp. 338-341.

[39] Pierre Maxime Schuhl, *Maquinismo y filosofía* (Buenos Aires: Editorial Galatea-Nueva Vision, 1955), pp. 122 *passim*.

[40] Alberto Wanger de Reyna, *Destino y vocación de Iberoamérica* (Madrid: Ediciones Cultura Hispánica, 1954), pp. 124. *See* especially p. 37.

[41] Gustavo Adolfo Otero, *Sociología del nacionalismo en Hispano-América* (Quito: Ediciones del Grupo América, 1947), *passim*.

[42]*See* Carlos de Moyano Llerena, "El desarrollo industrial en América Latina," *Revista de Ciencias Económicas,* Universidad Nacional de Buenos Aires (no. 311, junio de 1947), pp. 395-412; (no. 312-313, julio-agosto de 1947), pp. 465-494; Jesùs Silva Herzog, *El pensamiento económico en México* (México: Fondo de Cultura Económica, 1947), pp. 199; Aníbal Sánchez Reulet (Ed.), *La filosofía latinoamericana contemporánea* (Washington, D. C.: Unión Panamericana, 1949), pp. 370; Luis Roque Gondra, et al., *El pensamiento económico latinoamericano* (México, D. F.: Fondo de Cultura Económica, 1945), pp.

333; Eugenio Gudin, *Ensaios sobre problemas economicos da atualidade* (Rio de Janeiro: Ed. Civilizacao brasileira, 1945), pp. 235; Julián Alienes y Urosa, *Características fundamentales de la economía cubana* (La Habana: Banco Nacional de Cuba, 1950), pp. 405.

[43] Conference on Twentieth Century Diplomacy, University of Kansas, August 1957, paper on: "Ideological Bases of Anti-Americanism in Latin America."

[44] Vicente Saenz, *Hispano américa contra el coloniaje* (México, D. F.: Unión Democrática Centroamericana, 1949), pp. 77, 128-129, 209, 217, 222, 226, 251. I do not wish to duplicate documentation on this point which I have made available elsewhere (see footnote 43 above), but some of the following references might be particularly useful: Samuel Gorban, *Integración económica de América Latina* (Rosario: Editorial Rosario, 1951), pp. 166; A. Pinto Santa Cruz, *Hacia nuestra independencia económica* (Santiago de Chile: Editorial del Pacífico, 1953), pp. 219; Alberto Cornejo S., *Programas políticos de Bolivia* (Cochabamba, Bolivia: Imprenta Universitaria, 1949), pp. 373. The Cornejo volume contains the programs of the MNR, which has been governing in Bolivia since 1952, and other leftist parties. Fernando Morales Balcells, *La industria del cobre en Chili* (Santiago: Tall. Gráf. Santiago, 1946), pp. 152; José Humberto Hernández Cobos, *Crisis de la democracia. Su preservación y defensa* (Guatemala: Universidad de San Carlos, 1950), pp. 77; Baldomera Sánchez Camacho, *El problema colonial de América* (México, D. F.: Universidad de México, 1950), pp. 108; Andrés Ponte, *Como salvar a Venezuela* (New York: Carlos López Press, 1937), pp. 339; Julio V. González, *Nacionalización del petróleo* (Buenos Aires: El Ateneo, 1947), pp. 336; José Domingo Lavín, *En la brecha mexicana* (México, D. F.: E.D.I.A.P.S.A., 1948), pp. 305.

[45] Javier Márquez, "Remarks on Some Aspects of the Economic Relations between the United States and the Latin American Countries," *Some Economic Aspects of Postwar Inter-American Relations* (Austin: University of Texas Press, 1946), p. 62.

[46] Alain Turnier, *Les Etats-Unis et le marché haïtien* (Washington, D. C., 1955), pp. 354. *See* preface, which is written by Kernisan.

[47] Pablo González Casanova, *La ideología norteamericana sobre inversiones extranjeras* (México, D F.: Escuela Nacional de Economía, 1955), pp. 190.

[48] Lucás Ayarragaray, "Las universidades coloniales," *Revista de Derecho, Historia y Letras* (Buenos Aires, agosto, 1904), pp. 245-261; John Tate Lanning, *Academic Culture in the Spanish Colonies* (London: Oxford University Press, 1940), pp. 3-33.

[49] Fernando de Azevedo, *Brazilian Culture* (New York: Macmillan Co., 1950), p. 388.

[50] J. V. Freitas Marcondes, *A Sociological Study of The First Brazilian Legislation Relating to Rural Labor Unions*, M.A., University of Florida, 1953, p. 67.

[51] Pan American Union, *Chiefs of State and Cabinet Ministers of The American Republics* (Washington D. C., No. 30, Revised to August 7, 1953), pp. 1-2, 6-7.

[52] Gino Germani, "La clase media en la Argentina con especial referencia a sus sectores urbanos," *Materials Para El Estudio De La Clase Media En La América Latina* (Washington, D. C.: Unión Panamericana, I, 1950), p. 20.

[53] Theodore Apstein and Theo R. Crevenna, *The Universities of Paraguay and Uruguay* (Washington, D. C.: Pan American Union, Vol. 7, 1947), p. 46.

[54] George Pendle, *Uruguay* (London: Royal Institute of International Affairs, 1952), p. 31.

[55] W. O. Galbraith, *Colombia, A General Survey* (London: Royal Institute of International Affairs, 1953), p. 58.

[56] Cameron D. Ebaugh, *Education In Ecuador* (Washington, D. C.: Federal Security Agency, 1947), p. 80.

[57] República de Ecuador, *Educación, Ecuador: Informe a la Nación,* 1948-1949 (Quito: Talleres Graficos Nacionales, 1949), pp. 203-207.

[58] Theodore Apstein, *The Universities of Mexico* (Washington, D. C.: Pan American Union, Part I, Vol. 5, 1946), p. 20.

[59] Harriet Bunn and Ellen Gut, *The Universities of Cuba, The Dominican Republic, Haiti* (Washington, D. C.: Pan American Union, Vol. 4, 1946), p. 10.

[60] *Ibid.,* pp. 59, 83.

[61] Theodore Apstein, Ben F. Carruthers, Ellen Gut, *The Universities of Costa Rica, El Salvador, Guatemala ,Honduras, Nicaragua, Panama* (Washington, D. C.: Pan American Union, Vol. 6, 1947), pp. 42, 58, 98. *See* also Cameron D. Ebaugh, *Education in Nicaragua* (Washington, D. C.: Federal Security Agency, 1947), p. 45; Ebaugh, *Education in El Salvador* (Washington, D. C.: Federal Security Agency, 1947), p. 70.

[62] A list of these institutions is available upon request.

[63] George W. Ware and Lincoln Monteiro Rodrigues, *Report On The Agricultural and Veterinary Colleges of Brazil* (Rio de Janeiro: Escritorio Tecnico de Agricultura, 1954), p. 2.

[64] Ralph L. Beals, "The Social Sciences in South America," *Items* (Sosial Science Research Council, Vol. 4, Number 1, March, 1950), p. 1.

[65] John Gillin, "La situación de las ciencias sociales en seis países sudamericanos," *Ciencias Sociales* (Washington, D. C.: Unión Panamericana, febrero de 1953, num. 19), pp. 11-18.

[66] There are many works which describe the stigma attached to manual, productive, or technical kinds of employment during the colonial period. In preparing the chapters on the social classes in Latin America for a forthcoming volume on *The Nature of Power In Latin American Politics,* I found a voluminous literature. Some of the useful works are: José Antonio Saco, *Historia de la ésclavitud de los indios en el nuevo mundo seguida de la historia de los repartimientos y encomiendas* (La Habana: Cultural, 2 volumes, 1932);Silvio A. Zavala, "Evolución del régimen de trabajo en Hispanoamérica durante la época colonial," *Derecho del Trabajo* (Buenos Aires, junio de 1944), pp. 261-268; Sergio Bagú, *Estructura social de la colonia* (Buenos Aires: Librería "El Ateneo" Editorial, 1952), pp. 283; Affonso de Toledo Bandeira de Mello, *O trabalho servil no Brasil* (Rio de Janeiro: Ministerio do Trabalho, Industria e Commercio, 1936), pp. 90; Miguel Mejía Fernández, "El problema del trabajo forzado en América Latina," *Revista Mexicana de Sociología* (México, D. F., septiembre-diciembre de 1952), pp. 341-375; José de Barrasa y Múñoz de Bustillo, *El servicio personal de los indios durante la colonización española Aola en América* (Madrid, 1925), pp. 206; Hildebrando Castro Pozo (Ed.), *El yanaconaje en las haciendas piuranas* (Lima: Compañía de Impresiones y Publicidad, 1947), pp. 112; Pablo Enrique Cárdenas Acosta, *Del vasallaje a la insurreccíon de los Comuneros* (Tunja, Colombia, 1947), pp. 442.

[67] *See* Juan Agustín García, La ciudad indiana (Buenos Aires: A. Estrada y. cía., 2 ed., 1909), pp. xiv, 375; José Ingenieros, *El hombre mediocre* (Buenos

Aires: Vaccaro, 6 ed., 1918; first published in 1903), pp. 317; Manuel González Prada, *Horas de lucha* (Calloa: Tip. "Lux," 2 ed., 1924; first published in 1908), pp. 362. Many other sources use similar terms to show that work is debasing and degrading. *See* Olen E. Leonard, *Bolivia: Land, People and Institutions* (Washington, D. C.: Scarecrow Press, 1952), Ch. 6; Margaret A. Marsh, *The Bankers In Bolivia* (New York: The Vanguard Press, 1928), p. 22; E. Reginald Enock, *The Republics of Central and South America* (New York: Charles Scribner's Sons, 1913), pp. 349, 387; Luis E. Valcarcel, *Ruta cultural del Perú* (México, D. F.: Fondo de Cultura Económica, 1945), p. 26; Fernando de Azevedo, *Brazilian Culture, op. cit.,* p. 125; Donald Pierson, *Negroes In Brazil* (Chicago: University of Chicago Press, Third Impression, 1947), pp. 18, 161; Charles Wagley (Ed.), *Race and Class In Rural Brazil* (Paris: UNESCO, 1952), pp. 66, 133; Harry B. Hawthorn and Audrey Engle Hawthorn, "Stratification in a Latin American City," *Social Forces* (October, 1948), pp. 26, 28; José Ingenieros, *Sociología Argentina* (Buenos Aires: Editorial Losada S. A.., 1946), pp. 138, 140; Julio Vega, "Algunas características fundamentales del pueblo chileno," Revista *Geográfica de Chile* (abril de 1942), pp. 47-54; John Biesanz and Luke M. Smith, "Race Relations in Panama and the Canal Zone," *The American Journal of Sociology* (July, 1951), p. 9; Lowry Nelson, *Rural Cuba* (Minneapolis: University of Minnesota Press, 1950), p. 159; Lowry Nelson, "The Social Class Structure in Cuba," *Materiales Para El Estudio de la Clase Media en la America Latina* (Washington, D. C.: Unión Panamericana, II, 1950) pp. 51, 70; Paul Blanshard, *Democracy and Empire In The Caribbean* (New York: The Macmillan Company, 1947), James Bryce, *South America, Observations and Impressions* (New York: The Macmillan Company, 1914), p. 433; Albert Hale, *The South Americans* (Indianapolis: The Bobbs-Merill Company, 1907), pp. 280, 185.

[68] Sérgio Buarque de Holanda, *Raices del Brasil* (México: Fondo de Cultura Económica, 1955), p. 17. *See* review by G. Somolinos d'Ardois of the Sociedad Histórico Médica "Francisco Hernández" in the *Revista Intermericana de Bibliografía.*

[69] T. Lynn Smith, "Observations on the Middle Classes in Colombia," *Materiales Para El Estudio De La Clase Media En La America Latina* (Washington, D. C.: Unión Panamericana, VI, 1951), p. 13.

[70] Fernando de Azevedo, *Brazilian Culture, op. cit.,* pp. 93, 167.

[71] In Wagley, *Race and Class In Rural Brazil, op. cit.,* pp. 100-101.

[72] Ralph L. Beals, "Social Stratification in Latin America," *The American Journal of Sociology* (January, 1953), p. 339.

[73] Quoted in George C. A. Boehrer, *From Monarchy to Republic: A History of The Republican Party of Brazil,* 1870-1889 (Washington, D. C.: Catholic University of America, Ph.D., 1951), p. 13.

[74] Robert Redfield, *Tepoztlan, A Mexican Village* (Chicago: University of Chicago Press, 1931), p. 91.

[75] Roger Caillois, "Economic Quotidienne et Jeux de Hasard en Amerique Latine," *Cahiers Des Annales* (Paris: A. Colin, 1949), pp. 35-44. See also Efrén Araya Vergara, El juego y su repercusión en la vida económica y social del país (Santiago, Chile, 1951), pp. 47.

[76] Samuel Pizer and Frederick Cutler, "The Role of U. S. Investments in the Latin American Economy," *Survey of Current Business* (January, 1957), pp. 2-12 (reprint).

5: *The Envy Barrier*

Helmut Schoeck

Professor Stokes has described one type of intellectual—the pensadores—whose love for gracious living, whose disdain for technology and applied science contribute to the economic difficulties in Latin America. Yet there abounds also a more recent type of intellectual. He shares with the Latin pensadores a certain affinity for the seats of government, but in a different sense. And he is quite unlike the pensadores when it comes to dreaming grandiose thoughts. He does not care for sweet music and patios. His ideals are vast irrigation schemes, powerhouses, and steel mills. He might be called the restless intellectual. He is an aggressive technocrat. And yet, it is possible that his role in undeveloped countries is as unfortunate as the one of the pensadores. He is likely to try too much in the wrong places and directions with the wrong means. Moreover, he is likely to express himself to the population and its local and regional leaders unwittingly in terms which tend to strengthen their negative attitudes toward enterprise. These attitudes, of course, preceded the era of capitalism, but they must be suppressed by the ethos of a culture before a chain-reaction of self-sustained economic growth can get started.

By anti-entrepreneurial attitudes I mean a hostility to foreign and domestic individuals, families, and firms who work toward development.

This is not simply an "anti-capitalistic attitude," a hatred against foreigners who "extract the riches of the undeveloped country." The record of these nationalistic sentiments, their exploitation by domestic politicians, their effect of discouraging international investment, is well established. And so is their very reinforcement by Western aid—often misunderstood as gestures of atonement. [1]

By the anti-entrepreneurial attitude I mean more. It includes the spontaneous hatred in many communities against their own members who are about to become unequal due to their imagination, their hard work, or their acceptance of methods offered from outside. What makes the situation in many specific regions of the undeveloped world so unpromising is the apparent blending, and mutual reinforcement, of these attitudes.

Let us have a look at community life in the Near East. In this area of the world, it is said, Western economic development aid is required for political stability. But we lack a tenable theory explaining why these people stayed poor so long. Could it be that human groups are doomed to poverty as long as the emotion of envy remains overly excitable? In a recent article on the fellahins of Syria, Raymond E. Crist emphasizes the dysfunctional mechanism of social control:

"The rural villages seem permeated with an atmosphere of general malaise, the peasants in even the most remote areas being prey to suspicion and jealousy. A missionary doctor of nearly half a century's experience in the Near East told a revealing story. When he returned on one occasion from home leave in the United States he brought back with him some Golden Bantam seed corn, which he gave to a friend of his, a Moslem farmer in a small village. When the doctor saw his friend several months later he asked him how the corn was doing. Then the farmer had to confess: You see, I didn't plant the corn, because if I did my neighbors would pull it up. If I gave some of the seed to my neighbors, the other villagers would destroy it. If the whole village were given seed for a new crop, the next village would burn the new-fangled and superior crop. And so I thought it best not to plant it at all, and thus avoid trouble.

"The peasant imbibes with his mother's milk hatred, jealousy and mistrust of his neighbor." [2]

I have examined data from a wide range of cultures as well as consulted a number of experts on selected tribal cultures. To date nothing has come to light to weaken the following hypothesis. [3]

One of the major general brakes on economic growth is the envy barrier. It is partly due to the failure of a culture or civilization to offer non-invidious—even though perhaps irrational and mythological—explanations of differential success of its individual members. If I, myself, do not know, or at least suspect my neighbor of not knowing, why my crops or works are superior to his, I am inclined, in such cultures, to do as little as possible of what could make me an unequal.

Reo F. Fortune in his study of the people of Dobu gives a classic description of this "envy barrier". In Dobu ". . . a person who harvests a better crop of yams than his neighbors thinks of himself, and is thought of, as a successful thief." "Jealousy of possession is the keynote to the culture." "Towards the last months of the garden season . . . jealousy towards everyone else intensifies. The whole atmosphere is most closely related to the jealous watch over each other of man and wife."

And then Dr. Fortune makes a very interesting observation: ". . . it is not possible to say whether poverty has created the jealousy or vice versa. Either point of view could be put forward. Accordance is all that can be demonstrated, and in truth it is probable that the more accordance there is in the elements of a culture the stronger an intensification of the mutually agreeable elements will result. They will react upon one another."[4]

My own research with the Human Relations Area Files (Cross Cultural Survey) produced phenomena in dozens of cultures comparable to those which Fortune found in Dobu. Human groups and societies which have succeeded in de-emphasizing the mutual envy are rare exceptions. It seems highly probable that the envy barrier—the compulsion to observe strict conformity—is even more crucial than the population barrier in undeveloped countries for it takes a very determined family to limit births in the midst of a happily fertile community.

Western Intellectuals perpetuate envy barrier

If we can show that the people in undeveloped areas need most of all to acquire a certain indifference to envious neighbors, we can also show that the restless, socially agitated intellectual is not a very useful teacher for them. In his own rebellion against what he thought were the evils of laissez faire individualism he regressed—mentally and emotionally—to an adoration of the "whole society", the group, the community. His world view has become strikingly similar to the creed of the average native caught in a tribal tradition. This intellectual may use the jargon of modern economics, but his tenor, his implicit social philosophy are often in accordance with the tribal ethos of the preliterate culture. And it is this accordance of basic motives between the self-appointed messengers of Western progress and their audiences in undeveloped countries which can produce a climate even more hostile to creative economic behavior than the climate provided by the non-western culture itself.

Gunnar Myrdal, for instance, tells "poor countries" that they are getting poorer because the "rich countries" are getting richer. He encourages their politicians to fan blind nationalism as an instrument of economic blackmail. Myrdal told Egyptians that "the dissatisfied members of the world community have available blackmailing powers which they will increasingly learn to use to their own advantage.[5] Nasser certainly did learn in due time.

When such persistent messages reach men whose cultural ethic already holds that a man can get ahead by theft only the results must be disastrous.[6] The average person in undeveloped areas is ever less able to define differential success in non-invidious terms. Yet without this change in attitude toward possible and unpredictable inequality in a given culture it will be extremely difficult to adopt the organizational and physical methods on which the West's wealth was founded. But why did our restless intellectuals turn toward the "under-developed countries" - as if on cue - shortly after 1945?

INTELLECTUALS NEED POOR COUNTRIES

The foreign aid ideology and its apparatus intrigues Western intellectuals probably for these reasons:

(1) Again, he has an underdog whose cause he can champion. This is important not only for reasons of political power but it also helps the intellectual salve his own social conscience: he can ethically accept his own higher standard of living, his membership in an invidious society — by pretending to be necessary for the uplifting of the masses of the earth.[7] That he may actually help them stay near where they are now, does not occur to him.

(2) The intellectual — say, a professor of economics or political science — has always resented his insignificant role in the distribution of wealth. He assumes that the man who plans and commands the allocation of millions of dollars not only actually has, but also enjoys a sense of power which he, the intellectual, does not have. The foreign-aid-concept, after the failure of the intellectuals to gain such power through nationalization of industries in sufficient numbers and permanence — now promises them an almost unlimited field of employment where they can, for the next half century at least, as errand boys between East and West, free from annoying controls, manipulate billions, and still have a good conscience while doing it.

For the first time in history, the foreign aid apparatus affords thousands of intellectuals an opportunity to taste the rare pleasures which they imputed to the master-dispensers of millions of dollars, while at the same time striking a pose of pure altruism.

REDEMPTION OF INTELLECTUALS BY THE "UNDERDEVELOPED" WORLD

Moreover, for decades Western intellectuals have envied and

hated the men who first owned, late merely controlled, great corporate wealth. They seldom made a secret of their sentiments. But they also must have felt secretly ashamed of their own jealousy. In many countries they succeeded in putting over instruments of their envious aggression and revenge, such as confiscatory income tax progressions. But even so, some of them must have felt uneasy knowing that the only justification of such extreme progression of the income tax, for instance, was "ethical," never fiscal, necessity. It was the claim that the income tax should bring about greater equality. These intellectuals also knew that it was their own envious hearts, and not so much the population at large, which insisted on punishment by steeply progressive income tax rates.[8] Occasionally, they must have felt like heels. This feeling was bound to increase as soon as in Western countries the pockets of genuine poverty were reduced. It became ever more difficult for intellectuals to rationalize their aggressive envy toward the successful members of their own societies in the guise of fiscal equalizations by referring merely to domestic poverty. At this moment, the idea of a world wide equality of living standards occurred as the logical solution.

Gunnar Myrdal represents this type of international intellectual very well when he writes:

"What, in the end, are we going to do with our wealth, except to increase it all the time and make it ever more certain that all of us have an equal opportunity to acquire it? . . . . What shall we strive for? . . . . While the dreamers, planners, and fighters of earlier generations are finally getting almost all they asked for, somehow the "better life" in a moral and spiritual sense, the craving for which was their supreme inspiration, is slow in developing And there is an uncomfortable and deep uncertainty concerning how we should attain it. To my mind, there is no doubt that our moral dilemma is related to the fact that the "welfare state," which we have built up, with which we feel deeply identified, which we are not going to give up, and which we are bent upon constantly improving, is nationalistic.

". . . . Not merely to save the world, but primarily to save our own souls, there should again be dreamers, planners, and fighters, in the midst of our nations, who would take upon themselves the important social function in democracy of raising our sights—so far ahead that their proponents again form a definite minority in their nations and avoid the unbearable discomfort for reformers of a climate of substantial agreement. This is only possible if they enlarge the scope of their interests to encompass the world scene. They must again become internationalists, as they were when the reform movements started in the wake of the Enlightenment and the French Revolution." [9]

The issue of economic development aid to "underdeveloped" nations offers frustrated Western intellectuals an opportunity to mesh redistributive economic theory and policy with a tolerable personal conscience. They now can feel again as champions of the underdog—the world over. This alone would not be sufficient cause for objections. But it is possible that if this type of intellectual is given undue influence in the so-called underdeveloped countries— by intergovernmental capital transfers and ill-advised foundation activities—he will help to incite unrealistic aspirations, on the one hand, while, on the other, contribute to a cultural climate hostile to real economic growth.

If economic development is sought by means of intergovernmental loans and grants, the intellectuals both of recipient and donor countries, as well as internationally free-floating secularized missionaries of the Gunnar-Myrdal-type gain a disproportionate influence over the whole process. The ideas, methods, plans, and public utterances of such intellectuals tend to hamper whatever potential for long-range real development might have existed in an area and in a people.

By very virtue of being a modern intellectual such men and women are disinterested, probably *incapable,* and at any rate much too impatient, to encourage and foster the multitude of minute changes in human attitudes and practices which form the basis of economic and technological improvement. On the contrary, nearly all these intellectuals, being part of the general statist traditions, merely reinforce, on a sophisticated level, the awe of "society," of the "community," the "general good" with which the native population was filled in the first place and thus kept in bondage to a stifling and jealous tradition of envy of all against all.

It is inconceivable to have invention, initiation or acceptance of new ideas and methods for economic, technical, agrarian and sanitary improvements unless the more energetic individual feels relatively freed from the pressures toward conformity, toward egalitarian community standards. But it is precisely the twentieth century type of intellectual with his latter-day communitarian primitivism called "social responsibility" or "socialism" who perpetuates the web of social controls which keep the individual in fear of imaginary "big brother" who happens to be a failure. When we say a society is backward or stagnant because of its tradition we have said very little. The word "tradition" is merely a descriptive label for a vaguely recognized state of affairs, for a certain pattern. We must go beyond that with questions aimed at a causal explanation. Tautologies will not do.

Why is there tradition instead of change and acceptance of change? Why is it easier for a majority of people always and everywhere to follow tradition rather than risk pilot-ventures of change? What are we afraid of when we abstain from initiating change whose benefits we can well visualize? Who frightens us into subservience to tradition? It is surely not enough to say that it is tradition which does all those things.

Most of us have met the American college professor who shies away from buying a car in the medium or higher price class or who does not dare write a book without footnotes, although he knows that both deviations from tradition might be rational actions indeed. Is this man not ill prepared to tell undeveloped communities that they can have a higher standard of living before long if they toss out part or all of their tradition? [10]

Effect of the Intellectuals' Intervention

In a superb article on "The Politics of Underdevelopment", Professor Brzezinski, of the Russian Research Center of Harvard University, advises against "a policy of competing with the USSR in extending aid." For one thing, he holds, and I agree, that "the dominant aspirations of the new states are largely a product of the thinking and activity of a small minority of leaders, drawn from and supported by a relatively restricted intelligentsia. These intellectuals . . . chiefly Western-trained but also containing a sprinkling of Communists, are on the whole elitists, depite their protestations." [11]

Professor Edward Shils, of the University of Chicago, in an article titled "Intellectuals, Public Opinion, and Economic Development," reminds us of the fact that economic development in the West, until the latter part of the nineteenth century, came about without the aid of intellectuals. Shils then portrays the dominant men of letters in today's underdeveloped world. [12] They love, almost without exception, "Big Government." They are as fond of government service as they are contemptuous of the business man and his "concrete everyday reality." They seem controlled by an invisible jury of fellow intellectuals in the United States and England. In the field of economics, this means mostly the extreme socialism of *The New Statesman* and similar Western journals. A number of travelers, among them Dr. Gideonse, have noted that Prime Minister Nehru and his circle consider *The New Statesman* the last word on just about everything.

These Westernized intellectuals in India, the Middle East, Africa, and Asia suffer a "form of blindness to the capacities and incapacities" of their fellow-countrymen. They know little of and contribute nothing to the hard work required to make economic institutions functional. Worse still, Shils finds, the statism of these intellectuals, their emotional commitment to the central government, is especially detrimental in countries marching toward socialism. India, Indonesia, Ghana, and similar new nations, are committed by their leaders to a socialist future. The reason for this is that most of these intellectuals received their education in Western schools during the time between the two World Wars when academic socialism had not yet faced certain experiences of the years 1945-1958. [13]

For instance, T. A. F. Noble, analyzing "an experiment in food grain procurement" as a "case study in planning in an underdeveloped area" reaches sobering conclusions from the fact that the planners and action-minded people in those areas are so often concerned with the displacement of the market mechanism. What those "backward" countries would need most, however, is an improvement of the market mechanism.

Noble also points to the "cultural lag" which enables socialism to have a revival in countries which can least afford it:

"In many underdeveloped countries, the danger of recurring food scarcity is one of the most important concerns of Government, and plans are constantly having to be made to anticipate or overcome famine . . . . Methods of compulsory procurement of foodgrains are therefore often tried, backed by legislation and the complicated apparatus of its enforcement, but experience shows that even in Communist countries in recent years, with all their equipment of authoritarianism, these methods are less successful in bringing in adequate supplies of food than in antagonizing the rural population and reducing the scale of future cultivation . . . . There is nothing new in this conclusion, which is now commonplace in the literature of post-war planning in 'advanced economies.' But it may be important to illustrate it in the context of experience in 'backward' economies, since there is probably a natural time-lag in their adaptation of policy to new ideas, and they may sometimes be slow to learn to abandon policy shibboleths which have been discredited by experience in the countries that invented them." [14]

In a similar argument Shils shows that because of their socialist bent the "emergent" nations are in much greater need of an intellectual elite, with mass media of communications, critical of government to provide the check of public opinion on the economic experiments of the government. The ideological commitment to a society with a minimum of a competitive market needs more watchdogs in press and radio than countries where the market mechanism can still put a government enterprise to shame, if necessary.

Unfortunately, according to Shils, this criticism is not provided if the intellectual elite fanatically supports and executes the policies of the central government. Thus, India or Indonesia can afford the luxury of socialism much less than England or the Netherlands where an old tradition of public criticism of government policy may have prevented the worst effects of policies hostile to human enterprise.

For these reasons, I think, people in the United States, hearts bursting with altruism, should not delude themselves by believing that they can really — through loans and grants from government to government — help the 400 million Indians. What they are called upon to subscribe and finance is the political career of a marginal intellectual minority. [15] Conceivably, the most promising thing that could happen to the long-range economic chances of the Asian masses would be for their top planners to run out of Western funds. Otherwise, there is little hope that the "emergent" nations, within the next generation, would have domestic political arrangements capable of stopping socialism by the ballot. This is even less likely if the West continues to write financial life insurance for ambitious politicians in underdeveloped countries. [16]

THE NEW SUMPTUARY LAW

For the past ten years Miss Barbara Ward (Lady Jackson) has devoted nearly all her writing and public speaking to the advocacy of capital transfers in the name of morality. At the same time she seems to have given little thought to the causes of relative economic and innovative differences between peoples. According to her, "the group of nations round the North Atlantic Ocean are the privileged aristocracy of world society. They live in areas which not only are the most pleasant to live in from the point of view of climate and temperature . . . . but also possess the richest resources for industry and agriculture."

Miss Ward is obviously unhappy that we are "heirs to a range of resources and opportunities that today enables us, some sixteen per cent of the world's population, to enjoy steadily about seventy per cent of its annual income." Without apparently realizing whose envy she is fanning and which side in the cold war she is supplying with propaganda slogans, Miss Ward calls us "the lords of the earth" who are "as wealthy in relation to the rest of the world as Andrew Carnegie in relation to his steelworkers."

Miss Ward realizes that we share this globe with potential or actual robbers: "We can keep our seventy per cent of the world's income until somebody else comes and takes it away from us." But she hopes to placate them: "If over the next fifty years — I suggest fifty years, because, after all, our imperialism lasted four hundred years and this is the length of memory we have to counter — if, over the next fifty years, the Asian nations could come to depend upon Western help given generously, intelligently and cooperatively, to the tune of, say, one or two billion dollars a year, I think we should finally wipe out the picture of Western exploitation and imperialism." [17]

Is this not a bit naive? Have the splendid philanthropies of countless Jewish families over the past one hundred years yet wiped out the anti-Jewish stereotype of the egotistic money-lender?

We have to admit to ourselves that envious people do not want to be deprived of motives for their resentment and spite. Moreover, Miss Ward appears oblivious of the dubious quality of a Christian brotherhood which needs the income-tax collector for its basis. It seems to me on the evidence of many documents that the Christian concern with international economic "equalization" represents a resurrection of sumptuary laws. The mentality underlying earlier sumptuary laws both in Christian and non-Christian cultures now pervades much of the "liberal" writing about the dichotomy of developed versus undeveloped countries.

There is a peculiar contradiction in the social philosophy of those among our contemporaries who suggest increased foreign aid as a soothing poultice on undeveloped areas. The same authors often argue for what amounts to sumptuary laws domestically and for consumption-oriented reconstruction and stimulation of societies abroad.

At home the industry which entices and enables a man to own two or three cars to underpin his suburban way of life is condemned as unethical and materialistic. But the same authors who suffer anguish from the "economy of abundance" at home usually plead for measures which would be rational economics only if the people of poorly or undeveloped areas became aggressive consumers eventually.

When reduced to the essential proposition, I find it hard to see an ethical or psychological borderline between legitimate and illegitimate consumer wants. If Professor Galbraith [18] blames the family which works overtime for the second or third new car, how can he urge the peasant in Africa or India to change his work habits so that he may own two flashlights in place of a candle?

I cannot go into the history and practice of sumptuary laws. It is a most illuminating subject. But it appears to me that the authors who are most strongly emotionally involved in the dichotomy of developed versus undeveloped areas set themselves up as supreme arbiters quite similar to former monarchs and municipal authorities decreeing sumptuary laws.

Some "liberals," socialists, and unhappy intellectuals in general dislike the fact that capitalism made possible what David Potter of Yale calls "people of plenty" in the West.

When we study the concluding remarks of many articles and books favoring substantial foreign aid to undeveloped areas, it is difficult to ignore the implication by their authors that it would be desirable to transfer just about enough wealth to bring our own domestic economies down to a level of inconspicuous consumption.

The Rhetoric of Inequality

There may be good reasons for suggesting a less conspicuously consuming society, although this goal may conflict with a philosophy of full employment. But if someone thinks that we would be happier or more religious as soon as we forget our economy of abundance, this same man should not argue that we are morally or strategically compelled to bring about industrial and commercial processes in less developed areas of the world. For in the long run they must produce the same imbalances there that he now deplores in his own society.

Poverty and needs are relative concepts. If a Continental Mark III is said to be disruptive of fellowship in an American middle class neighborhood, so is a sewing machine in a primitive village in Africa. The sentimental proponents of aid to undeveloped areas reason in a circular fashion. Needless to say, some proponents of foreign aid to undeveloped countries do not include the sumptuary argument in their argument for such aid. However, even though Congress, for the most part, may still be immune to direct persuasion by the moralizers of aid, these sentimental proponents should not be deemed ineffective. When Western grants to undeveloped nations come under international jurisdiction — under a multi-government board — the influence of the sentimentalists is bound to grow. But even now they can bring pressure on the United States Congress by flooding the constituents with sentimental foreign-aid literature in the hope of inspiring corresponding letters to Congressmen.

For several years now in progressive and liberal circles a rhetorical question has become increasingly popular. The basic theme is always the same. We quote from *Social Action,* January 1955, a typical phrase: "Watch for opposition to the new program (i. e., a large-scale program of economic and technical aid to Asia) from those who do not know we cannot go on much longer with 6 per cent of the world's population (in the U. S.) producing and consuming almost 50 per cent of the world's annual output of goods and services." [19]

This is absurd rhetoric. We might ask just as well; How much longer can Harvard go on monopolizing half a billion dollars for the benefit of her students and faculty? And why should she be allowed to corner another 80 million dollars at a time when many poorer colleges barely hang on to life? The answer might be: Harvard men are so good, they deserve it. They can make the best use of scarce funds. Could it not be that the same answer would apply to the invidious dichotomy between developed and "under-developed" countries?

The often-heard statement that " international inequality" is bound to become ever more "politically impossible," as we grow richer and the century wears on, is an argument for aid that lacks logic as well as essence. It is difficult indeed to believe that the villagers in the interior of India or Africa should suffer from the fact of wealth in Park Avenue or Suburbia when, at the same time and for over a century, we have had inequalities as great within peaceful democracies. [20] There are Swiss mountain villages where people live in conditions not unlike those of primitive peasantry in undeveloped countries. Regularly some of their more vigorous members go to the cities, often Paris, make some money as innkeepers, but return, after a while, to spend the rest of their lives in the home village. And yet, the social harmony of Swiss democracy, a truly peaceful society, has not suffered from the inequality between a mountain peasant and the standard of living of a Swiss merchant in Zurich or Geneva. And all that takes place in a densely populated geographical area only two-thirds the size of West Virginia.

Is it therefore not meaningless in any context of sociological reality to lodge in the consciousness of Western populations the depressing image of village life somewhere in India or Afghanistan — as a kind of indictment: why don't you do something? The argument and assertion is simple and it is alluring for its obvious appeal to the emotion of envy.

(1) There are rich countries and poor *countries* in the world of today.

(2) The rich ones are growing richer and the poor ones poorer.

(3) The fact of (a) and the dubious fact of (b) must never be attributed to anything under the control of the poor countries.

(4) Possibly the rich countries are rich only or mostly due to what they have taken, or withheld, from the poor ones.

(5) World War III, the Soviet Union, the moon, or all three of these, will come down upon us unless we, the West, deliver quickly what is due to the poor countries: namely, a rising standard of living comparable to what we tell ourselves they see in Western countries.

(6) In any event, no matter who will do what, when, or where, it is of utmost historical urgency, so we are told, that the "underdeveloped countries" will catch up with the industrialized nations.

The use of words in most of these pronouncements is so superficial that they are worthless as analytical tools for designing economic growth. At the same time, such words become very potent and dangerous stimuli for pernicious policies and attitudes detrimental to genuine economic development.

"They" and "We," underdeveloped countries, poor and rich, slow and fast, urgent and necessary — all these words when applied to the artificial and invidious dichotomy of developed versus undeveloped countries are far removed from any ascertainable referents in social and cultural reality.

Several papers in this symposium have shown some of these semantic traps. Few have hinted to their rhetorical misuses in speeches and books by those who want an overheated concern for this dichotomy in order to exploit it as a generalized fear from which to draw a mandate for their own services as world-wide planners of economic programs and international equality. These activities of individuals and agencies are disruptive enough of what is left of sane foreign policies. But they are doubly harmful. The same individuals and groups, who stack American and Western foreign policy with the mystical load of "underdeveloped countries," love to address audiences in undeveloped countries with a rhetoric of envy. This ideological message must arouse and endorse sentiments and ideas which decrease the chances for those developments that could bring about a stability in the relationships between "older" and "emergent" nations.

Partly, the Myrdals and Barbara Wards speak to the "poor nations" in order to relieve guilt feelings. But they also have to pour out these frantic messages of concern in order to generate the "international steam" they need for persuading Western governments and legislators to satiate the needs created by the secular missionaries. By analogy, I might travel to a crude high school in an "underdeveloped" state of the United States, seek out a couple of teenagers whose aggressive tendencies are not matched by their scholastic achievements, and tell them about the glamor of student life in the Ivy League. I could tell them that these fabulous boys, on the way to fame and success in America, have stolen opportunities from the students in the "underdeveloped state" of the Union. Does anyone really think that such a message would help those students at the poor schools? And yet, my address may have whetted their resentful hunger for Ivy League esteem and environment. In other words, a message of pity combined with proffered assertions of self-guilt will not help people, in any circumstances, to reform their habits and life goals, as individuals, in the manner required for intellectual and economic progress.

It is conceivable that by a twist of motives and sentiments the Western intelligentsia has lost the sense of proportion in confronting the undeveloped areas. This loss may come from a psychological process (from a wrong perception of socioeconomic reality) which in itself is chiefly responsible for the lack of innovative actions and economic growth in areas whose poverty we now feel compelled to deplore so loudly.

Needed: A New Theory of Differential Economic Growth

At least in some minds, the guilt feeling of the West toward undeveloped areas will depend on the degree to which Western observers and scholars are incapable themselves of explaining the differences in economic achievement. Some believe that the "rich" countries are simply those which got the machines and capital first. Obviously this simplification will hardly balm our "social Conscience." A search for the causes of differential development of cultures is therefore not only valuable for scholarly or pragmatic reasons. It promises also new knowledge helpful in ethical or existential culture contact situations.

It is psychologically difficult, it seems to me, for Western negotiators to deal rationally with their opposite numbers from undeveloped countries as long as they themselves believe at least half of the theory of differential economic growth which native intellectuals took from Marxism. The members of an Asian delegation in Washington for discussions on United States loans to their development projects are likely to believe what an Indian author wrote a few years ago: "The nineteenth century witnessed the apogee of capitalism in Europe. That this was in large measure due to Europe's exploitation of Asian resources is now accepted by historians." [21] And a Western socialist stated several years ago that "the white West fails to bring emancipation and rationalization to the non-white peoples under its control or within its cultural reach, and thus leaves the job to communism. The fact that there are backward countries at all can be blamed on the advanced countries, and must be so blamed in the cases of the colonial and semi-colonial countries. The case is more complicated in a white country like Russia herself. Even there, however, it is perfectly sound to argue that, whatever the special explanation, the bourgeoisie failed its historical mission; weakness is no excuse in history. In any event, where the bourgeoisie has failed to do its liberal job, the liberal job is still to be done, in order that the communist unification, rationalization, and harmonization can be consummated. If liberalism fails, then communism must do the liberal job before proceeding to its own post-liberal job. It is not liberalism, it is communism, which comes as the liberator, the emancipator." [22]

Conclusions

Differences in economic achievement on this globe might be borne easier both by the intellectuals of developed and undeveloped countries if we can build a new theory of differential economic growth. Fashionable economic thought still implies, as does Marxist theory, a dichotomy of exploited and exploiters, or other invidious confrontations. We need a theory that can help explain economic and innovative inhibitions within a given culture with factors for which the members of such a culture, and their external friends, must blame primarily the people who suffer from the inhibitions.

We should also pay much more attention to the role of intellectuals —often marginal men in the true sense of the word—in the fixation of growth-impeding attitudes in undeveloped countries.

There is a rationally inexplicable intensity with which authors in the West insist on the sacrificial acceleration of economic growth in non-Western areas. I am tempted to explain this by the affinity between such Western intellectuals and the recipient natives. The intellectual feels compelled to urge aid to natives due to a universal human motive which also keeps the Asian or African peasant on a subsistence level. I propose to call this envy-avoidance behavior. This secondary drive—acquired mostly in the sibling group—is partly responsible for the existence of undeveloped or poorly developed economies. But further, this fear of being the target of envious eyes now underlies our own gestures of atonement toward those cultures. Our gestures and statements, if relayed and reinterpreted by local political leaders can thus strengthen growth-impeding values in underdeveloped cultures. People who are poor because they fear the envy of their immediate neighbors can hardly be helped by intellectuals who want to improve their situation because they fear the envy of these people.

Could it be that the *congruity of motives* causes the peculiarly insecure situation whenever representatives of developed and undeveloped countries meet? The acts and grants of atonement, which intellectuals in the West feel necessary, will inspire the intellectuals in undeveloped areas to address their peoples in a way which will assure the fixations that kept them near the subsistence level.

Innovative and economic behavior conducive to economic growth will be found whenever the invidious confrontation of the "haves" and "have-nots" has been de-emphasized. This can be achieved by a theory of good versus bad luck or certain forms of religion. But, unfortunately, today native leaders can reap political following most easily by fitting the invidious dichotomy of rich, developed, profit-seeking nations versus poor undeveloped "exploited" nations onto the ancient tribal envies. Inasmuch as Nehru, for instance, tries to inculcate his Indians with a secular, wholly agnostic veneer of socialistic philosophy—itself being in essence little more than a rationalization of envy—he reduces the chance for economic progress some parts of India might have had under an influx of individualistic values from the West.

The following processes seem to sustain the issue of developed versus undeveloped countries: Citizens in the developed countries are made unhappy, insecure, or frustrated with their economic achievements by methods—and due to motives—the equivalents of which operate the mechanism of black magic in primitive cultures. We are now literally resurrecting the fear of the evil eye, a fear which has the effect of a brake on innovative enterprise and economic growth. [23]

The economic and technological expansion we call capitalistic West was made possible, among other conducive factors, by the relative freedom from fear of the envious ones. Christian ethics and eschatology, the Protestant ethic, and other Western values, made it possible, psychologically and ethically, for the successful person to live with his success and with his less fortunate fellows. The ethos of our culture allowed a definition of success which did not imply that anyone's gain meant the loss or deprivation of another person or group. [24]

Regarding Guatemala, Sol Tax, one of our leading anthropologists, observes: ". . . that like us the Indians operate in terms of a complex of competing values, but the results are different partly because their ordering of the values is different from our own, and partly because the arena in which the values compete is different. The Indians live in small communities, where harmony and the good opinion of others is deemed necessary to life. Indeed, the Indians believe that without good relations with nature, with the supernatural, and with fellow men, health breaks down, prosperity is lost, luck is bad. Yet in a small society pretty much at a bare subsistence level, with a competitive economic system, it is impossible to rule out envy and the fear of envy; or accusations of greed, and the fear of such accusations. An Indian to whom fortune offers new alternatives must steer the old yet always new course between his individual needs and interests and those of the society, and must do so in a small community where all neighbors watch and where all are neighbors. The Indians respond to the challenge in part by establishing extraordinarily formal and impersonal social relationships, in a different way as stand-offish as (by reputation) are the privacy-seeking inhabitants of a London club. But they also respond to pressure by changing the proportions of their expenditures. In brief, they increase their expenditures for clothing and housing (as well as food) both for the pleasure of it and because miserliness is shameful; but much more than this they increase their contributions to religious, ritual, and community needs. Rich people take the more expensive obligations, and take them oftener. Indeed they sometimes become impoverished on this account! This is the respect in which consumption can be conspicious and also legitimate and safe. This could be considered a way of redistributing wealth except that in the process so much is consumed in the form of alcohol and perishable food that there is a considerable net loss; so although the rich man may go broke, no Indian gets a corresponding advantage."[25]

Is the dramatization of aid to poor countries not the global parallel to the rites of envy in rural communities of undeveloped countries? We talk ourselves into a frenzied fear of envious eyes staring at the West from all the poor countries. Often we prepare ourselves to pay ransom in ways which are economically about as realistic as the ritualistic expenditures of the Indians in Guatemala.

[1] As early as 1953 the London *Economist* understood the vicious circle produced by Western economic aid to undeveloped countries:

"Local myopia is often founded on beliefs and prejudices that have nothing to do with economics. The Arab, Persian or Egyptian, however keen to attract capital, judges that he can behave as loftily as he likes to the West because he has suffered at its hands and is owed compensation. A second premise is that he is indispensable . . . .

"In recent years the twin premises have been further encouraged One end-product of such enterprises as Mr. Bevin's Middle East Office, President Truman's Point Four, the United Nation's agency for the relief of the Arab refugees, and

President Eisenhower's recent grant of $43 million to Persia, is an enhancement of the conceit that western bounty is due as of right, and that, no matter how often western street names are torn down and American or British offices sacked, the West will turn the other cheek. Normally, the technique for a concern needing capital is to display the security and yield obtained by earlier investors. Underdeveloped countries, in their arrogance, offer no such attractions, and the would-be lender is understandably shy . . . .

"The American government's idea in launching aid programs for underdeveloped countries was that public aid would fade away and private investment step in. But what happens in Western Europe is not happening in the Middle East. Nor will it happen quickly. Especially in xenophobic countries, the private investor is not the man to whom to turn for basic requirements such as vast irrigation schemes or networks of communications. . . . Yet here, at least in the Middle East, is the threat of a vicious circle. The greater the public aid that is proffered from the West, the more lasting the Middle East's belief that the West is under an unredeemed obligation to it . . . .

"The remedy lies in the hands of the 'underdeveloped' peoples, but it shows too little sign of being used. Indeed, their rich men, far from setting the example for a local change of investing habits, are prone also to place their private investments in those countries of greater security." (November 7, 1953, pp. 403-404).

[2] "Land for the Fellahin: Land Tenure and Land Use in the Near East", *American Journal of Economics and Sociology*, 17, January 1958, p. 163.

[3] Specific analyses and documentation will be found in the following publications of the author: "Individuality vs. Equality", in *Essays on Individuality*, ed. by Felix Morley (Philadelphia: University of Pennsylvania Press, 1958; also published by the Oxford University Press in Great Britain, India, and Pakistan). See pp. 108ff, 116ff. "The Role of Envy in Soviet Strategy", *World Liberalism* (London: Pall Mall Press), 7 (2), Summer 1957. "Das Problem des Neides in der Massendemokratie", in *Masse und Demokratie*, ed. by Albert Hunold (Erlenbach–Zurich: Eugen Rentsch Verlag, 1957), pp. 239-272.

The following authors also give impressive illustrations of the "envy barrier" in simple societies: Allam R. Holmberg, *Nomads of the Long Bow: The Siriono of Eastern Bolivia* (Washington, D. C.: Government Printing Office, Smithsonian Institution: Institute of Social Anthropology, No. 10, 1950). See p. 36 and 60. Walter Dyk, *A Navaho Autobiography* (New York: The Viking Fund, 1947), p. 194. Eric R. Wolf, "Types of Latin American Peasantry", *American Anthropologist*, 57 (June 1955), see p. 460 and 461 for "institutionalized envy". See also Wolf's article "Closed Corporate Peasant Communities in Mesoamerica and Central Java", *Southwestern Journal of Anthropology*, 13 (Spring 1957). Edward C. Banfield, *The Moral Basis of a Backward Society* (Glencoe, Ill.: The Free Press, 1958), see references to envy, pp. 18-19.

[4] R. F. Fortune, *The Sorcerers of Dobu* (New York: 1932), p. 135f.

[5] G. Myrdal, *Rich Lands and Poor* (New York: Harper 1957), p. 74ff. This little book is a slightly tamed version of his lectures in Cairo under the title "Development and Underdevelopment: A Note on the Mechanism of National and International Economic Inequality," published in Cairo in 1956 prior to the seizure of the Suez Canal. The arguments are very similar to those he put forward in *An International Economy* (New York: Harper, 1956).

[6] Islamic countries suffer from a religious tradition which blends easily with socialistic clichés about the "guilt" of economically more successful persons and

firms. See, for instance, Mirza Mohammad Hussain, *Islam and Socialism* (Lahore, Pakistan: Muhammad Ashraf, 1947). Islam has "laid down certain rules which govern and determine the form and intensity of wealth-earning activities of man. They are so restrained as to be in complete harmony with the peace and well-being of society as a whole. At no stage are these economic activities to be free from the yoke of moral considerations. . . . A religion which regulates and con-trols even our menu . . . can never fail to build up an ideal society which has been the cherished dream of Utopian thinkers." (pp. 71-72). On p. 73 the author as-sures us that the holy Quran "raises an insurmountable barrier against the rise of the satanic system of Capitalism which divides and disintegrates society and concentrates wealth in a fewer hands and condemns the teeming millions to pov-erty and starvation." On p. 75 we read "Islam . . . arrests the growth of capital-istic tendencies."

[7] Socialists and American "liberals" often engage in almost amusing mental gyrations when they try to justify their own economic inequality, compared with the lower classes they champion. Perhaps the best illustration of that anguish is offered in the diaries of Beatrice Webb when she comments on the feelings of her socialist cabinet ministers in the twenties (*Beatrice Webb's Diaries*, 1924-32, ed. by M. J. Cole, published in 1956).

[8] See Walter J. Blum and Harry Kalven, Jr., *The Uneasy Case for Progressive Taxation* (Chicago: University of Chicago Press 1953), pp. 74ff comment specifi-cally on the connection between envy (rarely admitted) and the case for the progressive income tax. The authors believe, however: "Every experience seems to confirm the dismal hypothesis that envy will find other, and possibly less at-tractive, places in which to take root." (74).

[9] *An International Economy*, p. 322.

[10] See Bernard Barber, *Science and the Social Order* (Glencoe, Ill.: Free Press, 1952), "Among scientists, such symbols [expensive homes, fine cars, and costly clothes for wives] are considered inappropriate even when inherited income may make it possible for some few scientists to procure them." (p. 107).

[11] *World Politics*, 9 (October 1956), p. 57.

[12] *Ibid.*, 10 (January 1958), pp. 232-255.

[13] In support of this see, for instance, Henry M. Oliver, Jr., *Economic Opinion and Policy in Ceylon* (Durham, N. C.: Duke University Commonwealth-Studies Center Publications, 1957):

"Most Ceylonese legislators and publicists have assigned major economic roles to the state. In part this is attributable to nationalist ambitions; it has seemed unthinkable that the government do nothing to remedy this situation while for-eign capital and management commanded the economic heights, Ceylonese in-comes were far below Western levels, and national economic independence was only a dream. Nationalists have demanded that the state be promoter and pro-tector, that it take on much of the burden of transferring income, wealth, and economic power from foreigners to citizens. . . . "Nationalist ambitions are not, however, the sole explanation of interventionism's strength in Ceylon. Especially during the past two decades much Ceylonese opinion has favored measures to bring about a somewhat more nearly equal distribution of income and opportun-ity . . . Social conscience and group self-interest also led to demands for govern-ment action to transform the economy. Apart from special nationalist features, most of the argument for intervention has taken familiar European forms. Be-cause of their British tutelage, Ceylonese intellectuals have adopted or altered economic philosophies expounded at Oxford, Cambridge, and London; Ceylonese trends of thought have paralleled, although they have not exactly reproduced, trends in Britain. In general, economic opinion has become more interventionist and more egalitarian with the passing of the decades. During the interwar years a high percentage of university graduates emerged with views well to the Left of the modified liberals and conservative interventionists who were the legislators and spokesmen for the older generation. By the late 1930's the radical swing had become quite sharp, and in recent years most university students have been Left of the Gaitskell wing of British Labour; a high percentage have proclaimed themselves to be Trotskyists or Communists." (p. 35 f.)

[14] *Economic Development and Cultural Change*, 5 (1957), p. 175.

[15] And G. Myrdal is quite unconcerned that we shall finance a primitive and ruthless political elite. For one thing, Myrdal, in many instances of his writings, is in favor of the nationalism of underdeveloped countries. Yet he also writes: "And to foment these feelings [of nationalism] is often the most effective means, and sometimes the only means, of acquiring and keeping political power, which is the first obligation of every politician. The effect may easily be that the political leaders are virtually compelled to take policy steps against foreign interests which are not motivated by their country's true development interests but only by the intense nationalistic feelings of the people which the leaders have to cater to. And in this very process these feelings are usually prodded toward new heights of intensity." (*Rich Lands and Poor*, p. 74).

In view of this vicious circle I have serious doubts about the wisdom of recommendations offered by M. F. Millikan and W. W. Rostow: "This incentive [for economic take-off] cannot be created unless American resources available for economic development [e.g. in India] are sufficiently big and offered with a continuity and on terms such that a serious operating politician [!] can plot a long-period course with reasonable confidence." (*Foreign Affairs*, 36 (April 1958), p. 423).

[16] In response to this many people will say: But we can't do that because the uncommitted world will go communist if we fail to bail out their politicians each time they fall short of a five-year plan. I doubt it. See for instance: "The most important point to remember is that the basic problems of Asia cannot be solved either by us or by the communists. They were created by secular developments which antedate the conflict between democracy and communism by several hundred years. . . . That Soviet or American economic intervention, even were it many times larger than its present size, could effect any substantial alleviation of Asia's population problem, is, in the light of well-documented historical precedents, an untenable proposition. That problem can be solved, if it can be solved at all, only by the Asians themselves through initiatives of their own. Its magnitude severely limits the effectiveness of foreign intervention, economic or pedagogical. The admission of this fact implies neither a defeatist attitude nor an argument against American assistance in forcing the most rapid economic growth compatible with the underdeveloped countries' resources. In all cases, such assistance is justified by the claim of human suffering upon our generosity; in some cases, it is also good business and good politics. But when this line of reasoning is stretched to mean that American economic policies towards the "uncommitted" countries, bold and expensive as they may be, can achieve a decisive change in the balance-of-power between the Soviets and ourselves, then we are asked to reckon without the West's fundamental dilemma in Asia." (Robert Strausz-Hupé,

"Back to Sanity," *United States Naval Institute Proceedings,* 84, May, 1958, p. 27).

In similar vein, Charles Wolf, Jr., an economist on the staff of the Rand Corporation, suggests "that Soviet Bloc aid is perhaps not simply the threat we have assumed, but may entail some windfall benefits as well; that bigger and better aid offers by the United States are not necessarily warranted as a *counter* to Soviet aid, though they may well be warranted for other reasons." ("Soviet Economic Aid in Southeast Asia: Threat or Windfall?," *World Politics,* October 1957.

Strausz-Hupé as well as Wolf reject—for correct reasons—the political-strategic argument for massive economic aid to poor areas, but, perhaps in deference to the *Zeitgeist,* feel constrained to toss in the humanitarian argument—an argument which this paper as well as others in the Symposium have questioned on grounds of economics and social philosophy. Elsewhere, however, Strausz-Hupé is sceptical of a foreign policy based on altruism (*Power and Community,* New York: Praeger, 1956, p. 51).

The humanitarian obligation of the West to uplift poor countries at this time of history as a matter of morality is also questioned by Jacob Viner (*International Economics,* 1951, pp. 370-375), S. Herbert Frankel (*The Economic Impact on Under-Developed Societies,* 1955, pp. 83-86), and H. F. Angus (*Canada and the Far East 1940-1953,* 1953, pp. 77-79).

[17] All quotes from Barbara Ward, *Interplay of East and West,* pp. 91-95.

[18] John Kenneth Galbraith, *The Affluent Society* (Boston: Houghton, 1958.

[91] *Social Action* (New York: Council for Social Action), 21 (No. 5), p. 28.

[20] "It is difficult to see why knowledge of international disparities in level and range of consumption should have an especially powerful effect on the average person in poor countries." (Peter T. Bauer and Basil S. Yamey, *The Economics of Under-Developed Countries,* Chicago: University of Chicago Press, 1957, p. 139). Could it be that Western intellectuals impute their own envy of their affluent fellow citizens into the hearts of far-off peasants in poor countries in order to suppress unpleasant reflections on their own ethics?

[21] K. M. Pannikar, *Asia and Western Dominance* (London 1953), p. 484.

[22] Eduard Heimann, "Marxism and Underdeveloped Countries," *Social Research,* September 1952, p. 343.

[23] See my article "The Evil Eye: Forms and Dynamics of a Universal Superstition", *Emory University Quarterly,* 11 (October 1955), pp. 153-161. Compare the findings of Phyllis H. Williams in her dissertation *South Italian Folkways in Europe and America* (New Haven: Yale University Press, 1938). "Beliefs in witches and in the Evil Eye color the lives of even third-generation Italians . . . Americans are apt to assume that if an immigrant is given the opportunity to enjoy the advantages this country offers . . . he will seize them with eager hands. But this is not always true. The eager hands are not stretched out, and there is no gratitude for the offer. (p. XV).

[24] "In any society the aim must be to keep the less successful from blocking the creative activity of the more far-seeing. This aim is reached by making envy 'not-respectable' either to the envying individual himself or to his neighbors . . . The laissez faire ideology of the 18th and 19th centuries was very effective in dealing with these problems of envy and freedom to experiment." (David McCord Wright, "Moral, Psychological and Political Aspects of Economic Growth", *Särtryck Ur Ekonomisk Tidskrift* (Uppsala: Almquist & Wiksells, 1954), p. 193.

[25] "Changing Consumption in Indian Guatemala", *Economic Development and Cultural Change,* 5 (1957), p. 155.

PART III

ECONOMIC FACTORS

6: *Social Overhead Mythology*

WILSON SCHMIDT

American aid is justified to the public and to the Congress primarily on political grounds. Some proponents of aid, just for good measure, add a few economic arguments to support their case. These are like substantive footnotes—not important enough to put in the text, but helpful to the main contention. This paper considers one of those footnotes which has been promoted to the text in recent discussions of foreign aid for economic development. [1]

The argument to be considered is one of those evinced by some proponents of aid to show that private foreign investment is insufficient to the task of financing economic development and that, as a consequence, foreign assistance is necessary. They hold that certain projects or services, called social overhead, [2] are essential to economic development, but they are not attractive to foreign or domestic private investment.

The projects and services included, though not by all writers, in the social overhead are electric power generation, railroads, education, roads, harbors, airports, water works, housing, telephone communications, irrigation, public health, and agricultural extension services. In some quarters, "basic" industries such as steel are added.

Aid for such projects is thought to do more than compensate for a shortfall of private investment: it supports the growth of private investment, further speeding development. Social overhead assistance provides or cheapens services which are essential to private production and distribution. And, because the social overhead sector is not congenial to private development, the allocation of aid to it rather than other sectors minimizes government competition with private enterprise.

At least three issues are raised by the social overhead thesis, as we shall call this argument: (1) The amounts of social overhead services provided through private foreign investment. (2) The sufficiency of the flow of that investment. (3) The effect of foreign assistance for social overhead services on the level of both foreign and domestic private investment.

Analysis of these issues suggests that the social overhead thesis provides flimsy support for aid. But the following arguments do not constitute a case against foreign assistance, nor do they prove that private foreign investment can alone finance and stimulate the desired rate of foreign economic growth for that would depend upon the rate selected. Rather the succeeding analysis merely shakes, perhaps shatters, one argument for aid. If convincing, it should serve to help shift attention to the central issues in the foreign aid question—namely the international political effects and equity aspects of intergovernmental transfers.[3]

A. Private Foreign Investment's Contribution to the Social Overhead

The proponents of the social overhead thesis possibly underrate what private foreign investment has done and can do in the social overhead sector. No comprehensive study exists, but several examples will suffice to deny any claim that private investment provides no social overhead services or that it can provide no more.

The United Fruit Company operates 15 hospitals and 120 dispensaries in its tropical environment. It maintains 253 elementary schools at an annual cost of about $800,000. Eighty-seven percent of the service provided by its communications subsidiary is used by the public, and the Great White Fleet transports more than bananas.[4]

The Creole Company, owned by Standard Oil of New Jersey, provides social overhead services in the form of education, housing, medical facilities, roads, water, ports and others as a necessary part of its oil operations.[5]

Standard-Vacuum's contribution to social overhead in Indonesia starts ". . . when a new oil strike is made and development begins. For then, access roads, pipelines, airports, docking facilities—and later houses, schools, and hospitals—must be built. While the transport facilities are constructed in the first instance for the company's own purposes, they become available to the general public and reduce the load on central or local government budgets accordingly.

"For example, STANVAC has constructed over 775 miles of roads, all available to the Indonesian public, of which over 600 miles are still being maintained by the company. In addition, it currently has under construction in Central Sumatra a road from Lirik to Butan, following the route of the new pipeline, which is about 90 miles in length. The company has also repaired many miles of existing government roads and any number of bridges.

"Road-building activities are not confined to the producing areas: STANVAC has also provided municipal roads, such as the one from Palembang to the Sungei Lais landing across the river from the refinery at Sungei Gerong. Today this road is, in effect, about four miles of city street, although the adjacent land was jungle when the road was built. Similarly, the company has built about six miles of road in the Palembang suburbs of Bukit Besar and Kenteng.

"Thus far, STANVAC has built two airfields in Indonesia: one at Pendopo, and one at Djapura near the Lirik oil fields. The latter was turned over to the government when completed, and the government-owned airline, Garuda Indonesian Airways, runs five to seven flights a week from Palembang. Flights are so heavily booked that STANVAC has to make reservations for its personnel two or three weeks in advance. The Pendopo airfield, although owned by the company, is fully available to the government and, like the Djapura field, continues to be maintained by STANVAC.

"Another transport facility established by the company and later opened to public use, is the ferry service at the Teluk Lubuk crossing on the Lematang River. Also, a canal over one mile long connecting the Musi River with Kampong Bali, and a passenger dock at the end of the Sungei Lais road, have both been built by the company for the use of local population.

"The contribution of STANVAC to the stock of Indonesian social capital is not confined to transport facilities. The company has installed some 125 miles of telephone line in South Sumatra, which has been placed at the disposal of government departments. As the Central Sumatra fields open up, a similar development will occur there. In several Palembang suburbs the company has provided pipe for the municipal water supply, and even assumed part of the cost of installation.

"The company has also contributed in numerous ways to community services. For example, it has turned over to municipal employees, for use as a sports field, some 84 acres from one of the company's housing concessions in a Palembang suburb, and has released over eight and one-half acres to the government as a site for a school building." [6]

Some persons may contend that these examples are merely flukes—unrepresentative of American overseas corporations and the work of men who were particularly conscious of their social responsibilities.

Regrettably, the full record is not available. However, about one-third U. S. overseas direct investment in the postwar years has been in oil. Virtually all, if not all, of the American overseas oil companies have provided such services in some degree; hence, these examples are not isolated instances. Furthermore, despite talk among businessmen about their social responsibilities, it is evident that the reason for the provision of social overhead facilities by American overseas firms could be the same as the reason why the home office provides restaurants for its employees, i.e., they indirectly pay.

There is nothing indirect about the return to other types of private foreign investment which provide social overhead services. The American and Foreign Power Company, the Brazilian Traction Light and Power Company, and Mexican Light and Power Company for example all sell social overhead services directly for a profit. That investment of this kind is significant is evidenced by the projected construction expenditures of American and Foreign Power from 1956 through 1960 of $527 million.

Finally, private foreign investment indirectly contributes to the social overhead by increasing the tax receipts of governments, which may use them for overhead development. In 1955, American firms in Latin America paid over $1 billion in taxes. [7] Furthermore, by raising the real income of residents, private foreign investment increases the host nation's taxable capacity.

Few of the developing nations have done as much as they could to attract the private foreign investment which they could gain. The obstacles to the international flow of capital are legion. Consider just electric power generation. In this essential area of social overhead services, the rate policies of foreign governments have been exceedingly unfavorable to private foreign investment, as well as domestic investment. The International Bank for Reconstruction and Development has been obliged to carry on a campaign for the last few years to induce foreign governments to permit higher power rates, presumably in part to make it possible for the IBRD to make bankable power loans. The Economic Commission for Latin America noted that "Tariffs for electricity are far below over-all price levels in Latin America, especially in the countries where inflation is severe. . . . the discrepancy is so great in Latin American countries that it has completely discouraged private investment and is a very heavy drain on public capital." [8] In one Latin American city it has been recently said, only partly facetiously, that the citizens will be using candles in ten years.

Clearly, at least *some* developing nations have not exhausted the foreign sources of social overhead services.

B. IS THE PRESENT FLOW OF INVESTMENT SUFFICIENT?

The foregoing examples may prove little about the need for aid. The current flow of investment into social overhead services, or even the flow which would occur under the most favorable investment climate, may be judged inadequate against United States political objectives in under-developed countries or against criteria of equity. An inquiry testing the sufficiency of present or potential private foreign investment against such standards does not belong to the economist qua economist. But one criterion which falls within his purview relates to the benefits and costs of such services as seen by the recipient country. From this view there need be no special shortage of private foreign investment in the social overhead sector which would justify aid.

Nothing is gained—in fact, all is lost—by the provision of a given good or service unless the value to the community of the benefits in having that good or service exceed the true cost to the community of providing it. The true cost of a product is the sum which the resources required to produce that product could earn in alternative employment; and that sum, under competition, tends to equal the value of the benefits those resources would produce in their alternative uses. Hence, if the benefits to be derived from a commodity do not exceed its true costs, some other product is more valuable (provides more benefits) and should be supplied instead. Conversely, if the benefits do exceed the costs, the commodity should be provided.

If the market mechanism is working satisfactorily, private enterprises embark on ventures which create benefits whose value exceeds their true cost because the difference between value and cost provides a profit. If they do not undertake such activities, it must be that they cannot appropriate to themselves money receipts equal to the full value of the benefits produced and/or that the money costs of producing the commodity are higher than the true costs imposed on the community.[9] Ventures subject to these conditions must comprise in whole or in part what is meant by the social overhead (1) because an identifying characteristic of social overhead services is their unattractiveness to private investors and (2) because the proponents of the social overhead thesis would surely not urge the construction of projects whose true benefits fell short of their true costs.

To gain commodities whose benefits exceed their costs but which are not provided by private firms, a government may subsidize private firms to induce them to supply them, or it may provide the products itself at a loss—a loss because the government also will be unable to obtain money receipts through sales equal to the full value of the benefits provided and/or will be obliged to pay money costs higher than the true costs. The cost in taxes necessary to finance the loss or subsidy would be more than recouped by the community out of the excess of the benefits derived from having the commodity over the true costs of producing it so that the subsidy or loss does not impose a net burden on the community. [10]

Applying this to the problem of gaining foreign capital for social overhead projects, a government may sell securities to foreign individuals or private institutions and construct and operate the facilities itself at a loss. Or it may pay a subsidy to foreign firms to finance and operate them.

For both international techniques, there are ample precedents. Governments were the major borrowers in the three major capital markets of the 19th century. And, there are numerous examples of the successful use of subsidies to attract private foreign capital. Colonial India guaranteed a 5% return to British capitalists to build its railroads. About 50 million pounds was paid to them between 1850 and 1900. The result: "The companies, once the initial contracts with the virtually foolproof clause guaranteeing a 5% annual interest had been signed, were able to raise their capital with ease from the investing public in Britain." [11]

In Brazil, beginning in 1852, legislation was passed to attract foreign capital, particularly into railroads. The inducements included relief from import duties on construction materials, a privileged zone of five leagues on either side of the right of way from which other railroads would be excluded, and a 5% guarantee on invested capital. [12] In Venezuela, most railroads were constructed by foreign capital with a government subsidy or a guaranty of at least 7% return on the invested capital. [13]

The Argentine constitution of 1853 charged the government with the responsibility of "promoting industrial enterprise, immigration, the construction of railways and navigable canals, the colonization of public lands, the introduction and establishment of new industries, and the importation of foreign capital." Subsequently a policy of railroad concessions was established and the investor was assured of profits of 7% through guarantees by the state. [14]

Canadian economic history is replete with devices for stimulating railroad construction and financing. So is that of the United States.

American land grants, according to Professor Thomas Cochran "aided greatly in attracting domestic and foreign capital into railroad construction. Investors who might be skeptical about the immediate earning power of a railroad across the prairies had faith in the ultimate value of the farming land. This seemed particularly true of foreign investors. The land grants undoubtedly drew otherwise unavailable money from England and Continental Europe into projects like the Illinois Central and the Northern Pacific." [15]

It may be protested that the international capital market is a shadow of its nineteenth century predecessor, troubled by past defaults, threats of nationalization, artificial American obstacles to the export of capital by certain lenders, and so on. All this is valid. But there is some price for capital which will overcome these risks and obstacles.

The interest payments and/or the subsidies to foreign firms necessary to overcome the obstacles may be judged too high and aid may consequently be urged. This might be correct on grounds of equity or politics, but it has nothing to do with the social overhead phenomenon. By means of subsidies to private domestic investors and through the expenditure of borrowed funds and tax receipts, a government, in the interest of maximum economic welfare, should allocate resources so that the value of the benefits to be gained from an additional dollar of investment in the social overhead sector and in the private sector is the same. If they are not equal, resources should be shifted to the higher benefit area. If a government chooses not to borrow abroad for social overhead services or not to subsidize foreign private firms, it must be that the value of the benefits obtained from another dollar of investment in the social overhead sector would not cover the cost of obtaining the dollar abroad. But this would also be true if that dollar were borrowed by the government for relending to the private sector since, as a result of a government-induced allocation of resources, the value of the benefits to be obtained by another dollar of investment in either sector would be the same. Thus, when the price of foreign capital is too high, it is too high for all ventures—not just for social overhead services. Therefore, a case for aid based on the view that the price of obtaining foreign capital for social overhead services is too high has no special connection to the need for social overhead services. The need for aid is independent of the social overhead phenomenon.

Nor can it be contended that a need for aid stems from a shortfall of private foreign investment in the social overhead sector. As long as governments allocate resources properly, the existence of a social overhead sector makes no difference to the size of the flow of private foreign investment. This is shown in the following.

Suppose that a nation receives a certain flow of private foreign investment, all of which goes into the non-social overhead sector, and assume that the expected return on the last dollar of that investment is the same as the expected return on investment in the capital-exporting nation. Suppose further that the government of the recipient country, by borrowing capital in the domestic market, increases the quantity of resources devoted to social overhead at the same time. If it is doing its job perfectly, the value of the benefits gained by investing a dollar of capital in the private sector and a dollar in the social overhead sector will be the same, for otherwise the government should induce a shift of resources to the sector showing the higher return.

Next suppose that through some miraculous event, the deterrents to private domestic investment in social overhead areas are removed. That is, assume that private firms could charge for all the benefits provided by social overhead facilities and/or that private firms would no longer be subject in the social overhead sector to money costs of production which exceeded the true costs.

The government would cease to expand the social overhead sector because private firms could handle it, and the government would therefore cease to issue securities on the capital market to finance expenditures of its own for that purpose. Domestic private firms would borrow those funds released by the government on the capital market and provide the social overhead services themselves.

Private firms would tend to undertake no more or less investment in the social overhead sector than the government. A rational government would invest in social overhead services to the point where the true value of the additional benefits to be gained just equalled the true costs. To go further would waste resources because additional investment would produce benefits whose value fell short of their true costs. Private firms, now able to charge for all the benefits and now required to pay no more than the true costs, would cease to expand at the same point. To go further would bring losses because the value of the benefits (and thus the receipts) from still more investment would fall short of the costs. Furthermore, there would be no reduction in domestic investment in what was formerly the only private sector of the economy since the funds required for private investment in what was the government sphere would be made available to private enterprises by the government's release of funds.

Since there would be no charge in investment in either sector, the

incentive to invest in what was formerly the only private sector would
be the same as it had been before the deterrents to private investment
in the social overhead sector were miraculously removed. Consequently the flow of private foreign investment to the former private
sector would remain unchanged.

Exactly the same analysis would apply if a government denied entrance to foreign firms in, let's say, the shoe industry. The government,
however, must provide the same amount of shoes that private firms
would and, in doing so, withdraw resources from other fields. Private
foreign investment would enter the fields evacuated by the government and thereby sustain the flow of external capital.

Because the flow of private external capital is no different whether
a social overhead sector does or does not exist, no general economic
argument for aid can be sustained on grounds that there are limitations on private foreign investment in that sector of the economy.

This conclusion and the earlier view that the need for aid is independent of the social overhead phenomenon involve a key assumption, namely that the government allocates resources so that the
value of the benefits gained from an additional dollar of investment
in the private sector and in the social overhead sector are the same.
This allocation of resources is obtained by means of subsidies to private firms to induce them to provide social overhead services and/or
through the governmental provision of such services at a loss. But can
it not be argued (1) that developing nations are too poor to finance
such subsidies or losses, or (2) that their governments cannot raise
taxes or cut other government expenditures to finance them, or (3)
that they lack knowledge of projects which might profitably be undertaken? If so, the above conclusions would be placed in jeopardy.

(1) Poverty, per se, provides no obstacle to subsidies or losses. [16]
First, they merely reallocate a nation's resources; the capital, labor,
land, and management induced to move from the private to the social
overhead sector are not lost in transit. [17] Thus, only the allocation and
not the size of a nation's resources (its wealth) is involved. Second,
as indicated earlier, the value of the benefits to the nation in having
the social overhead services outweigh the true costs of providing
them by more than enough to recoup the subsidy or loss which is
necessary to shift resources. That is, subsidies or losses for worthwhile social overhead services cause a net addition to economic welfare and wealth; in effect, they are costless to the nation as a whole. [18]

(2) Unwillingness to raise taxes or cut government expenditures to
permit the payment of subsidies or to cover losses does not damage
the conclusions either. Such reluctance cannot be ascribed to the

cost for it was just noted that subsidies or losses to provide worthwhile social overhead services are costless. Rather, unwillingness suggests that further subsidies or losses are undesirable, i.e., the additional benefits would not exceed the cost. The reason lies in the fact that the benefits which private firms cannot appropriate are not bought and sold in the market place. [19] Nor are the true costs which they should be paying established through exchange. Consequently, an objective measure of them is lacking, and judgment of the value of the benefits and the true costs (and thus the appropriate subsidy or loss) must be left to the government. If a government refuses to raise taxes or lower government expenditures to finance subsidies or losses, it would seem that the government does not think it worthwhile to have the service which would be induced by the subsidy or loss. There are no perfect, objective measures with which to deny its conclusion.

(3) Finally, lack of knowledge presents no special problem. Information can be obtained by the allocation of resources to education and by hiring overseas experts. Private firms and individuals do invest in knowledge, and, to the extent that they fall short of investing enough in gaining information, governments can and do invest resources with profit to the nation as a whole. Resources should be devoted to gaining knowledge up to the point where the additional benefits just equal the additional costs. Any remaining ignorance is too costly to remove in the light of the benefits to be gained by removing it. It might be retorted that foreign governments may be too ignorant to search for foreign experts. But this is hardly a reasonable generalization and overlooks the fact that foreign consulting firms look for jobs to do, i.e., they go to the government.

C. Does Social Overhead Aid Stimulate Private Foreign Investment? [20]

Suppose that a government constructs a power plant or a road system. The resulting reduction in the cost of additional power or transportation services will have a favorable effect on private investment in industries using such services. But this favorable effect on total private investment may be partly, fully, or more than fully offset by a rise in other (non-social overhead) costs of production, though not necessarily in the same industries. The unfavorable effect may occur because higher rewards are paid to resources to induce them to shift into the social overhead sphere; substitute resources remaining in the private sector will therefore receive higher rewards, and these higher rewards raise costs of production and thereby deter investment in the private sector. By providing aid, the United States Government could help to minimize this unfavorable effect since the government of the underdeveloped country would find less need to divert resources from alternative employments if aid were available.

But the favorable effect of foreign aid for the social overhead may be partly, completely, or more than completely offset. First there is the possibility of a substitution of projects. One summer day in the early 1930's a ragged man begged for a dime for food at the back door of a neighbor's home. The housewife, a member of the W.C.T.U., concluded from his appearance that it would be better to make him a sandwich for she felt he would spend the dime for demon rum. As she brought him the sandwich, he pulled out his handkerchief to wipe his brow, and a dime fell from his pocket. But she gave him the sandwich anyway. He parted, saying "I needed some food, but now I'll get some beer." Because food was his most urgent need he probably would have spent the dime for a sandwich. By giving him a sandwich, she had made it possible for him to satisfy with his own funds his second-most important desire—beer. In fact, she gave him beer.

Like the gift of a sandwich, the provision of aid for social overhead facilities may allow the recipient government to shift funds from overhead projects which it otherwise would have financed with its own funds into second-choice opportunities. The second-choice may lie within the social overhead sphere, but it may lie in areas hospitable to private investment, both domestic and foreign; in the latter event, aid would substitute in some degree for private investment.

Evidence of substitution of projects is of course lacking. One would have to know what was in the minds of the planning staff of the under-developed country before they thought they might obtain some aid. This writer has never had a Minister of Finance on his couch and can hardly imagine the International Cooperation Administration requiring the Director of Planning to submit to the relevant equivalent of the California F test. However, fears of substitution in projects are found in the views of at least one group which in no sense opposed foreign aid. The committee appointed by the Secretary-General of the United Nations to prepare a detailed plan for the Special United Nations Fund for Economic Development (SUNFED) wrote:

"Although non-self-liquidating projects [social overhead facilities] may well constitute a significant part of the total operations of the Fund, its scope should not necessarily be confined to assistance with such projects, provided the assistance granted contributes to the economic development of the country. If the Fund were thus limited, we feel that it would have undesirable effects. *Governments applying for assistance from the Fund might be tempted to shift the use of their own financial resources* away from that combination of non-self-liquidating and other projects which would be most desirable for the promotion of their countries' economic development. *They might either be tempted to withhold their own resources from the category of projects assisted by the Fund;* or, alternatively, they might put too many of their own resources into this category of projects in order to obtain additional assistance from the Fund. [21]

Clearly, to sustain the contention that foreign aid for the social overhead will assist the growth of private foreign and domestic investment, the proponents of the social overhead thesis must show that a compensating substitution in projects does not occur. This is a formidable task. Unfortunately, it is not enough to say that the administrators of the aid program can watch the policies of recipient countries to determine if substitution has occurred. Even if the social overhead expenditures (exclusive of aid) of the recipient country rose, the administrators of the aid program would have to know that they would not have increased more in the absence of aid. And, even if the recipient government were found to have intervened increasingly in spheres congenial to private enterprise, the administrators would need to know whether or not this would have happened in the absence of aid.

A second possible deterrent effect of aid on private foreign investment is a substitution in sources of finance. Clearly, an underdeveloped country is wise to obtain foreign capital as cheaply as possible. In fact, it would be unpatriotic to do otherwise. If aid funds are provided on cheaper terms than private foreign investment, the country would be well-advised to substitute aid funds for private funds in some degree. [22]

Support for this kind of substitution effect also is found among some writers who favor aid for development. For example, the authors of *The Political Economy of American Foreign Policy* wrote "The only important deterrent effect on private foreign investment of large-scale investment of United States Government funds abroad is that it gives rise to misunderstanding of what is a reasonable return commensurate with risks. [23] We can logically conclude that governments of underdeveloped countries would therefore do less to attract private foreign investment than they would in the absence of aid.

Still another example is provided by the experts who wrote the

United Nations' *Measures for Economic Development of Underde-veloped Countries.* They noted that the removal of certain United States obstacles to the flow of American portfolio investment over-seas would increase the supply of capital available for export but "The demand may not, however, be large since only the borrowers with the best credit could hope to borrow more cheaply in the open market than they can borrow from the Export-Import Bank, or from the International Bank." [24]

A third deterrent may prevail even if foreign aid is not cheaper than private foreign capital. Suppose that the Prime Minister of an under-developed country has two goals, a greater percentage of the economy under direct state control and more economic development. Suppose further that these two goals—end-products—are in some degree substitutes for one another in the mind of the Prime Minister. He would, therefore, be willing to give up some of one product—control—for some additional amount of the other product—develop-ment. But he would admit additional private foreign investment to permit more development only up to the point at which the benefits from additional development just offset the benefits lost through the decreased control which is implicit in absorbing more private foreign investment. Having reached such a balance, if the Prime Minister is given a choice, at the same cost to the country, between aid for social overhead services (which came under his control) and private foreign investment, he would clearly choose the aid; assuming that both would assist development in equal amounts, aid would provide him with the same amount of development but with more socialism. [25]

A fourth interaction between foreign aid and private foreign in-vestment is found in the bargaining element which may accompany inter-governmental transfers. The United States Government could withhold aid as a device for bargaining for improvements in the cli-mate for private foreign investment. The International Bank for Reconstruction and Development, the Export-Import Bank, and the foreign assistance agencies have done this in varying ways and de-grees.

As long as the benefactor is entirely free to withhold aid at a net gain to himself, he can establish conditions on his gifts as he pleases. But economic development assistance is viewed by the United States Government as an instrument of foreign policy. The American gov-ernment is not so much interested in development per se as in the political benefits which development and the act of aid may bring. Hence, the way in which we give aid can be as important as the aid itself. To lay down unwanted conditions on aid to a country could

be the worst possible course of action in terms of our political goals
if those conditions would alienate the recipient. Conversely it might
be worthwhile to run the risk of incurring the displeasure of the current foreign government by imposing conditions if they would significantly advance, by stimulating private investment, the rate of development, which in turn might bring future political benefits.   The
grantor faces a tricky choice of policies.

Even if aid were a sure lever for lifting private foreign investment,
either through the provision of social overhead services or the attachment of conditions to improve the investment climate, it is not certain
that it would be worth it. Leaving aside any political benefits which
may accrue, the direct gain to the United States from increased private overseas capital flows consists of the additional dividends, profits, and interest receipts which they may earn abroad. Certain indirect benefits may also be obtained, from both expanded private
foreign investment and from the aid which stimulates it, in the form
of improved terms of trade and a greater gain from trade; private
foreign investment and aid may increase the supplies and reduce the
prices of foreign products, e.g., raw materials, required by the United
States and may stimulate the demand for American products by raising
foreign incomes.

Against these benefits must be set the cost of aid. The net balance
is obviously uncertain because it is impossible to predict how much
private foreign investment will expand (or contract) in response to
a certain amount of aid, as argued above. Furthermore, the existence
of the benefits is in doubt. It is often noted that American exports
are greater to countries which have higher per capita income. This
suggests that the demand for American exports is greater the higher
the foreign income, thereby improving American terms of trade and
gain from trade. But the premise on which this is based is such a
naive correlation that it requires no comment. [26] Foreign economic
growth financed by a transfer of resources from the United States
(private or government) can move the American terms of trade and
gain from trade in either an unfavorable or favorable direction. [27]

It is also contended that United States aid improves the American
gain from trade by protecting sources of supply. This relies mainly
on uncertain political equations, which cannot be verified by an economist. But an economic aspect should be considered: the provision
of aid may relieve a country of the need to depreciate its currency
in order to expand exports to buy capital equipment from abroad;
therefore, raw material supplies for the United States would be smaller than they otherwise could be.

In sum, it is altogether uncertain whether aid which induces foreign economic growth and expands private foreign investment will return net economic benefits. But suppose there were no uncertainty. Dean Edward Mason writes: "The economic growth of the United States is made somewhat easier if growth likewise takes place in the under-developed areas of the world. It is better for us economically if we can depend on low-cost foreign sources of raw material supply than to be forced to exploit high cost domestic sources or to develop synthetic substitutes. . . . But the favorable repercussion on the United States economy of an accelerated rate of growth in under-developed areas is not—in itself—likely to be such as to justify a large United States foreign aid program designed to promote this development. *We can obtain a larger return for our money elsewhere.*"[28]

Some approval is gained, no doubt, for aid programs because of the economic arguments provided. But one of those arguments—the social overhead thesis—cannot withstand scrutiny. It should be reduced to the footnotes. Its demotion would serve to return the debate on aid to the primary questions of the political benefits gained and to the equity issues involved in the foreign assistance programs.

---

[1] The following sources may be consulted for most parts of the argument. Committee for Economic Development, *Needed: A New Foreign Aid Policy,* (April 1957), pp. 6-7; Committee for Economic Development, *Economic Development Abroad and the Role of American Foreign Investment,* (February, 1956), pp. 16, 21; International Development Advisory Board, *A New Emphasis on Economic Development Abroad,* (March, 1957), p. 13; Raymond T. Moyer, International Cooperation Administration, *Hearings before the Committee on Foreign Relations, U. S. Senate, on the Mutual Security Program for Fiscal Year 1958,* p. 637; Roy Blough, "Foreign Policy and Investment Abroad," *Management Guide to Overseas Operations,* ed. by Dan H. Fenn, Jr. (New York: McGraw-Hill, 1957), pp. 213-214; Research Center for Economic Development, University of Chicago, *The Role of Foreign Aid in the Development of Other Countries.* A Study Prepared at the Request of the Special Committee to Study the Foreign Aid Program, U. S. Senate, (March, 1957), pp. 19-20, 54-55; The Center for International Studies, Massachusetts Institute of Technology, *The Objectives of United States Economic Assistance Programs.* A Study Prepared at the Request of the Special Committee to Study the Foreign Aid Programs, U. S. Senate, (January, 1957), p. 40; American Enterprise Association, *American Private Enterprise, Foreign Economic Development, and the Aid Programs,* A Study Prepared at the Request of the Special Committee to Study the Foreign Aid Program, U. S. Senate, (February, 1957), p. 55; International Development Advisory Board, *Partners in Progress,* (March, 1951), ch. 7.

[2] Sometimes, more fittingly, social and economic overhead.

[3] For a discussion of the difficulties of assessing aid in terms of these benefits,

see the writer's "Foreign Aid—Some Issues and Problems in Assessment," *Federal Expenditure Policy for Economic Growth and Stability,* Joint Economic Committee, November, 1957.

[4] Edmund S. Whitman, *Threefold Way to Western Hemisphere Unity.*

[5] See Wayne C. Taylor and John Lindeman, *The Creole Petroleum Corporation in Venezuela,* (Washington: National Planning Association, 1955).

[6] Center for International Studies, Massachusetts Institute of Technology, *STANVAC in Indonesia,* (Washington: National Planning Association, 1957) pp. 63-64.

[7] Even supposing that the recipient governments use all of the proceeds for social overhead services, the total of tax payments need not constitute a net contribution to the social overhead because the advent of foreign firms and the growth of economic activity which they induce will increase the need for social overhead services. Some American communities, after successful efforts to attract industry, have found that the additional tax resources produced were insufficient to finance the induced increase in required communal services. However, whatever doubts one may have on this count concerning the contribution of private foreign investment to social overhead, they are not relevant to the social overhead thesis. If added private firms do not bear the full costs of their activities, it is hardly their fault since tax policy belongs to the government. Furthermore, in view of the tendency of underdeveloped countries to discriminate against foreign firms in the administration of taxes, it is not at all clear that they do not bear the full costs and more. Incidentally, where foreign governments fail to impose appropriate taxes, the argument considered in this footnote would seem to support reliance on private foreign investment in extractive industries—the frequent whipping boy in many discussions of international investment. Investors in extractive industries, more often than in other industries, provide their own social overhead facilities.

[8] *Economic Survey of Latin Amreica,* 1956, II, p. 109 (mimeo.)

[9] Such is the case, in economists' terminology, where (1) external effects prevail and/or (2) where indivisibilities exist such that marginal cost pricing would bankrupt the firm unless each firm could act as a perfectly discriminating monopolist.

[10] Taxes levied to cover the loss or subsidy will misallocate resources which imposes a cost on the nation; hence, subsidies and losses should not be set so as to completely close the gap between the value of the additional benefits and the additional true costs. Support for subsidies is found, though on grounds largely irrelevant to this essay, in Economic Commission for Latin America, *International Cooperation in a Latin American Development Policy,* (New York: United Nations, 1954), pp. 99-100.

[11] Daniel Thorner, "Great Britain and the Development of India's Railways," *Journal of Economic History,* XI (Fall, 1951), p. 391.

[12] J. S. Duncan, *Public and Private Operation of Railways in Brazil,* (New York: Columbia University Press, 1932), pp. 22-23. There may be some very serious problems in constructing a subsidy which produces precisely the desired result. An example of one difficulty is the snake-like system developed in Brazil which resulted from the fact that the subsidy was based on a fixed amount of capital investment per kilometer so that the railroad companies were induced to avoid grades at all costs. *Ibid.,* p. 26.

[13] John C. Rayburn, "Rail Transportation in Venezuela," *Inter-American Economic Affairs*, (Spring, 1957), p. 23.

[14] H. S. Ferns, "Investment and Trade between Britain and Argentina in The Nineteenth Century," *Economic History Review*, Second Series, III (1950), pp. 205-206.

[15] "The Entrepreneur in American Capital Formation," *Capital Formation and Economic Growth*, (Princeton: Princeton University Press, 1955), p. 353.

[16] This assumes that the subsidies and losses, except as they increase real income and thereby permit more voluntary savings, are not allowed to effect the aggregate volume of domestic investment. If aggregate investment rose, an involuntary decline in consumption would occur, and any change in consumption resulting from the subsidies or losses would make the poverty of a nation a relevant obstacle to the use of subsidies or losses. Of course, devices are at hand to prevent the involuntary reduction in consumption.

[17] See, however, the first sentence of footnote 10.

[18] This hides a subtle issue. If the subsidies or losses lead to a rise in the aggregate volume of domestic investment, apart from the increase permitted by a rise in voluntary savings attributable to an increase in real income, compulsory development occurs. The current population suffers a reduction in its consumption and future generations benefit by having a greater capital stock. Members of the current population may give less weight to the interest of unborne generations in determining the current rate of investment than the members of the unborne generations would if they had a voice in the present. If one believes that unborne generations should be given more consideration in determining the current rate of investment and if the subsidies or losses do induce a rise in the aggregate level of investment, the statement in the text still holds but the nation is redefined to include unborne generations. Note that on such a premise the second sentence of footnote 16 is invalid.

[19] This paragraph applies only to external effects; see footnote 9.

[20] A brief but valuable discussion of certain aspects of this question is found in *Staff Papers Presented to the Commission on Foreign Economic Policy* (Randall Commission), (Washington: Government Printing Office, February, 1954), pp. 134-136.

[21] United Nations, *Report on a Special United Nations Fund for Economic Development*, (New York: 1953), p. 20. Italics added.

[22] No substitution would occur if the marginal product of capital were constant in the range of additional capital supplied through aid. If the marginal product were not constant the fact that aid monies and private capital might go into different projects (and would therefore seem to be imperfect substitutes) would be of little significance over the longer run since a void in private investment in certain fields could be made up through government investment in those areas.

[23] William Y. Elliott, *et. al.*, (New York: Henry Holt, 1955), p. 332n.

[24] United Nations, 1951, p. 80.

[25] A number of arguments have been adduced to show that the provision of social overhead services will deter private investment. S. H. Frankel argues in *The Economic Impact on Underdeveloped Societies*, (Cambridge: Harvard University Press, 1953), p. 105, that the construction of such facilities will lead to inflationary pressures which will foreclose transfer of profits to private foreign investors. This may be true as a matter of practical fact but, as he points out, it need not be so if the government pursues proper monetary and fiscal

policies. Furthermore, the contention is not relevant to the social overhead thesis since aid is, per se, deflationary.

[26] See Loreto Dominguez, *International Trade, Industrialization, and Economic Growth,* (Washington: Organization of American States, 1956) for a review of the literature and some statistical evidence which raises doubts.

[27] See James Meade, *Trade and Welfare,* (Oxford: Clarendon Press, 1955), ch. 27 for the models.

[28] *Promoting Economic Development,* (Claremont: The Associated Colleges, 1955), p. 19.   Italics added.

7: *Political Economy of Non-Development*

PETER T. BAUER

Proposals for accelerating the economic development of undeveloped countries by compulsory saving—that is, special taxation to accelerate capital formation, notably government investment expenditure—is a major issue of contemporary economic discussion. Its adoption is now influentially advocated as a principal criterion for the allocation of United States economic aid.[1] These policies state that government has to determine the rate of saving and investment by special taxation; and that the composition and direction of economic activity must therefore be determined largely by government action. These proposals are here examined in the light of economic history, of technical economic analysis, and of wider social and political considerations, proceeding from the more technical and special matters to wider and more general issues.

The term undeveloped is used here to denote countries in which real income and capital per head are low compared to those of North America, Western Europe, and Australasia; in which major output is for subsistence rather than market offering; and in which technological advances have been little applied to agriculture and industry. This agrees with current usage, except for the major reference to subsistence production.

Compulsory saving as a major element of comprehensive planning is now widely regarded and vigorously advocated as essential for the economic development of about two-thirds of the population of the world, to break the vicious circle of undevelopment, poverty, and stagnation. Yet not one of the countries now developed has advanced by such means. In the economic history of the highly developed countries (Great Britain, Western Europe, Scandinavia, North America and Australia) there was much government intervention, but no special taxation to speed capital formation, and no large-scale government control of the content and direction of economic activity.[2] All of these countries began as undeveloped.

It is in the Soviet countries that compulsory saving and government direction of the economy are essential characteristics of economic activity. These "essential" instruments of advance, now pressed on the undeveloped world, are precisely those of the Soviet Union. Whether they have been effective there is a much debated question, but in their general level of economic attainment the Soviet economies are undoubtedly still far behind those of the developed world. The proposition that no country has become developed by these measures is therefore not disturbed.

On the other hand, the forces which produced economic advance in the early history of the developed countries are already present in many parts of the undeveloped world. This is clear from the rapid development of many of them. Latin American countries are reported to have increased the gross national product by an annual increase in output per head of 2 per cent from 1935 through 1953,[3] and to have reached the annual rate of 2.4 per cent from 1945 through 1955.[4] West Africa and Southeast Asia have also advanced very rapidly during the present century. Although national income figures for these areas are inadequate or altogether absent, the rapid advance is clear from various statistics notably, but not only, of external trade, public finance, transport returns, and public health. For instance, a half-century ago there were no exports of such staples as Southeast Asian rubber, West African cocoa, groundnuts, or cotton, and exports of rice from Siam and of oil palm produce from West Africa were a fraction of their present volume.

In some other undeveloped regions, as the Middle East, South Asia, and East and Central Africa, economic development has occurred, but more slowly. Still other areas, notably many regions of Africa and Asia and parts of Latin America, have shown no significant economic advance.

Differences in rates of development reflect different combinations of the prerequisites of development such as possession of useful natural resources or accumulated capital, access to foreign contacts, institutional arrangements, economic qualities of the people,[5] and government policies. There is no general law or prescriptive right of development that all communities should ever attain the same standard of living or the same rate of progress. There is no more reason for expecting this for nations than for individuals, firms or industries. There is obviously no more reason for expecting economic equality than equality in height, appearance, or individual attainment for that matter.

Least of all is there any reason to expect that the different nations of the world would be caught up simultaneously and uniformly in the stream of material progress, even to be pushed at one time into it. It is just this difference in material progress which is reflected in economic attainment. It is misleading and naive to regard such differences as abnormal and reprehensible, and as reflecting selfishness and malice in the developed nations, rather than differences in the undeveloped nations themselves.

The proponents of compulsory saving find tenuous support in actual or apparent ignorance of important categories of capital and capital formation. Much capital formation has been in categories which are unrecorded in statistics and unrecognized in discussion. Cultivated agricultural properties under private non-corporate ownership, and their extension and improvement, are the most important of these neglected categories; others are livestock, various types of equipment, simple structures, and, in a related field, traders' inventories. This neglect leads to the curious treatment of the East African groundnut scheme, which has not yielded any groundnuts, as investment, with the complete disregard of millions of small-scale agricultural properties in Africa producing a huge tonnage of groundnuts; and the equally strange recognition of rubber estates as investment and the exclusion of smallholdings, which cover an area in Southeast Asia about equal to that of the estates.

Spurious support is further gained for the compulsory saving device through drastically under-estimating or even ignoring the economic improvement which has occurred in many parts of the undeveloped world. This may reflect an unwarranted identification of poverty with stagnation, in order to support policies, or a belief that incomes are so low in undeveloped countries that they could hardly have been lower in the past.[6] It may also express a naive respect for conventional statistics.

Reductions in death rates, with differential rates of population increase, must be considered in international comparison of income per head. Because of changes in relative populations in different countries, the mean income per head may fall in the world as a whole, even if it has increased in every single country, poor or rich. Thus there is little validity or meaning to the frequent suggestions that mean income in the undeveloped world has declined in the last half-century, and that inequality with the developed world has increased. Yet this argument serves as a basis for radical policies both on a national and international level. Surely the familiar process of measuring economic advance by changes in real income per head understates economic progress when this is, as usual, accompanied by falling death rates and rapid population increases.

While economic literature has by and large emphasized the stagnation of the undeveloped economies, political, anthropological, and
sociological writings discuss frequently the rapid changes in many of
them. It is evident from general economic history and from recent
experience in undeveloped countries that low *levels* of income and
capital may be found associated with either slow or rapid *rates* of
development.

Even though the economic advance which has taken place in
undeveloped countries is generally under-rated, the recognition of
the development which has occurred, though highly relevant, does
not dispose of the proposals for even more accelerated development.
These proposals lean heavily on the demand for compulsory saving
and comprehensive planning with particular emphasis on compulsory
saving. The stress on compulsory saving is supported by the argument that it is required to increase income per head, which is said to
depend on the rate of investment, and that this increase in income
per head is the essence of desirable development. These propositions
are usually advanced as simple or even axiomatic. They appear, on
examination, to be misleading oversimplifications.

The relation between compulsory saving and capital is complex.
It is profitable to examine the consequences of compulsory saving
in terms of two sets of effects, which may not be entirely independent.
First are the effects of collection. [7] When the economy operates
partly on a subsistence basis, as is the case in all undeveloped countries, taxation falls on production for the market. Thus the attractive-
ness of market production declines, and there is relatively greater
advantage for the producer who reduces his market production in
favor of subsistence. This is movement *away from development*. To
the degree that compulsory saving pushes people into the subsistence
sector and out of the money economy they push the country away
from the possibility of remaining in the international market where
industrial capital goods must be obtained—if the undeveloped lands
are to have them.

While, as is well known, taxation often increases both the total
supply of effort and also the supply of effort to the exchange sector,
compulsory saving is overwhelmingly likely to reduce the volume of
private saving. It reduces net income (i.e., after taxes), and this typically results in reduction of saving out of proportion to the reduction
in consumption.

The second set of effects of compulsory saving are those derived
from disbursement of the taxes. In terms of general economic rea-

soning little can be said, and admittedly certain types of government investment can be highly productive both in capital formation and in economic development. Improvement of basic communications, water control schemes, or promotion of education are examples. However, there are various influences in the direction of uneconomic expenditure. Perhaps the most important of these is the facile and obviously unwarranted belief that development is a direct correlate of investment expenditure. This disregards variation in investment's contribution to output, let alone to desired output, and disregards also the time interval between expenditure and output, plus the uncertainty of the value of the uncertain output in the undefined future.

The proceeds of compulsory saving are not a net addition to the supply of capital, but a transfer of funds. To regard them as a net addition, as is usual in development plans, is to consider them costless. Such an approach ignores the inevitable repercussions on the private sector (i.e., non-governmental economic activities) of both the transfer or collection and expenditure of the funds. By ignoring the almost inevitable reduction in the private sector, gross capital formation is presented as net. It is even possible that excessive reduction in private capital formation may produce a net decline in a country's total capital accumulation. Whatever the outcome, the process of compulsory saving cannot be rationally considered except as a transfer of funds.

Even if compulsory saving increases the net supply of investable funds, this does not guarantee a like growth of income. Income is not a simple product of investment expenditure. Other factors may be even more important in increasing income, such as the supply of complementary resources, suitable institutional arrangements and government policies, and especially the quality and attitudes of the people. Heavy expenditure may produce no development, while slight expenditure may produce much—through the spread of technical knowledge, or the emergence or extension of the exchange economy.

It is far truer to say that capital is created in the process of development than that development depends on capital formation and especially investment expenditure. This derives from the presence of other influences, and also from the *composition* of gross investment. Gross investment includes important categories of items on which income is spent rather than promoting growth of income—of which housing is only one example.

Even if compulsory saving should increase income per head, if development has meaning as a desirable process, it must refer to an

increase in *desired* output. Governmental collection and investment
of saving effect production which is not subject to the test of voluntary purchase at market price, but is rather measured by cost. Increased output through this method is at best an ambiguous indicator
of economic improvement. For a substantial part of governmentally
enforced investment it is possible to go further. If the capital is not
provided voluntarily, this suggests that the population prefers an
alternative use of resources, whether current consumption or other
forms of investment. [8]

But beyond the purely technical economic considerations, an assessment of the processes of compulsory saving and comprehensive
development planning involves wider issues of a political character.
The effects of such comprehensive and far-reaching policies pervade
political and social life. Many consequences of alternative policies
can be identified, but reactions to these consequences depend on
ideological commitments rather than on logical analysis.

It is often suggested that, in the context of economic development,
individual choice and valuation are irrelevant because they depend
on social environment which will be radically changed by development. For those to whom individual choice is irrelevant, compulsory saving and compulsory planning are fully acceptable.

The right of some individuals or groups to force others to develop,
within a country or internationally, is not obvious. The proponents
of forced development assume that it is obvious—but they are very
different people from those who bear the cost whether in the sacrifice of income or the social strains involved. The proponents are
largely urban, while the cost falls on the countryside. Frequently
they are foreigners: foreign politicians, academic economists and
other social scientists, journalists, and above all, spokesmen for the
international agencies. Moreover, quite often the advocates enjoy
large incomes and influential positions created by the very development programs they espouse.

Since the widening of the range of choice is one advantage of
development, the consequences of compulsory development in this
area are of interest. [9] Compulsory saving implies centralized decisions
on the composition of the national income, so that the access of individuals to alternatives is severely restricted both as consumers and
as producers; and a heavy taxation, which greatly restricts the command of the individual over the fruits of his labors. The consequence
is unavoidable, but the advocates are not concerned.

Even if compulsory saving were to increase appreciably the national income conventionally measured, the political system and the na-

ture of society are likely to differ greatly from those whose development was not dependent on such processes. This obvious general consideration is borne out by the nature of Soviet societies where compulsory saving and comprehensive development planning are essential features of the economy. I repeat that in no now developed country have these processes been found necessary.

The nature of the process by which incomes are increased in undeveloped countries will undoubtedly greatly affect the character of the society which emerges, and thus determine the broader and more significant meaning and result of the process.

This discussion is not to suggest that the major undeveloped areas of the world should remain undeveloped, or that economic backwardness somehow creates happiness. Rapid change in these areas is inevitable, and on many different grounds may be desirable. But rapid change produces great strains and problems, and different methods of advance may produce different results in this realm. Although the strains appear whether the propellant of change is private enterprise or government investment, there is a distinct likelihood that they will be especially great under large-scale public investment financed by compulsory saving. Such a process of development assumes a homogeneity in the population of the affected country such as that of Sweden, which developed without using the techniques. Most of the undeveloped lands, however, are not of one nationality or one ethnic group, but are characterized by a cultural pluralism which would be unimaginable to the developed nations outside the Soviet territories. India, for example, has dozens if not hundreds of dialects, languages, and ethnic enclaves.

Private investment is undertaken in the expectation of profitable returns. These depend on adequate skills, as well as social institutions and attitudes not wholly unrelated to the activities stemming from the investment. Private investment implies decentralized decision-making, based on local differences in opportunities, costs and complementary resources. This allows adaptation of economic activity to local conditions and attitudes. [10]

Public investment is not linked to the expectation of profitable returns, and is not therefore closely geared to the presence of complementary factors. Thus the likelihood of acute social strain is much greater under large-scale public investment than under private investment. This conclusion is strongly reinforced by the necessarily centralized nature of investment decisions in public investment which therefore cannot be adjusted closely to the actual tremendous variations in local conditions. [11]

It is fair to suggest that the rapid spread of groundnut production by the establishment and extension of hundreds of thousands or millions of peasant holdings in West Africa, occurring so smoothly as to be barely noticed and producing a vast quantity of groundnuts, stands at one end of the spectrum, whereas at the other end stands the East African groundnut scheme which has yielded no groundnuts after the expenditure of £ 35 million, and at the cost of great local upheaval. [12]

Large-scale compulsory saving and comprehensive development planning as major instruments of economic policy in undeveloped countries are likely to encourage the development of totalitarian regimes. [13] This is not a matter of concern for those whose values are totalitarian, of course, but political contentment is not a function of the rate of economic advance or of the level of income. The lack of correspondence is particularly notable during periods of rapid social change accompanied by a disintegration of traditional communal life. Readiness to accept a totalitarian regime is very great when traditional communities and loyalties have been swept away, and the people have not yet evolved satisfying new relationships. [14]

Regardless of the social consequences intrinsic to the process, some people, usually spokesmen of the international agencies or governments, or university teachers or journalists, emphasize the need for a higher rate of development. But this postulates additional resources which the population is not prepared to make available voluntarily, either by loans or by gifts, that is either by voluntary saving or by charity or public spirit. Therefore they must be taxed for the purpose, that is they must be compelled to surrender the resources. This still does not yield sufficient investment, and additional resources have to be supplied from abroad. But again, foreign individuals cannot be induced to lend or to give voluntarily, that is to supply the resources by private lending or through charity. At the same time the government of the under-developed countries cannot tax the foreigners, so that it becomes necessary to persuade the foreign governments to tax their own people and hand over the proceeds. In short, neither the citizens of these countries, nor the foreigners, are prepared to supply the resources voluntarily. They have to be extracted compulsorily from the local population by taxation; and foreign governments have to be persuaded (or blackmailed) to make their own citizens contribute to the process. [15] The extent to which the process can be carried depends on political factors, such as the amenability of the local population to taxation and of the foreign governments to persuasion.

Compulsory saving and development planning imply extensive socialization of the economies of under-developed countries at an early stage of their development. This method is not advocated widely but is proposed as a condition of the receipt of foreign aid, especially American aid. Opinion about the desirability of this far-reaching process must be governed largely by one's political position. But it is clearly desirable that the principal relevant considerations should be understood before the resources of the most powerful developed economies are harnessed to measures designed to socialize the underdeveloped world in conditions in which any economic benefit is far more conjectural than the likely social strain and political upheaval.

[1] I use the term compulsory saving in the sense that has come to be generally accepted in both academic and popular usage.

[2] Japan, a country where in spite of rapid economic advance the standard of living is still very low compared to Western standards, provides an apparent exception to the argument of the text. There was some measure of compulsory saving in Japan in the decades following the Meiji restoration, but it was a comparatively minor feature in the economic advance, which moreover started from a higher level and in more congenial conditions than have prevailed in many under-developed countries in recent years. Nor was it accompanied by comprehensive development planning. Altogether the process was entirely different from that envisaged in current proposals for compulsory development in underdeveloped countries.

[3] These figures exclude the effects of the improvement in the terms of trade. If these are included the figures are raised to 4.7 per cent and 2.4 per cent respectively. The information is from Analyses and Projection of Economic Development, United Nations, 1955. This is a study prepared by the Economic Commission for Latin-America which is generally at pains to emphasize the disabilities under which under-developed countries are alleged to suffer, and on this ground its estimates are more likely to err on the side of under-statement rather than exaggeration of the rate of growth.

[4] *Economic Survey of Latin-America* 1955, United Nations, 1956, p. 3.

[5] It has even been seriously suggested that the absence of qualified personnel to undertake the work of economic programming is one of many vicious circles in which the under-developed countries are caught. Investment Criteria and Economic Growth, Center for International Studies, Massachusetts Institute of Technology, 1954, p. 25.

[6] This belief seems related to the suggestion that the position of underdeveloped countries is, or was until recently, comparable to that of Western Europe on the eve of the industrial revolution. In fact, however, Western Europe had by then reached a far higher level of social attainment than most of the under-developed world at present, or until very recently.

[7] These matters are discussed more fully in Bauer and Yamey, *The Economics of Under-developed Countries*, Chicago 1957, chapter 13, and in P. T. Bauer, *Economic Analysis and Policy in Under-developed Countries*, Durham, N. C., 1957.

[8] This does not mean that this type of expenditure is more or less likely to be

wasteful than other government expenditure, either in the sense that the population would have preferred a different use of resources, or on some other test, such as the cost of performing a particular service or producing a given volume of commodities. But it is in this type of investment financed by compulsory saving that it can be shown most clearly that the population would have preferred a different use of resources.

[9] This is a position which is apparently shared by Professor Arthur Lewis, since he writes "The advantage of economic growth is not that wealth increases happiness, but that it increases the range of human choice." *The Theory of Economic Growth,* p. 420.

[10] At times the rapid progress was so smooth that it remained unnoticed for some years, or even decades. The rapid expansion of the native-owned rubber acreage in Sumatra and Borneo in the 1920's (by means of adding rubber cultivation to the tradition shifting cultivation of dry rice) went unobserved for about six years, and was greatly under-stated in official estimates for another ten years. The establishment and growth of the kola-nut industry in Southern Nigeria received little or no official recognition until a few years ago, and its significance has come to be appreciated only quite recently. There are several other important cash crops, including West African cocoa and groundnuts, the progress of which was under-estimated for long periods.

[11] The decisions are necessarily centralized even if their execution can be decentralized.

[12] Even when the social and economic costs of such measures become manifest this will not induce their proponents to reconsider the principles from which their suggestions stem. Rather the reverse. The heavier the stakes and sacrifices the more reluctant people will be to reconsider the principles in the name of which the sacrifices have been exacted.

[13] A totalitarian regime must be distinguished from a dictatorship. The former refers to the area of human activity controlled by the state; the second to the processes by which the government can be changed. This vital distinction is much obscured in contemporary discussion.

[14] There are many suggestive remarks on this range of issues in Eric Hoffer, *The True Believer,* New York, 1951.

[15] The insufficiency of the combined supply of resources from compulsory saving locally, and from voluntary sources locally and abroad, strengthens the presumption that the society is not ready for the drastic measures envisaged.

8: *The Case for Minimum Interventionism*

Gottfried Haberler

The problem of economic development far transcends the competence of any one discipline. Sociologists, anthropologists, political scientists, and, above all historians should make their contributions. The economist cannot, in this matter, confine himself to the traditional limits of his discipline if he is to say anything useful about economic development.

Some current criteria of economic development deserve special attention in order to distinguish between factors accidentally associated with development and factors essentially associated. First we may consider the naive proposition that to be a rich country is to be a developed country. Saudi Arabia may be cited to show richness without development, since oil resources produce high per capita income without the other essentials of development.

The second fallacy examined is the causal association of high industrialization with high development. Although there are no undeveloped countries which are industrialized, there are clearly highly developed countries which are not industrialized. New Zealand, though predominantly agricultural, is among the most highly developed countries,[1] and, except for industrialization, it would be difficult to show that Iowa or Nebraska are backward. There is, furthermore, no industrial developed country without a highly developed agriculture. Many countries with a high percentage of their labor forces engaged in industry have remained major exporters of both food and raw materials: The United States, Australia, and Denmark, for instance.

The quality of the people in a country is of utmost importance as the basic index to development. A country is more highly developed as its people are better educated, trained, and more efficient in the use of modern means of production. Per capita output, as we can show, depends on many factors of environment in relation to numbers of population. There are, however, striking cases of countries which have offset poor endowment in natural resources. Switzerland, with no natural resources except scenery and water power, has through hard work, thrift resulting in capital accumulation, and full use of international trade, developed a real national income per head and standard of living higher than most countries in the world today. Even the major depletions and capital losses caused by war can be quickly repaired if the free capitalist economy is allowed to function —as is conclusively shown by the prompt recovery of the West German economy after World War II.

A comparison of the characteristics of presently developed countries at the beginning of their development with those which are yet undeveloped highlights significant advantages for development in the present situation. The world's most tremendous and rapid economic development has occurred in the capitalistic era, within the past two centuries or so. At the beginning of the nineteenth century all now-developed countries, except possibly England, were undeveloped. In what ways and to what extent are the presently undeveloped areas in a better or worse position to accomplish rapid economic development?

The whole of modern technology in industry, agriculture, transportation and communication, in addition to advances in preventive medicine furnish an "un-earned" advantage for the backward areas. It is not only possible for the undeveloped countries to leap over two centuries of technological growth, but also to participate in the current increasing rates of growth in the developed countries today. It is not necessary for India to duplicate English inventions, but merely to utilize them.

In fact, the very growth of technology has produced demand for new materials, as well as increased demand for others. This has made assets out of waste for those undeveloped countries in which the materials are located, and added tremendous amounts to their national incomes. The use to which this new income is put is not the present question; it could be allocated to capital accumulation.

These matters seem obvious, but merit attention because of the wide adoption of a theory, especially in UN quarters,[2] that the underdeveloped countries are largely being deprived of the fruits of technological advances of the industrial countries. The whole Economic Commission for Latin America theory is long,[3] but some major points can be refuted here.

A main foundation of the theory is the statement that industrial countries keep the benefits of technological improvements instead of passing them along to buyers abroad in the form of lower prices. This, it is said, is a consequence of the fact that wages are pushed up when productivity of labor rises, so that the price level of the industrial products remains unchanged, if it does not rise.

Now it is admitted that recently trade union activities and extreme full employment policies have combined to push money wages up as fast as productivity, and often faster. Earlier, the tendency was for money income to rise with increasing productivity, while prices remained constant, rather than for prices to decline while money income remained constant. The consequences of both recent and earlier trends are creeping inflation, deplored by some conservative economists because of damage to fixed-income consumers and economic stability. [4]

There is, however, absolutely no reason to believe that the actual wage and price policy reduces real demand for primary products whether produced in industrial countries themselves or in undeveloped countries. Since primary producers in the developed countries know how to protect their own interests, rising industrial wages serve only to raise the general price level higher than it would have been, without producing a general shift in the *relative prices,* as between primary products and manufactures, or in the ratio of export to import prices as between developed and undeveloped countries.

On occasion the criticized wage and price policy is cited as an instance of monopolistic exploitation of primary producers, in both developed and undeveloped countries, by the manufacturing industries in the advanced countries—a conspiracy of trade unions and industrialists. While England enjoyed a monopoly of industrial leadership (as a country) in the early nineteenth century, and attempted to prevent exportation of machinery and know-how to continental Europe and America, her efforts were clearly unsuccessful. Today it is fanciful to accuse developed countries of such restrictions. There is more competition now than ever in the field of capital equipment, machinery, and technological know-how. That there is no national monopoly is proven by the fact that several European countries, plus the United States, Canada, Japan and others, are all eager to supply customers such goods.

This is not to deny that some specific technological changes have hurt some countries, developed as well as undeveloped, just as they have hurt specific occupational groups. Easy examples are the invention of synthetic nitrate, and its impact on the Chilean monopoly of natural nitrate, of synthetic rubber and the changed demand for Malayan natural rubber. But there can be no doubt whatsoever that technological progress, greater availability of capital goods, and improved communicability of technological know-how put the now undeveloped countries in a better position for rapid development than were the developed countries a century ago, or than Great Britain at the beginning of the Industrial Revolution.

In some respects undeveloped countries are handicapped today in comparison with the original circumstances of the now developed countries. There is first the strong probability that European countries started from a higher level of economic development than many undeveloped countries have now achieved. National output, or national income per head was almost certainly higher in Western and Central Europe than it is now in most undeveloped countries.

Human resources were certainly better in Western and Central Europe. Unfashionable—and even taboo—though it be to mention national characteristics now, in certain quarters, the average degree of level of education, literacy, skill, health, energy, physical strength, and capacity for sustained work was higher 100 years ago, and is higher now in the developed countries than it is in the now underdeveloped countries.

Another unpopular but significant consideration is climate. Even the most advanced technology cannot overcome the handicaps of tropical climate. The relation of other natural resources to population was also more favorable in Europe and to European offshoots than it is now in the densely populated undeveloped countries, and in most tropical countries, regardless of population density.

Technological progress and demand for raw materials emanating from developed countries have led to discovery of or activation of previously unknown, unrecognized, or unutilized natural resources in many backward areas. There is, however, acute danger that spurting population growth will cancel partially or entirely such benefits. The Malthusian devil has not been exorcised.

While some of these basic handicaps are inescapable, some can be slowly reduced. Handicaps in natural resources can be overcome, but only by the slow improvement in human resources. All of these handicaps mean that the undeveloped areas cannot develop as fast as more fortunate areas, and that inequalities in income and standard of living will continue to increase. [5]

There are other handicaps, however, which are at least primarily the result of policies, and which may be reduced by policy changes. It is a common complaint that present undeveloped countries receive less help in the form of capital exports than was received by their forerunners. [6] A typical comparison is that of the British record over the period of fifty years before the first world war with current U. S. private capital exports. During this half-century it appears that "Great Britain invested overseas an amount equal to about 4 percent of her national income. . . If the U. S. today were to devote a similar percentage of her national income to the same purpose, she would be exporting funds to the tune of 12 billion dollars each year." [7] Professor Nurske adds: "These figures are almost absurdly large and tend to confirm the view that there was something unique about Britain's foreign investment."

It is unnecessary to treat at length the differences between the economic position of the U. S. and Great Britain which overweigh any apparent similarities that might produce an expectation of such capital exports from the United States today. Even if the external conditions of foreign lending had not changed as they have since 1914, [8] the United States continues an internal demand for capital far stronger than that in tightly-packed pre-war Britain. It is significant to note that British capital moved in response to market demand and the anticipation of highest profits.

But the external conditions of foreign lending and investment have rapidly deteriorated since 1914. Not only has the political climate changed all over the world to make capital exports to undeveloped countries very hazardous and unprofitable, but the foreign investor today has also to reckon with inflation, exchange control, price control, and confiscation, in addition to the normal business risks. [9] But even if these policies changed suddenly and radically, there would be no sudden flooding of capital into the underdeveloped countries. The confiscation of one major foreign capital investment can destroy confidence in many countries which will take years to restore.

The consequence is that basic structural changes in the world economy make it impossible for capital flows to play the same role in development which they played before 1914. Western capital surely could and would make a far greater contribution than it now does if it were not actively discouraged by nationalistic, anti-capitalistic, and generally interventionist policies in the great majority of undeveloped countries. Capital flows toward those opportunities in which potential profit and risk tend to balance, rather than toward unpredictable risks and uncertain, though minimal, profits.

The scope and results of these policies go far beyond the question of international flow of capital. The now developed countries achieved their early development under the comparatively liberal [10] if not completely *laissez faire* conditions of the nineteenth century. But many of the now undeveloped countries are attempting to begin their careers of industrial growth by adopting policies of massive government intervention into the price mechanism which took the West a century to develop. This involves a fantastic misreading of cause and effect, as if meeting an aging millionaire with cancer led one to decide the cancer was the cause of his wealth.

In some underdeveloped countries excessive and unjustified intervention by governments is a major obstacle to development. Having neglected and failed in many of the proper and vital functions of government, all essential to development, they have added the obstacle of an ineffectual effort to do those things which private business and the free market could do better and more cheaply. Then they have stifled the remaining private entrepreneurs with unnecessary restrictions and controls.

It seems that even those who are willing to give governmental economic activities a much larger scope than is justified must recognize that the backward countries are backward, too, in the art of honest and stable politics and efficient administration. While there are obviously great differences in this respect between the underdeveloped countries, the evidence shows that they are generally more backward in political arts and public administration than in industrial management and technology. This is not surprising, since it is far simpler to learn techniques than to act ethically or to establish effective governmental administrative systems.

It is difficult to see how the fact could be evaded, however ignored, that industrial development in the nineteenth century was made possible only by the rise of free enterprise. For brevity, three witnesses may be called—none of whom is by any interpretation an extreme *laissez faire* liberal. First is the famous English economist Alfred Marshall. Along with fixed physical conditions Marshall greatly emphasizes the importance of the rise of human freedom and "free enterprise" as fundamental determinants of eighteenth and nineteenth century industrial development. [11]

The next witness is Lord Keynes, surprising though it may be. He was fully convinced of the productive power of the free enterprise system. He did think that for smooth functioning the system must be supported by compensatory, mostly expansionary, monetary policies. It is held by many that Keynes went too far in this direction, and that his doctrine, particularly as perverted by his disciples, greatly harmed the free enterprise economy by introducing a chronic inflationary bias into financial policy. But Keynes himself never went so far, and rejected these perversions vigorously in the last years of his life.

The third witness is not known for his admiration of the capitalistic system—Karl Marx himself. But Marx, unlike many of his modern hangers-on, had an extremely high opinion of the productive power of capitalism. He describes the capacity of the *bourgeoise* (i.e., of capitalism) to develop underdeveloped countries with warmth and enthusiasm:

"It (the bourgeoisie) has been the first to show what man's activity can bring about. It has accomplished wonders far surpassing Egyptian pyramids, Roman aqueducts, and Gothic cathedrals; it has conducted expeditions that put in the shade all former migrations of nations and crusades.

"The bourgeoisie, by the rapid improvement of all instruments of production, by the immensely facilitated means of communication, draws all nations, even the most barbarian, into civilization. The cheap prices of its commodities are the heavy artillery with which it batters down all Chinese walls, with which it forces the barbarians' intensely obstinate hatred of foreigners to capitulate. It compels all nations, on pain of extinction, to adopt the bourgeois mode of production; it compels them to introduce what it calls civilization into their midst, i.e., to become bourgeois themselves. In a word, it creates a world after its own image.

"The bourgeoisie has subjected the country to the rule of the towns. It has created enormous cities, has greatly increased the urban population as compared with the rural, and has thus rescued a considerable part of the population from the idiocy of rural life. Just as it has made the country dependent on the towns, so it has made barbarian and semi-barbarian countries dependent on the civilized ones, nations of peasants on nations of bourgeois, the East on the West.

The bourgeoisie, during its rule of scarce one hundred years, has created more massive and more colossal productive forces than have all preceding generations together. Subjection of nature's forces to man, machinery, application of chemistry to industry and agriculture, steam-navigation, railways, electric telegraphs, clearing of whole continents for cultivation, canalization of rivers, whole populations conjured out of the ground—what earlier century had even a presentiment that such productive forces slumbered in the lap of social labour?" [12]

It is difficult to believe that three authorities who, if anything, are biased in the opposite direction, should be entirely wrong. If they are not entirely wrong, the underdeveloped countries of today need to learn from history that the free enterprise system has proved its capacity to raise productivity and develop the underdeveloped.

Since even these antagonistic witnesses support a rational policy of free enterprise for development, the lack of development must be examined in terms of flagrant deviations from free enterprise policies.

Perhaps the most serious menace to economic stability and growth in many underdeveloped countries is inflation, whether chronic, continuous, or intermittent. A symptom and consequence of wasteful and disturbing policies, inflation is the cause of serious and damaging distortions.

Inflation is a consequence of at least three policy errors, which produce their results in developed and underdeveloped countries alike. First is the overexpansion of governmental apparatus, vast bureaucracies and expensive armies which are wasteful and which are unsupportable by the poorer countries. Second are the massive wage increases which are directly ordered by governments or enforced by government-coddled trade unions. Argentina, Chile, and Brazil may be cited here. [13]

The third, perhaps most widespread cause of inflation, is the speed with which development is pushed. Impatience to get ahead, or to catch up, is met by the advice of many economists that capital investment is the necessary and sufficient condition for a rapid rise in output and income. So expenditure on capital investment is pushed ahead of the limited supply of capital from savings and imports, the rest of the economy is distorted, and inflation is the consequence—not development.

Now, what are the disastrous effects of inflation? A mere listing of some of them shows their impact on development. (1) Inflation produces social injustice for relatively fixed-income classes, such as teachers, government officials, bond holders, other creditors, and pensioners. (2) Secular inflation discourages thrift, and makes the development of a capital market well-nigh impossible. (3) It drives what savings there are abroad, i.e., encourages capital flight, and it (4) impedes capital imports.

Inflation (5) misdirects the remaining capital available. Open inflation produces excessive investment in inventories, while controlled inflation, if *really* controlled, may produce the opposite effect. Import controls worsen the situation, and lead businessmen to lay in reserves of parts, materials, and replacements which tie up capital in non-productive form.

Since even in underdeveloped countries prices are not entirely uncontrolled, (6) special problems are created by the existence of controlled and uncontrolled prices in a single economy. Public utility rates may, for example, be held down by government intervention below the point which allows maintenance and replacement. This leads to a deficiency in social overhead capital, which is constantly emphasized as essential to development by government planning advocates.

All efforts to repress inflation (7) lead to increasing interventions, controls and misdirected expansion of government. Thus the attempted cure produces further inflation, bigger government, less development.

The loss in income from inflation cannot be specifically measured, but one estimate has been made of the cost in Chile, by Professor Theodore W. Schultz of the University of Chicago. He concluded, after careful study, that "today Chile is operating about 20 or 25 percent below its normal output simply because of the way it is trying to live with its chronic inflation. If you go around in Chile and just assess the resources in agriculture, and in the shops in the cities, and so forth, you have rather a firm basis that if for a few years there was to be a stable price level, and expectations got adjusted, one would see that economy produce about 20 or 25 percent more than is now the case. There is that much slack in the economy, and the slack comes from the fact that there are price rigidities, price controls, and some factor prices, and product prices are held down, foreign exchanges are regulated, all sorts of devices are brought into play, and each distorts the economy a bit, and in Chile these distortions have become serious." [14]

Extended treatment might be given to the consequences of nationalistic restrictions on immigration, in addition to restrictions on foreign investment discussed already. This blocks the use of technical skills, for example, in Argentina and Brazil, and requires the importation of petroleum products into potential oil fields.

It cannot be stressed too much that, economically speaking, these policy obstacles to development are not unavoidable. *If faulty policies hamstring development efforts, the solution is to change the policies.* [15]

Now the "responsibilities" of developed countries to underdeveloped countries have received considerable attention. Not only has aid of all sorts been placed in the category of "responsibility," but Gunnar Myrdal has also presented an extraordinary theory that *the very existence of developed areas is a cause for failure of the backward countries to develop.* [16] The poor countries get poorer *because* the rich get richer. It is needless to add that this result is said to be produced by *laissez faire,* free trade regimes. Add a little planning, nationalism and protection, and the cause for poverty is no longer a cause!

Myrdal is not a Marxist, and it could be argued that he could learn much from Marx. But his theory transposes to the international sphere almost abandoned parts of the Marxian system—the theory of "increasing misery" (*Verelendungs Theorie*) and exploitation theory.

In addition to the handicaps considered above, Myrdal complains that the underdeveloped areas have no backward colonies to exploit. Where are the colonies of Sweden, Germany, and Italy?" Who did the United States exploit? Such statements are not only bad economics, but are also irresponsible utterances calculated to arouse the worst emotions among people already poisoned by nationalism, envy, and hatred for the West.

The whole position is the opposite of the truth. The developed countries have in fact made development possible for the backward areas. What would Malaya be without rubber, Brazil without coffee, Iraq and Venezuela, and Iran without oil, Ghana without cocoa, Argentina without beef? Remove contact with developed countries, and catastrophe would ensue.

I must refuse to follow Myrdal's example of absurd overstatements. Government does have a role in underdeveloped as well as developed countries. Development is slowed, or rendered impossible, not only because government attempts to do too much, but also because it tries to do the wrong things. This inevitably means that the governments of many underdeveloped countries, in the course of economic intervention, end by failing in the tasks they can and should perform, and which are unavoidable essentials for rapid economic development.

1. See John B. Condliffe, *Population and Economic Development in New Zealand*.
2. See especially publications of ECLA (Economic Commission for Latin America) e.g., *The Economic Development of Latin America and its Principal Problems*. 1950, *passim*.
3. It has been effectively criticized by Professor Viner, *International Trade and Economic Development*. The Free Press, Glencoe, Illinois, 1952, and Professor B. Rogge, "Economic Development in Latin America: The Prebisch Thesis," in *Inter-American Economic Affairs*, Spring, 1956, Vol. 9, No. 4. See also the present writer's forthcoming paper, "Terms of Trade and Economic Development," read at a roundtable conference of the International Economic Association in Rio de Janeiro, August, 1957.
4. Everybody agrees that if wages are pushed up so fast that it causes infla-

tion, economic stability is bound to suffer. But if money incomes (wages) rise only in proportion to the rise in overall productivity, many economists feel that stability can be maintained.

5. Professor Kuznets (*loc. cit.*) gives statistical evidence for that.

6. Gunnar Myrdal in his series of lectures *Development and Underdevelopment,* delivered in Cairo under the auspices of the National Bank of Egypt (Cairo, 1956) enumerates among the many handicaps of the present underdeveloped countries the fact that "they do not have at their disposal an international capital market as the now developed countries had at their time." (p. 76)

7. Ragnar Nurkse, "International Investment Today in the Light of 19th Century Experience." *Economic Journal,* December, 1954, pp. 744-5.

8. It is interesting that Keynes was very critical of the British policy of exporting capital. "To lend vast sums abroad for long periods of time without any possibility of legal redress, if things go wrong, is a crazy construction; especially in return for a trifling extra interest." "If a loan to improve a South American capital is repudiated we have nothing. If a popular housing loan is repudiated, we, as a nation, still have the houses. If the Grand Trunk Railway of Canada fails its shareholders by reason of legal restrictions of rates chargeable or for any other cause, we have nothing. If the Underground System of London fails its shareholders, Londoners still have their Underground System." This was written long before the second world war: *The Nation and the Athenaeum,* August, 1924.

9. One form of disguised confiscation is the case to which Keynes referred in the quoted passage, namely, legal restrictions on railroad rates which apply to other utilities as well. Under inflationary conditions in many underdeveloped countries legally permissible public utility rates have become ridiculously low in real purchasing power. This has made foreign investment in public utilities, including electric power, impossible, to the great detriment of the underdeveloped economies which are in great need of just that kind of investment.

10. I am using the word "liberal" in the old-fashioned sense of *"laissez-faire* liberal," absence of government regulations, not in the modern perverted sense in which it means exactly the opposite.

11. For Marshall's views on economic development as laid down in his *Principles of Economics* and other works see A. Y. Youngson, "Marshall on Economic Growth," *The Scottish Journal of Political Economy,* Vol.III, February, 1956.

12. *Manifesto of the Communist Party* by Karl Marx and Friedrich Engels. Authorized English Translation. International Publishers, New York, 1932, pp. 11-14.

13. Some of the Latin American dictatorships, e.g., the Peron regime in Argentina, had their principal supporters among organized industrial labor.

14. *Foreign Economic Policy.* Hearings before the Subcommittee on Foreign Economic Policy of the Joint Committee on the Economic Report, Congress of the United States, 84th Congress, First Session, November 9, 10, 14, 15, 16, and 17. Government Printing Office, Washington, D. C., 1955, pp. 581-582.

15. It is not easy to think of cases in which inflation is not the consequence of acts of public policy. An exception may be the case of imported in-

flation—inflation going on abroad and spilling over into a country through a larger export surplus. This is the case of Germany at present, but it would be hard to find an underdeveloped country in such a position. At any rate, no country can be forced against its will (except by physical force) to participate in world-wide inflation. All that it has to do to avoid it is to offset the export balance by open market operations or to let its currency appreciate.

16. See his Cairo lectures quoted above in footnote 6.
17. Germany and Italy had colonies but they acquired them late and it would be an insult to an economist to impute to him the belief that they were anything but an economic liability.

PART IV

INHERIT LIMITATIONS ON WESTERNIZATION

9: *The Population Barrier*

WARREN S. THOMPSON

A paper on this subject finds a place in this symposium for several reasons.

(1) Students of population quite generally recognize that death rates and birth rates, the two decisive variables in determining changes in the size of population, may be controlled by man, but that changes in these rates which are of basic significance may not be controlled independently of many other changes in culture patterns. At the same time, cultural changes which may significantly affect the level of one of these variables do not necessarily affect the other to any measurable extent.

(2) Economists studying economic development find a close relation between the rate of investment in underdeveloped countries and the rate of increase in production. It is obvious, therefore, that the rate of improvement which is possible in the level of living in underdeveloped countries, i.e., the increase in per capita income, is closely related to the rate of population increase—the higher the rate of population increase, the more difficult it will be to raise the level of living, other conditions remaining unchanged.

(3) Throughout human history, until quite recently, changes in the size of populations have been determined chiefly by variations or fluctuations in the death rate which were due largely to variations in the food supply and in the incidence of the contagious and infectious diseases. Although death rates fluctuated widely from time to time, even at their low points they were very high according to our present standards, and at their high points they frequently resulted in substantial reductions in the size of populations.

(4) On the other hand, birth rates as a rule have been much less variable than death rates and have averaged, except under catastrophic conditions, slightly higher than death rates. Until rather re-

151

cently in human history there have been few prolonged periods during which any fairly large population consistently enjoyed a death rate substantially lower than its birth rate. A steady and fairly rapid increase of population has been the exceptional human experience.

(5) We have recently entered a period when basic cultural changes have resulted in great reductions in the death rate. In parts of the West, these changes almost certainly began in the 17th century. In very general terms, these changes consisted at first almost entirely in small improvements in agriculture, and then in the development of slowly improving techniques in nonagricultural production; both of these kinds of changes made life a little easier. As a result, the death rate began to fall, but very slowly and over a rather long period. In the course of time, medical science also came to man's aid. In 1798, the year in which Malthus wrote his first essay, Jenner announced that small-pox could be prevented by vaccination. Eighty years later (1878) Pasteur announced his discoveries. Since that time a veritable flood of medical discoveries have given man an undreamed-of control over diseases.

The point of chief interest to us in this symposium is that all these medical advances can now be applied rather quickly and cheaply in the underdeveloped countries, and that they are being applied in varying degrees in most of them and are reducing the death rate very rapidly. In the West these changes in the death rate came slowly and, with a lag of 50 to 100 years or more, other cultural changes took place which resulted in the decline of the birth rate. This sudden change in the death rate in the underdeveloped countries has not been associated closely with such changes in the efficiency of the economy as actually initiated the decline of the death rate in the West, nor has it had any significant effect on the birth rate among the masses.

(6) This situation poses in an acute form the problem of the adjustment of population growth to probable economic growth. My task here is not to treat the entire problem, however, but rather to indicate some of the more important cultural problems involved in effecting those changes in the birth and death rates upon which the control of population depends. The significance of this discussion rests on the assumption that the rapid growth of population in the underdeveloped countries, or at least in many of the more populous of them, seriously endangers the success of their programs of economic development. Since there is no space to set forth the reasons for making this assumption, I shall proceed to the narrower task of in-

dicating some of the more important of the cultural factors which make population control in underdeveloped countries difficult and which are likely, therefore, to make it so slow as to endanger substantial economic improvement.

There has never been any people among whom cultural factors did not play an important role in determining the size of the population, in spite of the fact that at times uncontrollable physical conditions are the decisively determining factors. Thus some environments, because of the quality of the soil, the length of the growing season, the small annual rainfall, or other characteristics about which man can do little, definitely limit agricultural production and thus limit the population that can live in a given area. Many specific physical happenings which are still quite beyond human control, such as droughts, floods, and the onset of particular epidemics, also may temporarily have a profound effect upon the size of the population. But even many of these physical events and conditions which may be decisive during any given period of time do not act independently of the cultural patterns prevailing among a people.

There is a physiological limit to the birth rate, of course, and physiological factors such as the health of the people and their sexual vigor are important; but the fact is that cultural attitudes have always been very important in determining the birth rate, even more important than they have been in determining the death rate. These attitudes are embodied in marriage customs, in traditional ideas regarding the desirable size of family, in attitudes toward the practice of abortion, in the community's sanction or denial of the right of widows to remarry, and in many other traditional beliefs and practices. The cultural factors affecting the birth rate are usually so deeply imbedded in custom and tradition that people are not conscious of their operation.

On the other hand, most individuals and most peoples are well aware of the impact of immediate and unusual physical events on the death rate; but it is doubtful that they are equally aware that cultural factors also have a significant influence on the death rate. Is it generally recognized that the customary practices of child care largely determine the rate of infant mortality? Do the peoples who practice infanticide realize that it is being used to prevent change in the size of the population? Do the people living in cultures in which boy babies are much better cared for than girl babies realize that when the number of males substantially exceeds that of females, at all the ages which are of consequence for reproduction, that they are not only raising the death rate but reducing the birth rate?

The Cultural Control of the Death Rate

Let us now examine some of the factors effecting changes in the death rate. [18] As noted above, the death rate in underdeveloped countries has generally been high, and has also been quite variable over rather short periods of time. These wide variations in the death rate have usually been due in large measure to variations in those physical conditions over which man has had little control, such as drought and disease. However, even these physical factors seldom operate independently of the cultural factors. Thus, while it is true that the failure of the rains in any particular season, or the occurrence of floods, cannot be attributed directly to the culture of a people, the fact that they have done little or nothing to guard against recurrent disaster from such sources may be due, in part at least, to beliefs and attitudes which are an integral part of their culture. [12] On the one hand, these beliefs and attitudes may lead to indifference or fatalism as regards provision for the storage of water, the digging of wells for irrigation, and the building of dams and dikes to prevent floods; on the other hand, their beliefs and attitudes may encourage both individuals and communities to protect themselves, through such works, against catastrophes. Customs and laws may also determine to a considerable degree whether the new lands which are available will be occupied, and whether they will be used to the best advantage. The death rate, in fact, is much affected by such differences in cultural attitudes. [1]

Cultural attitudes also affect the readiness with which people will accept better farming practices and will provide for the safer storage of food supplies from one season to another. Effort, or lack of effort, in this direction determines to a significant degree the poverty of the people which, in its turn, reacts upon their willingness to risk change in customary practices and upon their physical ability to till their land more intensively. Thus a whole complex of cultural attitudes which may at first appear unrelated has a very significant influence on the level of the death rate, because it prevents vigorous efforts to make a more rational adjustment to the environment. The irregular but recurrent conditions of the physical environment could often be guarded against to a significant degree were it not for cultural attitudes which either cultivate indifference to, or directly forbid interference with, natural processes. The very acceptance of a high infant mortality as natural and inevitable, i.e., that one-fifth to one-fourth of all babies will die before they are a year old, is a factor which has inhibited efforts to reduce this terrific wastage. The same situation results from the customary attitudes toward most contagious and infectious diseases. But in addition to the mental attitudes of resignation, a widespread physical disability results from these diseases and prevents vast numbers of people from any vigorous effort to improve their economic condition.

Culture and Health. In addition to these cultural attitudes and patterns which have always encouraged or discouraged—usually discouraged—man's efforts to mitigate the economic hardships arising from the operation of the natural forces in his environment, we find among most underdeveloped peoples many cultural attitudes which directly obstruct any efforts to introduce new and more scientific controls over disease and illness. [13]

In spite of the repeated demonstrations of their effectiveness, Western medical practices are often rejected for relatively long periods. In general, the reasons they are not accepted lie in the cultural attitudes regarding the cause of disease. These views, in turn, determine the type of treatment which is acceptable. "Prayer meetings" to a god believed to have caused a cholera epidemic may be considered more efficient than inoculation and sanitation in a city in Southwest China because, from the standpoint of the cultural patterns prevailing there, such meetings go to the root of the matter. [7]

In Indian villages the Western-trained doctor does not occupy a position of respect, because he ignores the beliefs of the villagers regarding the causes of illness and the forms of treatment that they consider effective. [8] There can be little doubt that the adoption of a certain amount of what the Western-trained physician would regard as hocus-pocus and charlatanry would hasten the acceptance of Western methods of treatment in many villages. [11]

Western methods for the improvement of health and the consequent reduction of the death rate make headway quite rapidly, however, where they do not require the individual or the community to accept radically different beliefs and practices. Thus, the control of malaria by spraying areas in which germ-carrying mosquitoes breed is highly effective, because most of these areas can be sprayed without offense to the cultural attitudes of the people. But it often turns out that spraying the ponds and swampy areas is not enough and that the ditches along the village streets and the eaves and roofs of the houses also must be sprayed. If this is the case, serious problems may arise, since the villagers may consider such spraying equivalent to introducing new medicine into the village and the home; they cannot permit this, because they feel it may offend the deities which look after the welfare of the community and the family.

As we all know, Western medicine in its native habitat depends largely on an intimate personal examination of the patient by the physician; the results of this examination are not to be imparted by the physician to any other person, aside from parents and guardians, except as authorized. In India the family often, if not generally, accompanies the patient—even the adult patient—on a visit to the physician. The examination is public or semi-public, and usually consists of a mere glance at the patient. The diagnosis is likewise public and is generally very positive; the treatment is traditional and often rather spectacular.[8][11] Hesitancy, or a request for privacy, on the part of the doctor is often regarded with suspicion, as though the physician were concealing important information or lacked confidence in his own medicine, and therefore could not be trusted. Under these circumstances it should not be surprising that the Indian patient, with his traditional conceptions about the causes of illness and about the treatment needed once his particular illness has been diagnosed, is suspicious of Western methods of diagnosis and treatment.

Another important aspect of the maintenance of health, one on which the cultural attitudes of Indians and Chinese differ greatly from those of Western peoples, is the prevention of disease through better sanitation in the local environment. Everyone who has travelled in those countries has seen instances in which attempts to provide and maintain better sanitary practices have failed because the people did not accept the view that invisible organisms (bacteria or viruses) can cause disease. The writer has seen wells, which were efficiently sealed against pollution from surface drainage and which were provided with a pump so that there was no need to drop filthy buckets into them to draw water, re-polluted within a few hours after the pump became temporarily unusable. There simply was no effective belief that a polluted well could cause typhoid, dysentery, cholera, or other intestinal disease. Furthermore, there was no respect for community property to make it possible to keep a windlass, rope and bucket at the well for everyone to use, and there was no community or personal responsibility for keeping the pump in good repair.

The customs of a people can determine the survival rates of boy and girl babies. In both India and China the death rates of boy babies appear to be substantially lower than those of girl babies. This is the opposite of the experience of Western countries. Since there is as yet no evidence that this situation arises from a biological difference between the European and Asian peoples, it must be assumed that it results from the differential care bestowed on boy and girl babies because of the higher value placed on sons than on daughters.

Many other facts might be cited to show that differences in cultural attitudes and practices hinder the adoption of modern health practices.

Dwelling at such length on the difficulties of getting the villagers in India and China to make use of available Western-type health services may give the impression that the writer does not believe that these services are having any influence on the death rates of these countries, or that they will have any influence in the near future. This is by no means the case. As indicated in the introduction, there is abundant proof that the new practices aimed at safeguarding health are catching on rapidly, particularly when they do not require personal acceptance by the individual of new beliefs concerning the cause and treatment of his own noninfectious ailments. Even mass inoculation of a preventive character is making rapid progress, although there is much more opposition to such inoculations in many localities than one might suppose. In China, under an authoritarian regime, force is often used to secure immunization of whole communities. But in spite of rather wide differences between communities, control of the contagious and infectious diseases is taking place almost everywhere in the underdeveloped areas at a fairly rapid pace. Moreover, there can be no reasonable doubt that this rapid (as compared with the rate at which the decline took place in the West) decline in the death rate will continue for some time in most underdeveloped countries, if the necessities of life remain available even at their present low per capita levels. The establishment of maternal and child welfare clinics is proving an extremely effective way to spread better health practices and to increase the people's respect for trained health workers. As a consequence, infant mortality is being reduced and an increasingly large proportion of all the children born are surviving to contribute to further population growth in due time.

THE CULTURAL CONTROL OF THE BIRTH RATE

The control of the birth rate is even more intimately bound up with the most cherished cultural patterns of every individual's daily life than is the control of the death rate. For this reason changes in the birth rate are almost certain to take place much more slowly than changes in the death rate; changes in the latter, as has been pointed out, can often be effected directly and quickly by governmental and community organization of health work.

We are all aware that most cultures place great emphasis on reproduction adequate to insure their survival, and that this emphasis is shown in many and varying beliefs and practices in different cultures. Almost inevitably, in view of the high death rates prevailing everywhere until quite recently, this emphasis on survival led to the development of cultural patterns resulting in high birth rates. It is obvious that as death rates decline survival can be assured with a much lower birth rate; but this fact does not mean that the cultural patterns encouraging a high birth rate will change quickly to sanction the lower birth rate which is now adequate to insure survival. Thus, ancestor-worship among the Chinese makes it imperative that every family have at least one son who lives to maturity to carry on this worship and to see that the family does not die out. This cultural pressure for reproduction adequate to insure continuation of the family is very great in China, and only a little less intense in India. In the past, it has usually been necessary to produce two to three times as many children as were likely to survive in order to be reasonably certain of having even one son live to reproduce—hence the strong social pressure for many births.

There is also a very widespread belief among the farmers of India and China that many children are needed to insure enough help to carry on the farm work during rush seasons—planting and harvest—even though there is not enough work to keep them fully occupied during a considerable part of the year, even when two crops are raised each year. Then, too, children have provided the only possible insurance for care in old age. Thus, the cultural pressure to reproduce prolifically became a powerful factor in determining most of the customs relating to family life.

It is often assumed that because our own culture has come to accept the need for voluntary controls over fertility, other cultures will proceed to adopt such controls with comparatively little reluctance and in a short time. I do not believe that the findings of cultural anthropology justify this hope. The change to voluntary control of births may come quickly in India and China as compared with the rate at which this change took place among the Western peoples, because of the improved methods of communication and the changed attitudes of the leaders toward population control. But as we shall see below, we do not yet know how to break down quickly the resistance of the people in underdeveloped areas to those new ideas and practices which would result in the widespread adoption of birth control. If the example of the Western peoples' adoption of birth control is cited as evidence of how quickly this can be accomplished, we should remind ourselves that the recognized industrial revolution in England started more than two centuries ago, and that the century or more before it began had been a period of widespread "enlightenment." This period had been preparing all the Western peoples for great cultural changes, and yet more than a century passed after the industrial revolution was well begun (1750) in England before there was any noticeable decline in the birth rate (1880).

It is also important to recognize that most traditional cultural patterns have sanctioned practices which prevent the birth rate from rising to its physiological maximum and at the same time have encouraged a high birth rate. In India and China a number of such practices have existed. In India an ancient custom (suttee) made it obligatory for the widow to die on the funeral pyre of her husband. This practice necessarily meant that every year vast numbers of young women who might yet have borne children died prematurely. Since many of the young widows were mothers of young children, their death almost certainly reduced the chance that their children would survive. Even today when suttee is no longer practiced, cultural attitudes are highly unfavorable to the remarriage of widows. This is also true in China, though to a lesser degree.

Many other customary beliefs and practices which affect fertility and the birth rate are so deeply embedded in the cultural matrix that people follow them quite unconsciously. Thus the belief that every woman should marry—and marry at a very young age, by the time of puberty or very shortly thereafter—is supposed to encourage a large number of births per family. I say "supposed" because such early marriage may actually reduce total fertility by increasing the death rate of young mothers and by leading to relatively early menopause. It probably leads also to higher infant mortality among the children born to very young and immature mothers and thus tends to raise the death rate.

The form of sexual relations in marriage and the almost complete dominance of the male also have an important influence on the birth rate. Hence, it would appear that a marked change in the social position of women would be a prerequisite for any substantial decline in the birth rate. There are no prolonged periods of sexual taboo in India and China such as are found among many peoples, and only relatively short periods of purification of the woman after the birth of a child; these facts are probably favorable in general to a high birth rate. The length of time children are nursed by the mother also bears a definite relation to the interval between births, although the time is almost certainly determined by tradition and by the need of the child for its mother's milk rather than by any conscious planning for the spacing of births. If anything should happen in the near future to reduce the length of time children are nursed, it might very well raise the birth rate.

Up to the present the underdeveloped countries are devoting very little effort to the control of the birth rate, even those countries, like India and China, where there is official encouragement of birth control. It may be worthwhile, however, to note briefly what is being done in these countries.

Many of the leaders of India and China at the present time recognize the advantages which would flow from a slower population growth.[48] The proof of this in India is that for several years now the Government has openly advocated family planning as a means of reducing the birth rate, and has allotted a rather considerable sum (Rs. 40 million) in the second Five Year Plan to the furtherance of this purpose. There can be no question that the leaders of India are entirely sincere in their efforts to achieve widespread control of family size among all classes of the population. They see a real danger to all their plans for the improvement of the level of living of the masses in the rapid growth of population at the present time, and in the still more rapid growth to be expected in the near future if health work gains in effectiveness and if there is no conscious and deliberate control over the birth rate. They are fully aware that traditional cultural patterns will keep the birth rate relatively high as long as they operate. They realize that something must be done to reduce the birth rate quickly.

A number of studies have inquired into the attitudes of the Indian people, chiefly the women, regarding family planning, in order to find out what can be done. They seem to me to be so important that they should be described, although very briefly. One such study, which indicates official concern about the rapid growth of population, was undertaken in 1951 by the WHO at the invitation of India's Minister of Health. Its purpose was to ascertain whether the rhythm method of birth control was suitable for use under the conditions of Indian life, and how effective it might be both in reducing pregnancies in particular families and in reducing the birth rate of the community as a whole. Stated in very general terms, the findings of this study indicate to me that this method of conception control was shown to be unsuitable for wide use in India; very few women knew, or were willing to go to the trouble to ascertain, the occurrence of their menses over a period of several months, and the method did not fit into the traditional pattern of marital relations. But such general reasons are not very useful in the planning of an effective campaign to

secure widespread control of conception. The answer, then, was
that the rhythm method could not be expected to be quickly effective
in reducing the birth rate in India—although it seemed to have had
some effect in that *very* small percentage of families which used it
properly over a period of some months.

Furthermore, the reasons given by the women who were opposed
to the control of conception, or who were indifferent to it—"It is not
natural," "It is against the will of God," "We want more children"—
do not give any precise information about the cultural and personal
resistances which must be removed before these women are likely
to take positive action toward spacing their children while they still
want more, or to cease bearing children when the family has reached
the desired size.

Other studies have also found that a considerable majority of the
women said they would like to know how to control conception, but
that when it came to doing something definite about it their interest
quickly disappeared. [16][17] The attitudes of the males appear to be
much the same until they have six or more living children. [12] It seems
to me, in consequence, that these studies have not yet thrown much
light on the peoples' real reasons for not doing anything about controlling the size of their own families nor do they indicate any readiness to control its size before it is large enough to insure survival at
the death rates to which they have been long accustomed.

I would not leave the impression that I believe all efforts to reduce
birth rates in India are hopeless. I do believe, however, that it will
be two to three decades before such a reduction in the birth rate
takes place that the rate of population growth will decline significantly from its present level, to say nothing of stopping growth entirely. In the meantime there will very probably be a period in
which the population of India and, I may add, of most underdeveloped countries, will grow faster than it is now growing. It is my
fondest hope that I am greatly mistaken in my judgment of the time
it will take the people of India to adopt the contraceptive practices
which will result in a rapid and large reduction in the birth rate.

Regarding the time element, Puerto Rico presents an interesting
picture. The birth rate has shown a definite downward trend since
1950, but in spite of this decline the natural increase in 1954 (birth
rate 35.0—death rate 7.6 equals net increase 27.4) was much higher
than in 1932-34 (birth rate 40.6—death rate 21.1 equals net increase
19.5), and was only 3 points below the highest natural increase (30.4
in 1947) ever recorded (20, pp. 631 and 653). Furthermore, the
large movement of young adult Puerto Ricans from the island to the

mainland of the United States may be responsible for a significant part of this recorded decline in the birth rate.

As regards the control of population growth, China's situation differs in many respects from India's and is so unique that I cannot forego a very brief description. The revolution going on in China affects basic social and economic institutions much more directly than does the national development of India. The traditional Chinese family, which has been the basic social unit, is being deliberately destroyed as fast as the Communists can do so. The farmers are being collectivized under heavy pressures, both economic and social. The propaganda machinery of a strong authoritarian government is being used aggressively to break down all types of cultural barriers to the establishment of a new pattern of society. Apparently the leaders of Red China decided in about 1954 that the growth of population which was already taking place as a result of the health services then operating was so great that it endangered the economic success of the revolution. Furthermore, they saw that it would not be long before the rate of China's population growth would be substantially higher than it was in 1954.

The 1953 Census showed a mainland population of 583 millions, a figure larger about 100 millions than that which had previously been used. This information may very well have set off the official campaign for the control of population through contraception, although the first announcements of a need for population control— as far as I have been able to ascertain—preceded the official publication of the Census results by a few weeks. We are interested here in trying to assess the probable success China will have in securing the widespread practice of contraception in the near future. It is too soon, of course, to expect any noticeable results from the very vigorous campaign for population control which is now being carried on, but several facts about this campaign are very interesting. China's birth control campaign is aided greatly by the attempt to destroy the traditional Chinese family, an attempt which has been going on since before the "liberation" in 1949. Besides, the Government of China has a well-developed propaganda machine, and is apparently using it to disseminate information about conception control—both explanations of why it is needed and of the methods which are available for use. In addition, a hard core of Party members can be counted on to follow practices which are approved by their leaders and which are, therefore, considered among the criteria of a good Communist. Finally, it seems that the Government is ready to use the health clinics, which are already established, for instruction in contraceptive practices.

On the other hand, the traditional cultural barriers discussed above must be overcome, and these are bound to be strongest in the 110-115 million families living in the rural villages where health work is the least developed. Hence, even with the best efforts the Government can make, it may well take two decades or more to reach these people, to convince them that it is to their advantage to reduce the size of their families, and to make it possible for them to practice conception control under the conditions in which they live.

At present, official publications say that the rate of population increase is 2.0-2.2 percent per year, and they also claim constantly that great progress is being made in reducing the death rate. One need not believe all of these claims to be convinced that the death rate is falling rapidly and will continue to fall for some time. As yet, no direct claim is made that the birth rate is falling. However, the statements that there has been an increase in the use of contraceptive devices and a great increase of inquiries regarding the means of contraception, even from the rural areas, may be regarded as indirect claims to this effect. Personally, I shall be greatly surprised if there is enough decline in the birth rate in the ensuing decade to hold the rate of population growth at its present level, and if there is any substantial lowering of this rate before the end of the following decade. If China's population is now increasing by 12-14 millions a year, as is frequently claimed, and if a decline in the birth rate started in 1953 and held the numerical increase to 12 millions a year until 1978, the situation at that time would be about as follows: 583 million plus 12 million each year from 1953 to 1958 equals 643 million in June, 1958. Twenty years with an increase of 12 million annually equals 240 million plus 643 million, 883 million in 1978. This assumes, of course, a per capita subsistence at least as adequate as it is at present. Evidence regarding the results of this Chinese experiment in population control will be awaited with great interest everywhere, since it appears to be the most thoroughgoing effort to reduce population growth now being made anywhere in the world.

CONCLUSION

If the outlook for the control of population growth is that two or three decades will be required to reduce the rate of growth substantially below its present level, then improving the level of living of the masses of the people in the underdeveloped countries will be an even more arduous task than has generally been assumed. I believe

that many of the leaders in some of these countries recognize that
the rapid growth of population raises serious difficulties, and I realize that many outsiders are aware of these difficulties. But I also
believe that many of these same people underestimate the obstacles
which stand in the way of widespread adoption of contraception by
the poor and ignorant masses in underdeveloped countries. This, of
course, raises the question of what can be done about the situation.
How are the masses of the people to be made to realize that a smaller
family will meet the basic cultural demand for family survival? How
are they to be convinced that the traditional functions of the family
are changing and that it may not be long until the community takes
over many of them, thus relieving parents of their traditional dependence on children in their old age, and the children of some of the
duties which have been expected of them in the past? How can
men be persuaded to give their wives a larger share in determining
all matters of family concern, and especially in determining the number of children they will bear?

It might seem a simple task to make the mass of the people realize
that as the death rate declines through the improvement of sanitation, the increasing use of Western medicine and, let us hope, the
growing adequacy of the diet, the effective size of the family increases
if the number of children born remains unchanged. But such basic
cultural changes as those which are needed to insure widespread
reduction in the average number of births per family are not effected
among the masses merely by a demonstration that such changes are
rational. What is involved is the acceptance of new values of living,
and this will only happen gradually, as people actually come to live
a little differently, i.e., as they make adjustments to a changing
milieu which they have ceased to think of as new and, hence, as dangerous and subversive. There are as yet no mass methods, analo-
gous to those which can be used to reduce the death rate, which can
reduce the birth rate without doing great violence to the folkways.
Perhaps the methods being adopted in China, and others which will
no doubt be devised as time makes the need for population control
measures even more urgent, will give decisive answers to the questions asked above. I do not believe, however, that much progress
will be made in most of the underdeveloped countries unless they
devote far more effort than they are giving at present to the education
of the people as to the consequences of a rapidly declining death
rate.

Although it has been clear for years that one of the most serious
obstacles to the rapid spread of conception control is the unsuitability

of the methods now available to people who must live at the low levels now prevailing in India, China, and most other underdeveloped countries, little has been done about it. Research in this field could be pushed more vigorously. The invention of simpler, cheaper, and more effective methods of conception control may very well do more to improve the living conditions of the masses in the next few decades than all the expensive industrial research now being pursued. But there is also great need for research into methods of changing more rapidly the cultural patterns which for ages have encouraged a relatively high birth rate. Easy methods of conception control are not likely to render these patterns automatically ineffective. But such cultural patterns can be made ineffective much more quickly if adequate support is given to the study of how to persuade people that it is important to reduce the size of their families.

Fortunately, a number of underdeveloped countries still have enough land to care for a rapidly increasing population for some time to come. Even these countries, however, if they do not soon try to control their population growth, will find themselves within a relatively short time—at a guess, from two to four decades—in much the same situation as China, India, and some of the other densely settled lands.

Of course, some of the aid now being given to underdeveloped countries could be used to educate these peoples to the need for a voluntary reduction of the size of their families. It is highly improbable, however, that such aid would be welcomed, or that political conditions in the more developed countries would make it possible for them to offer it. Outsiders can probably do little to help this situation until the leaders in the underdeveloped countries themselves recognize the rapidly increasing difficulties connected with their increasing rates of population growth. Never has population increased as fast or as steadily in most underdeveloped areas as it is doing now; never has there been as little new land available to many underdeveloped peoples as there is now; never has there been such a demand by the masses for improvement in their economic conditions.

One must also recognize, it will be said, that never has there been so much knowledge of how economic production can be increased, and so much willingness to help the underdeveloped countries use their resources more effectively. This is quite true. But we should remember that even if capital were fairly abundant (and it is not), and even if *adequate* technical assistance from abroad were available to help these countries train their own young men for the new economy (and such assistance is not available), an economy can become efficient as a whole only when it is an integral (organic) part of the culture. The Western peoples took from 150-200 years to make all the complex adjustments which many of these underdeveloped lands are trying to make in a few years. Furthermore, the Western peoples were not particularly concerned about death rates which were 20-25 or even higher, because they did not know that lower rates were possible. In the West the increase in production was slow for several decades. But it provided the wherewithal, in the early decades of development, for a slow reduction in the death rate and for the growth of population which was also slow in the early decades. This particular situation is now reversed in the underdeveloped countries. We cannot be certain that production can increase fast enough to care for the rapid increase in these vast populations; they are increasing much faster than did the populations of most Western lands from 1700 to about 1850, the exceptions were countries like the United States in which there was an abundance of new land and a very rapid increase in numbers .

I am not saying that production cannot be increased faster than the population is growing in many of the underdeveloped countries; but I do believe that a careful study of the present demographic situation, and an unbiased effort to look ahead even a generation, will show that success in raising the level of living in many underdeveloped countries depends on population control as well as on the most strenuous efforts to increase production by the best means now available.

As was noted above, there are degrees of urgency in the undertaking of population control. In the two countries to which most attention has been given here, however, the problem is very urgent; their success in achieving a better living for the masses may very well depend in considerable measure upon how fast the birth rate can be reduced. Indeed, it must be candidly recognized that in these countries great catastrophes due to a scarcity of the bare necessities of life are by no means impossible. This possibility is recognized even more clearly by the Chinese leaders than by the Indian leaders, if one may judge by the measures which the Chinese are actually taking. They are working to acquaint the people with the need for reducing the birth rate, to make available to them the means by which they can do this, and—especially—to make the people feel that it is *respectable* to use these measures, i.e., they are attempting to modify the cultural patterns of family life so that people will keep the effective size of the family (the number of children surviving to adulthood) at about the customary level.

This whole situation which centers around the relationship between population change and economic development carries many implications both as to policy and action, and concerns both the underdeveloped countries and the more developed countries which would aid them, but these implications cannot be explored here. In closing, I will say again that I believe the study of current demographic changes and of the probable changes during the next 15 to 25 years indicates the very urgent need that the reduction of population growth to be made an integral (organic) part of all development plans in underdeveloped countries.

1. Beals, Alan, "The Government and the Indian Village," *Economic Development and Cultural Change,* V. 2, No. 5, June 1954, pp. 397-407.
2. Blacker, C. P., "The Rhythm Method: Two Indian Experiments," *The Eugenics Review,* Vol. 47, Nos. 2 & 3, July and Oct. 1955.
3. Carstairs, G. Morris, "Medicine and Faith in Rural Rajasthan," pp. 107-134 (see 14 below).
4. Chou En-lai, An Interview in the *Report of the Indian Delegation to China on Agricultural Planning and Techniques,* pp. 22-30, Ministry of Food and Agriculture, New Delhi, 1956.
5. Dandekar, V. M. and Dandekar, Kumudini, *Survey of Fertility and Mortality in Poona District,* Gokhale Institute of Politics and Economics, 1953, v. XII, 191 pp.
6. Hanks, L. M. Jr., Hanks, Jane R., and Others, "Diphtheria Immunization in a Thai Community," See 14 below, pp. 155-195.
7. Hsu, Francis L. K., "A Cholera Epidemic in a Chinese Town," See 14 below, pp. 135-154.
8. India, Planning Commission, *Second Five Year Plan* (A draft outline) New Delhi, 1956.
9. India, Report of the Indian Delegation to China on Agricultural and Planning Techniques, Ministry of Food and Agriculture, New Delhi, 1956.
10. Kirby, E. Stuart, "The People of China, Birth Control for 600,000,000?" *Family Planning,* London, V. 5, No. 2, July 1956, pp. 3-8.
11. Marriott, McKim, "Western Medicine in a Village of Northern India," See 14 below, pp. 239-268.
12. Morrison, Wm. A., "Attitudes of Males Toward Family Planning in a Western Indian Village. *Milbank Memorial Fund Quarterly,* July 1956, pp. 262-286.
13. Opler, Morris E. and Singh, Rudra D., "Economic, Political and Social Change in a Village of North Central India," *Human Organization* 1952, v. XI: 2, pp. 5-12.
14. Paul, Benjamin D. (Editor), *Health, Culture and Community,* Russell Sage Foundation, N. Y., 1955.
15. Shao, Li-tsu, Peking Jen Min Jih Pao, Sept. 18, 1954, a speech at the National People's Congress.
16. Shao, Li-tsu, New China News Agency (English), Mar. 18, 1957, Chinese People's Political Consultative Conference.

17. Sovani, N. V., *The Social Survey of Kolhapur City, Part I—Population and Fertility,* Gokhale Institute of Politics and Economics, 1948, IX 82 pp.
18. Sovani, N. V. and Dandekar, Kumudini, *Fertility Survey of Nasik, Koloba and Satara (North) Districts,* Gokhale Institute of Politics and Economics, XVI 167 pp.
19. Stycor, J. Mayone, "Birth Control Clinics in Crowded Puerto Rico," See 14 above, pp. 189-210.
20. United Nations, *Demographic Yearbook,* 1955.

10: *Semantic Traps*

ALFRED G. SMITH

The tough minded temper of our age, proud of its practicality and realism, is embarrassed by any sentiments of tender ideals. We feel obliged to conceal all our susceptibilities to soft heartedness. The hero types of today wear the masks of tough, laconic cowpokes and detectives to disguise the romance of chivalry in our time. And in the world drama we do not speak of knight errantry, but of Point IV.

We would like to be the rugged realists, as hard headed and shrewdly austere as our puritanical forebears, but we cannot realize these aspirations of our age because we were not made that way. When we try to take a brass tacks approach to reality, we often rationalize our ideals as long range self interests, and infer our self interests from our ideals, rather than the other way around. We often explain our programs of aid to undeveloped countries as attempts to create new markets for our goods and new allies for our war against war, without analyzing our markets first and developing our ideals afterward. Our big hearted generosity often leads us to surmise what a country needs from what we can give it. In short, we often think of benevolence before we think of needs and interests. This is simply a heritage of our school book maxims, a component, not a criticism, of our mask of tough mindedness.

Our actual tenderness is well illustrated by our common interpretation of the phrase "aid to undeveloped countries." In popular periodicals, governmental publications, and professional journals, the idea of aid is delineated in great detail, while the idea of undeveloped countries is practically ignored. We have voluminous discussions of the nature of foreign aid and of the different forms it takes. Foreign aid can be military, economic, or technical. It can take the form of airplanes, factories, plows, hospitals, food parcels, and literacy programs. In comparison, the discussions of undevelopment and of the different forms that it takes are scurvy and perfunctory. We gen-

169

erally don't even bother to define the term; but when we do, our definitions are vague and casual. We use so many different yardsticks for characterizing undeveloped countries that no two of our conceptions are commensurate with one another. The fact is that our primary concern has been aid and not undevelopment. This is the image of our tender and acquisitive society in the mirror of the world.

When we speak of aiding undeveloped countries we must make sure that we know what we are talking about. We must know not only what aid is, but also what an undeveloped country is. Is it the same as a backward country, or an area of low standards of living? It is particularly important for our symposium to define these terms because we participants represent such widely different backgrounds as anthropology, economics, political science, sanitation, and sociology. We speak many different dialects of jargon. For us to talk to one another and achieve some measure of mutual understanding and pertinence, if not agreement, we must be explicit and above board in our terminology. The characteristics and diversities of undeveloped countries are the crucial concepts of our symposium. We must define such terms as "standards of living" and "undevelopment."

This paper will first examine the idea of undeveloped countries in general, and the assumptions that lie behind this idea. It will then analyze specific meanings of the term "undeveloped." Thirdly, it will consider a specific geographic area to test these general and specific meanings, and to introduce some new considerations that have been sadly neglected. Finally, this paper will present summary conclusions and suggest some implications.

The current idea of an undeveloped country is like the old idea of a primitive people. "Primitive" like "undeveloped" generally connotes something backward; but it often implies something more, and thereby it instigates a serious semantic confusion. A backward people or country can be either contemporary or ancient. Thus a primitive people sometimes means a primeval people. This confusion between primitive and primeval was rampant a hundred years ago when we thought of primitives as brute cave men like our own ancestors before the dawn of history. We thought that contemporary primitives were unchanged survivors of our own antiquity. We had progressed, evolved, and developed from that stage, while the primitives had not. The semantic shift from primitive to primeval instigated an assumption of evolution. Today, by a parallel confusion, undeveloped often means an earlier stage of creation.

Social evolution was the countersign of optimism in the nineteenth century. In our less confident age we speak of social change instead.

Our tough minded social sciences are skeptical of the simple evolutionary schemes of Comte and Spencer. Yet our social ideals for upgrading backward areas are often predicated on these schemes. We often think that an undeveloped country is on the first rung of the ladder going up.

If we reject the idea of social evolution, we must beware of throwing the baby out with the bath. We may say that no people are "backward in the context of their own culture." [1] We may also say that no one culture is morally or psychologically superior to any other. "Just as the physical anthropologists have ceaselessly combatted the concept of racial superiority, so cultural anthropology has . . . documented the essential dignity of all human cultures." [2] We may recognize that the idea of progress is an expression of our own cultural dynamics, and alien to the more static views of the world that are held in many other cultures. We may admit that when anthropologists began to see cultures as complex wholes, they could no longer rank different cultures along one-dimensional evolutionary sequences. Nevertheless, these anti-ethnocentric maxims do not make cultural comparisons impossible.

The culture of the wandering blackfellow of the Australian bush is much more simple than that of an African kingdom on the Guinea Coast. We can, with Kroeber, compare cultural intensities and judge one culture to be more elaborate than another. [3] We can legitimately say that there is progress with the "quantitative expansion of total human culture; the atrophy of magic based on psychopathology; the decline of infantile obsession with the outstanding physiological events of human life; and the persistent tendency of technology and science to grow accumulatively." [4] We cannot reject the notion of development completely.

Nor can we accept the grand schemes of social evolution. The sweeping historical syntheses of a Marx or Morgan may resemble great achievement, but "minds that discriminate what is achieved from what is attempted must dissent." [5] Organismic laws of cultural development are too simple. They must stretch themselves and stretch the facts to explain all they attempt to explain. They emphasize indigenous development to the neglect of foreign borrowings. They often assume that all societies evolve along the same line, that the course of history for arctic cultures follows the same pattern as the course for tropical ones. These schemes are too simple because they ignore cultural diversity and variability.

It is a part of our traditions in economic thought to assume a single line of evolution. It is an assumption that such differing economists as Marx, Marshall, Veblen, and Schumpeter hold in common.° Yet it is a stumbling block to the creation of economic principles for undeveloped countries.

When we speak of these countries we must avoid the assumption that they can develop only in a single direction. The next step up the ladder may lie along a variety of paths. Different countries may have to develop in different ways, one toward industrial capitalism, another toward agricultural diversification, and a third may not be able to develop at all. One country may need better hand tools, and another, new machinery.

We often do not recognize the full possibility of such variations because our vision is also blurred by a second traditional assumption in our economic thought. We often assume that Western economic principles have cross-cultural validity. This is an equally precarious assumption that we often take for granted with a guileless ethnocentrism. It often leads us to look at undeveloped countries as if they were or should be like our own.

Our Western economic principles describe our Western ways of life. They describe our own economic behavior. They describe how we try to satisfy our desires, for such things as three meals a day and social recognition, by producing wealth. We try to do this efficiently, as described by the principles of marginal utility and of supply and demand. We try to do this through free enterprise, which implies that our economic behavior is intimately connected with our political behavior.

Our ways of meeting our needs are not the only ways or the only needs. Peoples in other societies often have different needs. Some of them are conditioned to two meals a day instead of three. They often have different ways of meeting their needs.

In the complex cultures of some countries one cannot gain social recognition by producing wealth. That is only gained through politics, which may be a completely different orbit of behavior. Our concept of wealth is meaningless to the nomadic Negritos of the Sumatran swamplands. In their peregrinations almost all tangible property is an unnecessary burden. Most of our economic principles of marginal utility are inoperative among the potlatching Indians of the Northwest Coast. Indeed, our economic passwords are like a mariner's compass. They do not point to true north, and their error changes from place to place.

When we apply our systems of analyzing our behavior to any other culture we encounter, we are transcendentally promiscuous. Our principles of economic analysis, like the Freudian principles of psychoanalysis, cannot assume that human behavior is everywhere the same. It is in some respects, but not in others. Our dreams, no matter who we are, may be the guardians of our sleep, diverting our frustrations and anxieties from keeping us awake. Yet the substance of our problems, and how we dream them away, vary with our culture. The symptoms and the kinds of human maladjustment vary too, although we may be able to regard all maladjustments generally as a turning away from problems rather than a facing up to them. So too, the universal problems of making a living entail differences as well as common denominators. We should recognize that these differences do not spell undevelopment, just as differences in cultural psychologies are not maladjustments. A country is not undeveloped because it does not fit our system of economic analysis. [7]

So far we have considered undeveloped countries generally and negatively. They need not plow the same furrow of history that we have plowed to harvest power and prosperity. They are not undeveloped just because they differ from the West. They are not undeveloped in their own context, but only when they enter the twentieth century arena of world commerce and communications. Let us now turn from the general and the negative to the more specific and positive.

Undeveloped is a relative and comparative term. It is also a crude term. In physics we do not speak comparatively of hotter or longer. We use discrete units of measurement and speak of fifty degrees or fifty meters. These units define what we measure, and they distinguish one kind of measurement from another. When we measure "longer" we distinguish length in time from length in distance by using either minutes or meters. Thus when we want to measure development we must first determine what kinds of units we want to use, and we must make distinctions in terms of our units of measurement. We must know what we want to do.

We shall first distinguish between symptoms and causes. For just as a chemist may ask what water is, rather than why water is, we ask what, not why, an undeveloped country is. Most discussions of these countries recognize their geographical location as a common characteristic. All these countries lie in the Southern Hemisphere. [8] They lie in tropical climates, outside Huntington's higher energy zones. [9] "Geographically, the underdeveloped countries lie to one side of the vast confrontation of power between the United States and Russia." [10] These statements generally imply a causal theory of environmental determinism. If we speak of causes, however, before we speak of symptoms, we are likely to jump to conclusions. We should first determine that a man is drunk, before we determine why he is drunk.

We shall also make a second distinction, between common symptoms and definitive ones. It may be a common characteristic of fishermen to exaggerate, but for them to be fishermen at all, they have to fish. The many studies of undeveloped countries have found an endless series of common characteristics among them. It is common for these countries to have authoritarian regimes, and to practice child labor and the subjection of women. [11] On the other hand, we also hear that the discipline of their worker is self-imposed, and not imposed by others as in the West. [12] The population profiles of these countries commonly exhibit a high percentage of dependents, of old people over sixty and children below fifteen. [13] These are common symptoms of undeveloped countries, but they are not definitive ones. The population profile of the United States may soon resemble that of Indo-China. Our boom in babies and our increasing numbers of old people would not, however, convert us into an undeveloped country. All exaggerators are not fishermen.

What then is a definitive symptom of undevelopment? In the tradition of our economic thought, the most prevalent and popular measurement of backwardness is per capita income. [14] This is "the best available yardstick for arranging the countries according to their stage of economic development." [15] Let us then construct an index of per capita income, and compare different areas by their indices. Given the population and the income of the world as a whole, and of each of its seven principal areas, let the index of per capita income for each area be its percentage of the world income divided by its percentage of the world population. [16] Is this an index of development?

INDICES OF PER CAPITA INCOMES (1949)

Areas	Index of Per Capita Income (% inc./% pop.)	Per cent World Population (2,370 million)	Per cent World Income ($542 billion)
North America	4.844	9.0	43.6
Oceania	3.000	0.5	1.5
Europe	1.645	16.6	27.3
U.S.S.R.	1.358	8.1	11.0
South America	0.777	4.5	3.5
Africa	0.313	8.3	2.6
Asia	0.198	53.0	10.5
World	1.000	100.0	100.0

Thus, by comparing their respective indices, it would appear that

Oceania is almost a 100% more developed than Europe. Here we have a definitive symptom that is eminently measurable.

This popular line of reasoning perpetrates an orgy of errors: the mismanipulation of measurements; the reduction of complex conditions to a single variable; the promiscuous application of Western systems of economic analysis; and the assumption that development is merely a matter of degree.

An index to three decimal places is no more accurate than the figures from which it is derived. Yet we know the per capita income only for areas that have a cash economy. The figures for other areas are highhanded translations. They assume that values in a subsistence economy are negotiable for Western cash, and that the rate of exchange can be quoted. The fact is that the per capita incomes of Asia and of Europe do not mean the same things and do not represent comparable symptoms. Moreover, the income of a country like Malaya may go up and down with industrialization at home and the development of synthetic rubber overseas. Under such complex conditions the differences in Malaya's income would not express differences in her development. We cannot measure development by a single variable.

Per capita income is also a one-dimensional variable. It can only go up or down. Thus it is an index of one dimensional development, and it commemorates the old theory of straight line evolution. Per capita income is also a continuous variable, and it implies that development is a continuous and quantitative change. It cannot represent the possibility that quantitative changes can become qualitative ones. We can make a liquid hotter and hotter, until it reaches the point where it is no longer a liquid. Such transformations may be the milestones of economic development. Indeed, the difference between Western and undeveloped countries need not be just a difference of degree; it may also be a difference of kind.

Per capita income is the popular yardstick of development because it wears the laurels of a quantitative variable. We could establish it as the measure of development, but then Oceania would be a hundred per cent more developed than Europe. Besides, we need more than a single variable. [17] Therefore let us consider a group of symptoms that may fall under the headings of production and consumption.

Production in undeveloped countries is primarily for subsistence. This can be measured by the percentage of farmers and fishermen in the total population. The extent of a subsistence economy can also be measured by its exports. In undeveloped countries these are raw materials rather than finished products. These countries have small scale economic enterprises which cannot mechanize effectively. Therefore we often say that their production is inefficient, and that each individual operates at a low level of performance. [18] The consumption pattern of a country is what we often regard to be its standards of living. The average diet in undeveloped countries is low in total calories and particularly low in proteins. The people eat grains, not meat. Public health and medical facilities are inadequate by Western standards. The provisions for mass communications are meager, and the literacy rate is low. These are common characteristics of undeveloped countries.

When we speak of these deficiencies, however, we often assume that Western standards of production and consumption are the absolute standards. Moreover, we can find the full syndrome of all these symptoms in a given country and still deny that it is an undeveloped country. One definitive symptom has been ignored, here and generally in the literature. We often lose sight of a country's potentialities.

Let us turn to a specific geographic area for a concrete test of the variables we have considered so far, and for a test of the importance of potentialities. The Trust Territory of the Pacific Islands is located in the western Pacific just north of the equator. It consists of three Micronesian archipelagos: the Mariana, Caroline, and Marshall Islands. This territory extends over a vast expanse of ocean which is as large as the land area of the United States: some 3,000,000 square miles. The tiny islands that dot this watery expanse have a total land area of about half the state of Rhode Island: some 687 square miles. This insignificant amount of land is so dispersed that communication is a major problem.

There are two kinds of islands in this territory: high islands and low islands. The differences between these two are related to some of the differences in island life. The high islands are of volcanic or ancient continental rock formation. They generally have better soils than low islands, and a more variegated vegetation. They generally support a greater number of inhabitants per island, although the density of population is sometimes greater on a low island. Low islands seldom rise to more than a few feet above sea level. They are generally small, only as large as a few city blocks. Basically they consist of the skeletons of a variety of marine organisms which form what we generically call coral. Accordingly, the soils of low islands are shallow, low in humus, and low in water retention capacity. Tropical heat and heavy rainfall decay and leach away much of whatever nutritive values these shallow soils contain. Thus the low islands have limited potentialities for agricultural production. While high islands generally have several plant zones, low islands generally have only one. We see, therefore, that the territory is disperse and diverse physically. This limits the pooling of its poor resources for its economic development.

The basic economy of the Islanders is local subsistence farming and the gathering of marine foodstuffs. They cultivate root crops such as taro and yams, and tree crops such as coconuts, breadfruit, and bananas. In some areas, maize, citrus fruits, and other crops that were introduced by Europeans are moderately important. None of these crops is simply gathered. They must be planted and cultivated. To this otherwise starchy diet of the Islanders, farming also adds some pork and chicken. The principal sources of protein, however, are the fish, lobsters, and shellfoods that abound in myriad and colorful varieties. Yet by present means of exploitation, all these food resources are just adequate to maintain the present population. [10]

These are the only significant resources of the territory. Before World War II, sugar and its derivatives, syrup and alcohol, were the principal exports, and were valued at more than $6,000,000 per year. This was a Japanese enterprise, operated with Japanese labor. Since the wartime devastation of the islands, and the postwar repatriation of the Japanese, the territory has grown no sugar except for isolated family clumps. This resource has disappeared. A second resource has fared better, but its future is uncertain. Copra, the dried coconut meat that is used as fodder for cattle and as "palm-oil" in the manufacture of soap, has long been the major cash crop of the Islanders. Several factors have combined to diminish its resource value in the territory. First there was the complete disruption of copra purchasing and shipping during World War II. In the territory this lead to a neglect of the coconut palms and a failure to replace aging trees with new plantings. A second factor was the rise of synthetic substitutes, such as detergents, which made copra obsolete. A third factor was the increase in world production of other fats and oils. Finally, the less dispersed and more highly organized copra producers on the larger land masses of the Pacific, as in the Philippines, put the territory in an unfavorable position competitively.

The non-agricultural resources of the territory are no more plentiful. Mineral resources consist only of some phosphate, principally on Angaur, and unexploited bauxite further north in the Palaus. Marine resources are abundant but can hardly compete with the richer marine areas of the world. Trochus shell for making pearl buttons is the only significant marine export, and that is a very small enterprise. Forest resources are generally limited and poor. There are no industries. Island handicrafts have been exported for gift-shop sales, but they have never been a commercial success. Their quality is not standardized; their supply is not reliable; and the costs of transportation and distribution are prohibitive. New crops, such as cacao, are being introduced to boost the economy, but their value and significance are by no means assured. The territory is so poor in its resources that economic pump priming has little it can prime.

The human resources of the territory are also meager. There are only 57,000 Islanders scattered over this far-flung sector of the Pacific. Many islands have only a few households on them. Several of them have a total population of less than ten. Others, generally high islands, have several thousand inhabitants. This dispersal and uneven distribution of the population makes it difficult to administer the territory. The Islanders have few commercial or technical skills, and the rate of literacy is very low. This then is a commodious description of a specific area. Is the Trust Territory of the Pacific Islands an undeveloped country?

It does have most of the definitive symptoms. The Islanders have a low per capita income, based on exports of raw materials, and on work as helpers and houseboys for American administrators. The territory has a subsistence economy, and it is not industrialized. It has practically no facilities for mass communication, and its literacy rate is low. There is one symptom, however, that is barely visible in Micronesia: the potentiality of development. It is a poor and backward area, but it has no place to go. It has little to develop, and that can only develop a little. We can increase its consumption by promoting literacy and public health; but its population is too small and too dispersed to be a productive labor force competing in the arena of world trade. Thus we may doubt that this territory can even develop as a shipping center or a resort area. It is simply an area of meager potentialities.

When we assess a country's development, we must consider its potentialities. We must relate its actual backwardness to its possible growth. Although it is easier to see present conditions than to predict future possibilities, we should recognize that possibilities may differ just as conditions do. This is basic to our general recognition of diversity. Different countries can go up different ladders, and some ladders may be longer than others.

Nevertheless, we cannot measure these potentialities. We can only measure actualities. We may try to predict the future from present facts, but we cannot know fulfillment until it has been fulfilled. Moreover, potentialities can change. The Trust Territory probably had greater potentialities twenty years ago under the Japanese than it has today under limited American operations. Although potentials are peculiarly intangible and variable ingredients of development, they cannot be ignored.

This paper has urged that we look tough mindedly at undeveloped countries before we look at aid. We should consider national differences in condition, need, and potentiality, before we consider global relief. Some countries are more developed than others, but we should not think that an undeveloped country is on a lower rung of a single ladder of evolution. Nor should we confuse economic differences with economic undevelopment. Nor can we identify an undeveloped country by a single symptom, for the meaning and the nature of economic symptoms vary with the general economy of a country. An undeveloped country exhibits a syndrome of many symptoms. Its production and consumption are at low levels in relation to its potentialities. After we have considered the various characteristics of an undeveloped country, then we can consider the issue of aid.

In popular discussions, however, that issue is sometimes unrelated to undeveloped countries. Sometimes it is primarily an issue of the domestic economy of the United States. Then the arguments in favor of Congressional appropriations for aid follow Keynes and Keyserling in an emphasis on spending and consumption, and the arguments against follow Adam Smith and the Protestant ethic in an emphasis on saving and production. These are our economic problems, and they can muddy the waters of our understanding of most of the countries of the world.

[1] Melvin M. Knight, "Backward Countries," *Encyclopaedia of the Social Sciences*, New York, 1931.

[2] Melville J. Herskovits, *Man and His Works*, New York, 1948. p. 653.

[3] A. L. Kroeber, *Cultural and Natural Areas of Native North America*, Berkeley, 1947. p. 222.

[4] A. L. Kroeber, *Anthropology*, New York, 1948. p. 304. (Cf. pp. 296-304).

[5] Robert H. Lowie, *History of Ethnological Theory*, New York, 1937. p. 66.

[6] See for example the opening pages of Thorstein Veblen's *Theory of the Leisure Class*, New York, 1899, and the concluding chapter of J. A. Schumpeter's *Capitalism, Socialism, and Democracy*, New York, 1942. See also Melville J. Herskovits, *Economic Anthropology*, New York, 1952. pp. 55 ff.

[7] The essential and tacit implication of Boeke's studies on Indonesia is an economist's skepticism of the cross-cultural validity of Western economic principles. See J. H. Boeke, *The Structure of Netherlands Indian Economy*, New York, 1942.

See also J. S. Furnivall, *Netherlands India: A Study of Plural Economy*, New York, 1944.

[8] Willard R. Espy, "Blueprint for the Backward Areas," *New York Times Magazine*, March 6, 1949. p. 12.

[9] W. S. Woytinsky and E. S. Woytinsky, *World Population and Production*, New York, 1953. pp. 395 ff.

[10] Owen Latimore, "Point Four and the Third Countries," *The Annals*, 270:2, July 1950.

[11] Federico Chessa, "Depressed Zones and Economic Progress," *Kyklos*, 6:193-210, 1953.

[11] Federico Chessa, "Depressed Zones and Economic Progress," *Kyklos*, 6:193-in Bert F. Hoselitz, ed., *The Progress of Undeveloped Areas*, Chicago, 1952.

[13] Chia Lin Pan, "Demographic Aspects of Underdeveloped Countries," *The Annals*, 270:42-50, July 1950.

[14] W. S. Woytinsky and E. S. Woytinsky, op. cit., pp. 417 ff. See also Colin Clark, *The Conditions of Economic Development*, 2nd ed., New York, 1951; U. S. Department of State, *Point Four*, Washington, D. C., July, 1949; etc.

[15] Howard S. Piquet, "Point Four and World Production," *The Annals*, 268: 148-159, March, 1950.

[16] The figures cited are from Jacques Mertens de Wilmars, "Les soucis démopraphique des pays sous-developpés et des pays sur-developpés," *Bulletin de Statistique de Belgique*, 11:1506-07, November, 1952. Allowing for differences in reference years and in presentation, they jibe well with figures given by the Woytinskys, *op. cit. passim.*

[17] P. T. Bauer and B. S. Yamey, "Economic Progress and Occupational Distribution," *The Economic Journal*, 61:741-755, 1951.

[18] Alfred Bonné, "Towards a Theory of Implanted Development in Underdeveloped Countries," *Kyklos*, 9:1-26, 1956.

[19] United States Navy Department, Office of the Chief of Naval Operations, *Handbook on the Trust Territory of the Pacific Islands*, Washington, D. C., 1948, pp. 127 ff.; United States Commercial Company, Economic Survey of Micronesia, Vol. 1, *Summary of Findings and Recommendations*, Honolulu, 1946.

11: *The Case Against Profferred Aid*

H. G. BARNETT

Both the United States and the United Nations provide technical assistance only on specific request of responsible authorities of the host country. Additionally, in providing such aid there is the expressed or implied understanding that it be in the nature of assistance and not support: that the recipients also contribute something substantial to the project and thereby help themselves. These principles are sound—diplomatically, economically, and psychologically—but they often result in people getting something they never dreamed of wanting, much less asking for. The principal reason for this irony is that recipients of the assistance have not been parties to the request for it. In view of this fact, and without impugning the motives of those who make the requests, it is not unfair to inquire in each case: who is seeking what for whom?

The question is most pertinent when welfare planning is undertaken at the national or regional level, mainly or solely on the initiative and council of government officials, whether elected or appointed. The rationale for this procedure is that the people who are to benefit from the planning are, for one reason or another, unable to do it for themselves or cannot be trusted to undertake it in the national interest. However justifiable this reasoning may be, it cannot be denied that projects thus set in motion frequently encounter misunderstanding, apathy, or opposition on the part of their alleged beneficiaries. Consequently, officials and technicians find themselves working either alone or against rather than with those they presumed to serve.

Three examples of such an impasse in human relations will suffice to establish the point. One concerns the United States foreign aid program under the direction of the International Cooperation Administration (I.C.A.); another a UNESCO operation in Haiti; the third a rural development program presently underway in India.

American expenditures on foreign developmental programs have recently come under severe attack by spokesmen for public and private agencies. The critique aims at the extravagance of the system, waste which stems from several causes. One frequent complaint is the offering of technical advice and material aid at the discretion of its administering authority—the imposition of assistance. A much publicized example was the attempted construction of a hydro-electric dam on the Karadj River in Iran by the I.C.A. According to a U. S. Senate Appropriations Committee investigator, the project was undertaken at the insistance of the director of the International Cooperation Administration's mission without the support of its beneficiaries, the residents of Tehran. Indeed, they opposed the venture, countering it with a plan of their own. The latter called for the installation of additional steam driven generators to supplement an existing power output which was fueled by a plentiful oil supply. The Iranian request for a $500,000 advance to implement their proposal was rejected, and the building of an access road and other preliminaries to the construction of the dam went ahead. The dam was not completed, and presumably will not be; but $3,500,000 was spent on the project. In the denouement, an anonymous Iranian guide at the dam site is reported as slyly consoling a visiting American official with these words: "But perhaps you should not worry too much for us. You must understand that we are getting our generators after all—later than if you'd helped us with that down payment we wanted, but they're now being installed." [1]

In 1947 the Republic of Haiti, upon its request and through its Minister of Education, entered into an agreement with UNESCO to establish a fundamental education project in the Marbial Valley in Southern Haiti. The location of the project was chosen by representatives of the national government in cooperation with UNESCO officials. The choice was made because the valley encompassed in one small watershed some of the most acute problems to be found in the country and in similarly underdeveloped areas elsewhere in the world: land shortage, over-population, illiteracy, famine, and soil erosion.

It is the purpose of fundamental education, and therefore of the Marbial project, to: "help men and women to live fuller and happier lives in adjustment with their changing environment, to develop the best elements in their own culture, and to achieve the social and economic progress which will enable them to take their place in the modern world." [2] This ideal constitutes a charter for action by anyone on the basis of what "fuller and happier lives", the "best" in a culture, and social and economic "progress" mean to him. Clearly in the present instance the definition of what comprised these goals, the means of achieving them, and the selection of their beneficiaries, came from the sponsoring and administering agencies. This is evident from the procedure; it also appears in the working plan declaration that "every effort will be made to enlist the active cooperation of the local people, and by concentrating on the training of Haitian personnel to make the project self-supporting as rapidly as possible." [3] It is equally manifest in the reaction of the Marbial people to what was being done to or for them: "When the UNESCO team first came into the region many of the peasants imagined the program to be a vast charitable enterprise of which they were to be the beneficiaries and which, for reasons unknown to them, was being organized by some rich man named '1' Unesco', or by some agricultural company. But once informed about the actual situation, they welcomed with real pleasure the modest beginnings and the simple help which it was possible to provide." [4]

The Indian government, in part on its own and in part through cooperation with the American Foreign Operations Administration, has been engaged in a comprehensive program called community development. Its purpose is to increase India's agricultural production, extend her rural transportation facilities, and raise her mass standards in health and education. "This program, based on a self-help approach, uses modern methods adapted to local needs in attacking the problems that beset India's villages." [5]

In some parts of India efforts have been made to integrate village assemblies, called *panchayata,* into this program. Anciently these councils were composed of respected villagers who were accorded status and authority by informal consensus, not by election, inherited right, or appointment. Their function was to maintain tradition and minimize internal dissension. Under British rule they lost much of their influence and power. Following India's independence, their authority was in some places restored by legal action and new duties were thrust upon them. "Today (1952) the United Provinces government is making these *Gaon Panchayats* the center of its efforts to introduce modern programs in improved agriculture and education." [6]

PROGRESS BY DECREE

This obligation to initiate reforms at the behest of the state government has created an entirely new conception of the *panchayat* itself and has injected difficulties into its successful operation. Its members must answer to the state government and at the same time justify themselves in the eyes of their fellow villagers, one consequence of their new role being that they must campaign for election. Meanwhile the old *panchayats* continue to function by popular demand, in competition with their official counterparts and often rent by internal conflicts. "The new *panchayats* tend to operate in the shadow of the old. Some do nothing, others are used to carry out the will of the old *panchayat,* or of one village faction or another. Still others are neither totally inoperative nor wholly in the hands of old power groups but try to make some headway on their own." [7]

These three exhibits are not to be construed as an argument against national planning or as evidence for a wholesale indictment of externally conceived reforms. The issue is not whether ultimate success is achieved, for often it is. Neither is the question whether the designers of assistance have incorporated the needs or wishes of its recipients in their plan; it is quite probable that the Haitian and the Indian programs have done so, directly or indirectly. The point is that there are practical difficulties inherent in the approach to assistance through unilateral decision. The illustrations also involve a delicate question concerning the "rights of man" about which so much is heard these days. The notion of universal human rights is essentially ego- or ethno-centric and paternalistic, no matter what good it accomplishes. It is progress by decree, regardless of the measure of consent it meets with or engenders.

An obvious alternative, and one which is more in accord with American and Western European tradition, is to enable people to realize the goals they set for themselves. This has been tried, sometimes with notable success, both with and without foreign aid. Unfortunately, no unequivocal term exists to designate precisely this concept of assistance and no other. There are several partial approximations, among them community development, fundamental education, mass education, cultural mission, action research, and operational research; but they may mean this or something quite different, depending on the user. [8] Perhaps the term "aided self-help" is as expressive of the essentials as any, and it is the least committed to contradictions. [9] At any rate, this term will be used in the following discussion, which examines the idea in detail.

The key feature of this design for assistance is the requirement that the group of people to be served must be given the freedom to frame their definition of their needs and be granted the right to accept or reject such help as may be offered to satisfy them. It is necessary to phrase and to act upon this requirement in a permissive rather than in a mandatory way in order to acknowledge the realities in technologically underdeveloped areas and to permit some positive action on the part of well-intentioned outsiders.

Many people who live in accordance with a venerable tradition do not conceptualize their needs as problems; or they are unaware that anything can be done about them, if they do so envisage them. Some, living in isolation, do not even know what they lack, for this awareness comes only by comparisons between themselves and others. They therefore do not have the opportunity to acquire new wants by contact. Whether or not this is a desirable state is a debatable question; but it is being answered in the negative by aggressive reforms in many parts of the world and by undirected events in others. [10] Stimulated desire is a fact to be faced; and from the standpoint of the aided self-help design it does not matter where wants come from as long as they are internalized. The essence of the plan is mutual agreement on means and ends and not their imposition. Three examples will serve to illustrate its flexibility and the range of its application.

The Purari Delta is an extensive swamp land lying to the west of Port Moresby in the Southwestern part of Australian New Guinea. It is inhabited by some 10,000 natives, mostly illiterate, who live by hunting, fishing, and collecting wild food plants. Suddenly, in 1946, these people decided to alter radically their way of life. The instigator of the movement was a man who had seen something of the outside world and wanted its advantages for his people. During the war he served in the Australian Navy and later spent two and one half years on the Australian mainland. Upon his return he traveled around the delta, urging the people to break abruptly with the past and emulate the Australians. He denounced native custom, sacred and secular, and advocated thoroughgoing social, political and religious reforms. His key idea was the formation of a collectively owned enterprise, called the "Kompani," which was to produce, transport, and sell vegetable goods for the Port Moresby and Australian markets. Although his reforms were profound and extensive, they were accepted with enthusiasm. Local authorities and missionaries, foreseeing a collapse of the economic venture, attempted to induce its supporters to adopt a less ambitious program. Their advice was rejected. It was said that they were seeking to suppress native initiative and maintain their superiority. It was not until the scheme seriously faltered through the loss of capital invested in a boat, that their proposals were reluctantly given a hearing.

As hopes for the full fledged commercial operation faded, the Australian government's efforts to gain the confidence of its proponents bore fruit. Under the guidance of a specially trained officer, concrete steps were taken to work out a more realistic and manageable plan for the Kompani's activities. The funds of the amorphous organization were made subject to an audit, its excess of inexperienced employees was reduced, and its clerk began to attend a school for instruction in the management of cooperatives. The leader himself also attended this school. In addition, the government instituted a community development project to promote other cash income activities, to extend adult education, and to improve health conditions. [11]

The Koror Community Center was less urgently and spontaneously conceived. It is located in the Palau Islands of Micronesia, an area which was formerly mandated to Japan but is now administered by American civil personnel under a trusteeship agreement with the United Nations. Under the Japanese regime the Palauans were fairly prosperous and not altogether unhappy. The war and its aftermath gave a major reorientation to their social and economic system. The shift from Japanese to American ideals was accompanied by varying degrees of confusion, frustration and demoralization. These emotional disturbances expressed themselves in the failure of traditional authority, personal and group rivalries, anti-American sentiments, intra-family difficulties, emigration, general apathy, and in many other ways. These symptoms of unrest were evident to American observers. Moreover, the Palauans spoke freely about them to anyone sympathetic enough to listen. In other words, the affected individuals were consciously troubled and could name the causes of their discontent. Some thought they knew what should be done, others had no solution. There was no general agreement and no commanding insight or leadership.

In 1952 the American authorities decided to take one relatively minor step to alleviate Palauan discontent. They proposed a community centered program which aimed at the following objectives: a recreational program designed to occupy the leisure time of the Palauans; the formation of interest groups, such as community planning committees; integration of the intellectual interests of school graduates with community welfare plans; the establishment of an information center for non-English speaking adults; the unification of parent and child interests through community emphasis; the inspiration and support of Palauan group pride; the erection of a building as a physical focus for group activities; and the employment of an American director of the program whose function was to get it underway and at the same time train Palauans to take it over when he departed.

The proposal was explained to as many Palauans as possible and their reactions elicited. It was emphasized that the United States government would give any necessary assistance which was beyond Palauan capacity to supply, but that the acceptance of the proposal and its successful outcome rested entirely with the Palauan people. Unquestionably most of them did not understand how the scheme could resolve their difficulties; but many of its specific elements, such as the community building, did appeal to them. They accepted the idea and made a surprisingly good showing on their own initiative. [12]

A similar but more sustained and systematic approach has been employed in the community education program in Puerto Rico. [13] Its aim is to extend adult education in rural and urban districts "until it covers the whole island". Field workers are trained especially for the job. They establish community centers and make use of audio-visual materials along with problem discussions "to awaken the interests and initiative of the people in securing the economic and social welfare of their districts."

The burden of the Puerto Rican program rests on the field workers. They are very carefully selected, after many interviews and close observations of the way they fit into the social situations in which they must work. During a seventeen month sifting process, beginning in 1949, 1,200 candidates were interviewed. Forty were chosen, though many more were needed. After receiving instruction at a central point, each worker was assigned a district which in some instances included several towns or municipalities. His role is a very restricted one. He is described as a "catalytic agent", which means he is not a leader or an organizer of opinion; neither does he tell people what their problems are or what to do about them. He listens more than he talks. He makes suggestions only when he is asked or when it seems expected of him. "He is alert to see that the people do not look to him to solve a problem, to make contacts for them, to plead special privileges with influential people or lean upon him for the kind of help customarily expected of a service agency." [14] He is not a technical specialist, but knows men in medicine, agriculture, and other professions, whom he can contact if called upon for their assistance. Most of the time he spends getting to know the people of his district intimately and informally so that he is accepted as one of them. Out of close association with them he discovers what they want and are willing to work for, in part as a result of his educational displays.

The Purari, Palauan, and Puerto Rican cases exemplify three forms or degrees of external stimulation. In the first case it is indirect and its action is about as independent of outside influences as will occur. In the Palauan case the motivation for change was certainly present, with confused and conflicting manifestations, but the solution was entirely an American conception. In Puerto Rico, while the field worker is only a catalyst, his announced purpose is to "awaken" individual initiative and a desire for community improvement.

It appears that most cases of aided self-help fall in categories two and three above. A United Nations mission sent to study Caribbean and Mexican community development projects found this to be so in the thirty instances investigated. "It was the mission's repeated observation that people living in isolated rural communities either were not aware of some of their basic needs, or if aware of them they lived in the belief that fate had destined them to continue with unsatisfied needs. In all cases where local communities were seen vigorously attacking their local problems in an organized way, some agent or agency from outside the community had stimulated the people to the new undertakings. In practically all cases it was a person skilled in group organization who had provided the stimulation." [15]

It is not a coincidence that the term "community" crops up repeatedly in naming or describing aided self-help projects of the sort described. The actual or potential existence of a relatively small group of people who have common interests is a condition essential to the success of projects premised on internalized wants and requiring coordination of effort. A community in the social sense is not a geographical phenomenon. It is a way of behaving. "All communities are networks of human relation between persons who know and count on each other. They remain such only when they meet together, formally or informally, think together, and work together. Without these interaction processes, there is no guarantee that people and families living in the same geographic area are a community. When, however, they plan and do things together, they not only become aware of the fact that they are a community, but they develop sentiment about, and pride in, themselves as a group and actively seek new community undertakings." [16]

What are the advantages of a total community approach to change—that is, of a relatively small group of individuals concertedly undertaking to realize goals set by themselves and accepting help only if they feel they need it? There are several, including some already stated or implied.

(1) The decision to take action is group determined. This circumstance not only safeguards against the imposition of the values of some outside agent; it also minimizes, if it does not remove, the possibility of one or a few members of the group forcing their wishes on the rest. There are no guarantees against internal dictatorial coercions or partisan maneuvers; but if a group acceeds to them it does so on its own volition. At least it does not, as in India, have to contend with a "progressive leadership" established from without. [17]

The requirement of group adoption of a move also disposes of a common difficulty in societies undergoing forced change. It was at one time generally supposed that the way to bring a people out of heathendom was to educate a few selected individuals who would then lead the rest. This method seldom worked. Usually this strategy created social isolates, or perhaps a class of them, who belong neither to their own people nor to their adopters, "a special class of skilled craftsmen for running the apparatus of civilization, who stand outside their native social order both in terms of economic function and in terms of personal goals." [18] Frequently these alienated individuals leave their communities, unable to tolerate their backwardness or to find a niche in the outgrown system. Their training is imperfect, their abilities lost to their communities and they augment the dreary company of second class citizens in labor compounds and slum areas in urban centers.

Usually the individuals selected to teach the others—in time—are children. The reason for their selection is evident. Children are more malleable than their parents, and it is easier to teach the young than to re-teach the aged. But in the process, as some teachers later have the insight to realize, children are inevitably alienated from their parents. Instead of leading their elders to the light—a difficult assignment for youth—children part intellectual company with their parents and the two generations come to live in different cultural universes. Hence, the more successful the educator is the more social wreckage he leaves behind him. [19] If his efforts have only superficial effects, his pupils, as they grow older, become more like their fathers, as they must in order to live with them.

So, in the end, not only does the strategem of educating a chosen few fail in its overall purpose; it leaves a shaken or factionated society incapable of functioning on its own. Even more disastrous is its emotional toll: the hard choices it forces upon the individual who takes the path that parts him from his kin and kind. When all move together these disabling facts are avoided and the transition from custom to innovation is made in the security of mutual support. Much bolder moves can be made under such circumstances than when a lone individual must break with tradition, often in the face of contempt or ridicule. Then, too, parents teach their children—as they everywhere think they should—rather than the other way around. Furthermore, there are many changes that cannot be initiated by lone individuals simply because they are social phenomena, that is, group involved. Thus it would be impossible for one person or a few to adopt an alien monetary system or a political ideology without creating a separate society. [20]

Finally, it must be noted that a group decision, if it is genuinely such, has a self-fortifying psychological effect. When people as a group commit themselves to a course of action they are more securely bound to it than when they do it privately or singly. All the social pressures recognized in such terms as integrity, good faith, honor, and promise are brought to bear upon the individual as a consequence of his publicly committing himself along with his associates. A step in the ranks establishes a point of no retreat, unless again by group action.

(2) A voluntary decision to undertake something new is an act of proprietorship. When a person or a people freely espouse a course of action it is *theirs,* and this fact has important psychological consequences. One has already been alluded to; namely, that imposed technical or material assistance is no assistance at all. It begins as and remains an alien scheme; and its advocates assume and maintain the burden of putting it into effect. It is their baby; they have fathered it, and they soon discover, sometimes with dismay, that they are its sole means of support.

When, as an alternative, people decide their own future they accept the responsibility which a free choice assumes. This is an entailment too often overlooked, particularly in these days of marketing political ideologies. It may be necessary for us to advertise our way of life in competition with the Russian or some other; but there is no question that we, like the Russians, are overselling ourselves. In particular, we urge our ideals, including our technology, upon the uncommitted half of the world in all their impressive trappings. The appeal is great, and it should be so; but we fail to tell our customers that these goods we offer cost something—not just in money, but in effort, emotional stress, self-discipline, patience, cooperation, and other linked demands on the human machine. People, when they accept this super-salesmanship, later find that they have bought only a romantic's dream of a free choice, a bargain with the concealed price tag. On the other hand, when they make their own decisions they do so within the limits of their enabling capacities, assuming risks for which they alone are responsible, and for which they can blame no one else. In short, self-determination is constrained by self-obligation.

Along with self-obligation goes the reward of an independent position, a linkage which does not escape people who have recently emerged from colonial status or are striving to do so. A self-determined course of action, whether it be in state building or road building, frees a nation or a community from the importunities of conflicting advice and theory. People in backward areas are presently being bombarded with claims and counter claims for individualism,

collectivism, centralization, de-centralization, and many other con-
traries. [21] Many have ceased to listen, preferring their own counsel;
and others may be well advised to extricate themselves from the confusion by striking out on their own. This resolve has the further con-
solation that it shields them from things they do not understand or
cannot control. The peasant who adopts a new fertilizer, or the patient who swallows a strange pill often feels that he is placing himself at the mercy of occult forces; or, at the least, in thrall to persons
and situations from which he has no recourse. [22]

Granting people the unmanipulated right of self-determination has
advantages for the granter too. Giving is a delicate social mechanism. It is susceptible of all sorts of interpretations, intended or not.
It can be insulting, as it is in India and Burma when attended by publicity to honor the benefactor. It is widely suspected today as a form
of bribery, which is not altogether an unfounded suspicion. Even
when assistance is paid for, it is not above suspicion of an ulterior
motive, the more so the more competitive or insistent the offer of assistance. In any event, the charge of imperialism is latent and the
surest way to escape it is to wait until help is requested.

(3) Aided self-help is an educational process. It is a means by
which a group can come to realize both its capacities and its limitations. Starting with the discussion which must precede a commitment to action, members of a group learn to cooperate and plan together. Furthermore, with practice the group learns to isolate and
define its problems through giving expression to its needs. [23]

In both the talking and the action phases of this bootstrap procedure, other knowledge comes with trial and experience. Hidden
human resources are often exposed. New leaders and unsuspected
skills emerge under the challenge of an unfamiliar situation. Most
communities soon learn, if they do not know it already, that success
is limited. It is wisest, in the beginning, at least, to concentrate on
one specific problem or on a closely related few. [24] For a community
to work in this fashion, on its own initiative and resources, is the best
possible way for it to realize its potentialities. As with any inexperienced individual, so with communities undertaking new ventures:
both learn the difference between talk and action, theory and practice, the ideal and the attainable. And to repeat a previous point,
they realize what it means to take the responsibility for their decisions.

In brief, learning to help oneself in mutual adjustment with others
is a maturation process. The longer it is delayed or the more it is
delayed or the more it is discouraged the more habitual does the at-

titude of dependence become. Paternalism is acceptable in its proper place; but if the aim is self-reliance, the technical assistant, like the parent, will do well to think and act with, and not for, the overgrown adolescent.

(4) Aided self-help is most often a democratic process. The vigor of a group commitment is dependent upon the support given it by individual members of the community. When all are free to express their views and concur in the decision, the maximum support is assured. However, the supravention of authoritarian power does not in itself weaken the force of a decision. In many non-equalitarian societies leaders are expected to act for their subordinates and do so with no loss of group strength. Yet in connection with the present discussion, it must be remembered that the issues at stake involve departures from tradition; and without precedent or experience to guide them, authoritarian spokesmen may feel the need of more advice and concurrence than they are accustomed to acknowledge. When confronted by alien mysteries, it is not unusual to find rank and privilege giving way to ambition and adaptability.

A particular aspect of this fact is worth noting. Aided self-help schemes can induce an almost insensible, painless shift of leadership because a new situation calls for new skills, and this fact is evident and acceptable to everyone. Traditional leaders, those who are masters of familiar situations, may readily defer to others more capable of dealing with alien ideas. This concession can occur with remarkable ease among illiterate people, a few of whom have had some outside contacts. [25] To be sure, conflicts are always possible; but they can be avoided, without loss of face or power, by traditional leaders if they are willing to be cooperative. The chance of conflict developing can be greatly reduced if there is a community field worker on hand who understands the principle of cultural compartmentalization; that is, leadership in old and new activities can function compatibly if they are kept clearly distinct. [26]

The tendency toward equalitarian participation can be expected to be furthered if there is a community field worker or participant advisor on the scene who functions as a catalyst, as in Puerto Rico, or as a disguised leader, as in Koror. Such persons, to whom democratic procedures are congenial, are inclined to nudge the people they are trying to help in the direction of free but responsible speech; or as one author phrases it, "cooperative individualism." [27] Again, knowing the creative value of the interchange of ideas, unhampered by barriers of rank, sex, or protocol, they cannot fail to show some signs of favoritism for informal discussion by an unorganized assembly. "It helps people learn to build formal organizations for specific purposes, but it focuses on the individual as a member of a free society." [28] It also helps to prevent domination by self appointed leaders and self serving obstructionists as well as puppets controlled by outside interests.

(5) Community action is a grass roots approach to change. It does not benefit the minimum number of individuals possible, for a family decision can do that; neither does it benefit the maximum number, for this ideal has indefinite limits. It does serve the greatest number with common problems that can be worked out through face to face discussion and cooperative labor. It is therefore the optimum, judged in terms of a minimum of conflict to reach maximum benefits for a maximum number.

Like any action directly expressive of people's needs and desires, there can be no question of its acceptability. It matches satisfaction to aspiration as nearly as can be done on a group or societal basis. That is to say, there is no delegation of authority, no surrogation of responsibility. Needs and points of view, and the responses to them, are not relayed through spokesmen. There is no higher authority, hence no necessity for collective representation. The community is the deliberating, enacting, and implementing body. This combination of functions and their intimate linkage eliminates an otherwise fertile field for misrepresentation, compromise, special pleading, and plain political skulduggery.

(6) Community action is local and particularistic. It is adaptable to special and specific needs, and it automatically takes local human, cultural, and natural resources into account. It is a generalized concept with many concrete manifestations. Reports on projects in Australian New Guinea, for example, "demonstrate a variety of approach to and content of community development programs within the territory. Nowhere is a 'pattern' approach to be found, and this is an added reminder that development takes place 'where the spirit listeth.'" [29]

The adaptability of the concept deserves emphasis in view of the fact that most Americans regard technical and material achievements as measures of progress. Many tend to feel that if the underdeveloped areas can be stocked with *things,* the problems of the world will be solved. No doubt the people of some of these regions do want *things,* but many want non-material changes along with or in preference to the material ones. Thus, in India, the replacement of English by Hindi as the *lingua franca* of the country has been considered to be as important as increasing the food supply. [30] This is a nationalistic severing of the navel cord, not an instance of aided self-help; but language or any other change prompted at the community level could be such.

Community initiated action does not require any grand design—unless it be the decision to encourage the proliferation of the concept itself. In fact, it does not harmonize well with national or broad regional planning due to its dependence upon spontaneity and local peculiarities. It consequently settles some issues while raising others. It dispenses with the need, inherent in other approaches, to organize and coordinate developmental activities and the supervision of them. [31] It obviates the necessity of explaining or selling regional or national programs to unsympathetic or unsophisticated elements in the population. Community action by-passes an issue in the philosophy of assistance; namely, whether aid should be extended to the under-privileged classes primarily or invested so as to contribute indefinitely to the process of capital formation—the "humanitarian" vs the "aristocratic" viewpoint, to use Viner's terms. [32] The aided self-help approach permits the people, whoever they are, to answer this question for themselves because it is local and particularistic, community action contributes to diversification. At the same time its effects are expandable.

(7) Aided self-help projects are self-limiting. Since the projects belong to the community, from their inception in discussion to their fulfillment and use, they cannot go beyond the understanding or physical mastery of those they serve. This does not mean, of course, that their physics, chemistry, or logic must be understood; only that their importance is appreciated and that their management falls within the scope of local skills. This is so even when outside technical assistance is rendered, for it must be geared into the community resources.

An important aspect of this situation is that it embodies continuity with the past. In contrast to imposed schemes, aided self-help begins wih existing knowledge and its growth potential. In further contrast, the projects it envisages are short step and "next step" changes. That is, they are tentative and cautious, progressing under control, one step at a time. The growth they stimulate is evolutionary and less disturbing than externally forced changes or explosive internal ones.

Such growth also involves a minimum of experimentation and a minimum of delay in rewards. These are extremely important considerations for many people in underdeveloped areas. Where earning a living is a precarious pursuit, men are not inclined to stake their fate on new methods. "The average Indian farmer, raising barely enough to feed himself and his family in the good years and close to starvation in the bad years, could not offord long range experiments."[33] Any long range program, experimental or otherwise, is less acceptable to most people, especially if they are not accustomed to planning, than is an immediate return on effort and money expended. In the nature of man, a succession of short step rewards is a more certain incentive than is the lure of distant goals.

There are other features which recommend the aided self-help approach to change, among them the economy of its operation; but enough has been said to justify its serious consideration as one effective means of accomplishing progress, however that term is defined. It is not supposed that it is a universal panacea. There are many situations in which other approaches will inevitably be preferred and justified on contrary grounds. It is vulnerable to criticism on many counts; in fact, on any criterion which posits a value assumption. It can be argued that the aided self-help process is inefficient, time consuming, and minuscule; that it blocks national planning, is expensive in the long run, is unsuited to urban development, and is manipulative no matter how the fact is disguised. A good case can be made for all these complaints. It can also be maintained that slow change, social cohesion, cultural continuity, and even democratic processes are ideals to be sought only if one deplores their opposites.

In the last analysis, any position is supported by no more than a conviction of its worth. No matter how far it extends, or where it begins, the reasoning for it is threaded on a web of value judgments. Aided self-help appeals or fails to do so as one credits or discredits certain value assumptions which are inarguable.

[1] Van Rensselaer, Bernard S., "How *Not* to Handle Foreign Aid." Readers Digest, Feb. 1957 (pp. 25-30), p. 29.

[2] UNESCO, "The Haiti Pilot Project." Monographs on Fundamental Education IV. Paris, 1951, p. 61.

[3] *Idem.*

[4] *Ibid.,* pp. 41-42.

[5] Foreign Operations Administration, Statistics and Reports Division, "India— the FOA Program." Washington, April 5, 1954, p. 12, the FOA contribution to the program in the fiscal year 1952-53 was $11 million; India's was equivalent to $84 million.

[6] Opler, Morris E., "Selective Culture Change." *The Progress of Underdeveloped Areas,* Bert F. Hoselitz (ed.), Univ. Chicago Press, 1952, p. 134.

[7] Mandelbaum, David G., "Planning and Social Change in India," *Human Organization,* Vol. 12, No. 3, 1953, p. 9.

[8] Foster, Ellery, "Planning for Economic Development Through Its People". *Human Organization,* Vol. 12, No. 2, 1953, pp. 5-9; Thomsom, R., "Educational Aspects of Community Development," *South Pacific Commission, Technical Paper*

No. 74, Noumeo, 1955; Belshaw, H., "The Communities Project Approach to Economic Development," *South Pacific Commission, Technical Paper,* No. 84, Noumea, 1955; Dickson, A. G., "The Concept of a Team," *South Pacific,* Vol. 6, No. 2, (Sidney), 1952, pp. 308-312; Batten, T. R., "The Community and the External Agent." *South Pacific,* Vol. 6, No.11, 1953, pp. 557-60; Thompson, Laura, "Action Research Among American Indians," *Scientific Monthly,* Vol. 70, No. 1, 1950, pp. 34-40; Bonilla y Segura, Guillermo, "Report on the Cultural Missions of Mexico." Office of Ed. Fed. Sec. Agency, Washington, *Bulletin 11* 1945; Ruopp, Phillips. (ed.) *Approaches to Community Development.* The Hague. 1953.

[9] Crane, Jacob L., "Huts and Houses in the Tropics," (United Nations) Unasylva, Vol. 3, No. 3, 1946.

[10] Foster, George M., "Applied Anthropology in Modern Life," *Estudios Anthropologicos,* Publicados en homenaje el doctor Manuel Gamio. Mexico, D. F., 1956 (pp. 333-41, Spanish), pp. 338-39, English.

[11] "The Purari Delta. Background and Progress of Community Development." South Pacific Commission, Social Development Notes, No. 7, Nov. 1951.

[12] Barnett, H. G., *Anthropology in Administration,* Springfield, Illinois, 1956, pp. 143-150.

[13] "Community Education in Puerto Rico," *Occasional Papers in Education,* No. 14, Education Clearing House, UNESCO, Paris, July 28, 1952.

[14] *Ibid.,* p. 9.

[15] Hussein, Ahmed and Carl Taylor, "Report of the Mission on Rural Community Organization and Development in the Caribbean Area and Mexico," *United Nations Series on Community Organization and Development,* ST/SOA/ Ser 0/7, ST/TAA/Ser 0/7, March 1953, pp. 30-31.

[16] *Ibid.,* p. 35.

[17] Mandelbaum, *Op. Cit.,* p. 8.

[18] Fortes, Meyer, "An Anthropologist's Point of View," *Fabian Colonial Essays.* Rita Hinden (ed.), London, 1945, p. 231.

[19] Barnett, H. G., *Innovation,* 1953, p. 94.

[20] *Ibid.,* pp. 374-75.

[21] Opler, *op. cit.,* pp. 129-130.

[22] Mandelbaum, *op. cit.,* p. 6.

[23] Batten, *op. cit.,* p. 560.

[24] Hussein and Taylor, *op. cit.,* p. 33.

[25] "Further Education in the Cook Islands." *South Pacific Commission,* Social Development Notes, No. 9, July, 1952, pp. 1-5.

[26] Barnett, *Anthropology in Administration,* pp. 138-39; 141.

[27] Foster, Ellery, *op. cit.,* p. 8.

[28] *Idem.*

[29] "The Purari Delta . . .," p. 13.

[30] Opler, *op. cit.,* pp. 126-27.

[31] Belshaw, *op. cit.,* p. 1.

[32] Viner, Jacob., "America's Aims and the Progress of Underdeveloped Countries." In *The Progress of Underdeveloped Areas,* (pp. 175-203), pp. 188-191.

[33] "Point Four Pioneers," *Department of State Publication* 4279. Oct., 1951, p. 33.

PART V

REGIONAL CONFLICTS AND
ECONOMIC DEVELOPMENTS

12: *Indonesia: Centrifugal Economies*

JUSTUS M. VAN DER KROEF

The chain of revolts of outlying provinces and districts against the central Indonesian government during the months of December 1956, through March 1957, have focussed attention on the wide differences in social structure and developmental dynamics between the various parts of the world's largest island republic. It is clear that the principal reason for the revolts was the long endured and widespread dissatisfaction in various areas with the economic policies of the national government in Djakarta, which, so it is widely alleged, tended to drain the component regions of the nation for the benefit of a corrupt, inefficient central bureaucracy and thus retarded the implementation of regional as well as national development projects. In retrospect there can be little question that such "draining" indeed took place, and that the various provinces proportionally contributed far more to the national fisc than they received in return for regional advancement. But in the heat of the political crisis that followed the revolts, the deeper socio-economic reasons for the local uprisings have become obscured. Partisan and ethnic prejudice have come to becloud the main issues and the revolt is seen as a party struggle or as an explosion of resentment on the part of other Indonesian population groups against the Javanese who are said to allow a policy of "imperialistic exploitation" of other Indonesian areas. [1]

This paper will seek to analyze the recent rebellions in Indonesia in terms of seemingly inexorable consequences of the difference in local social structure in the country, and the antagonistic economic processes dependent on them. Though the data are limited to Indonesia, it is believed they may be relevant to other underdeveloped countries, for reasons which will become clear at the close of the argument.

I

Our point of departure is the cause of the rebellions commonly accepted in Indonesia itself, namely a political and cultural hostility of various regions toward the Java-centered and Java-dominated national government in Djakarta. Probing beyond this hostility one encounters first of all a marked distinction in economic structure and process between Java and other Indonesian islands like Sumatra, Kalimantan (Borneo), Sulawesi (Celebes) and Nusa Tengara (the Lesser Sunda Islands). The latter islands exhibit the characteristics of a "frontier society," less densely populated by far than Java,[2] with vast reaches as yet uncultivated. Though both Java and the other islands are predominantly agrarian, the structure of the rural economy shows a marked contrast. In Java the extremely labor intensive, flooded field (*sawah*), land fragmented form of production prevails. On the other islands, while *sawah* cultivation is by no means unknown, the labor extensive, dry field(*ladang*) form of production on cleared or burned forest and brush land, is as yet more common[3] Many variations of these two systems are known and practiced, but in general this observation holds true that in overcrowded Java the *sawah* form of agriculture has reached horticultural standards of labor intensivity in food crop cultivation, (e. g. rice) while on the more "open" outer islands the slash and burn technique of *ladang* cultivation appears much more haphazardly labor extensive, while it has allowed for a greater tendency in experimenting with the cultivation of commercial crops.[4]

The differences in the socio-economic development between Java and the other Indonesian islands are closely related to the respective dominance of *sawah* or *ladang* types of agricultural production. First it is necessary to emphasize, however, that both types came to be embedded in their particular environment many centuries ago and in time became inseparably interwoven with the warp and woof of the cultural fabric of their milieu. It is clear that well before the emergence of Hindu-Indian cultural influences in the Indonesian archipelago shortly after the beginning of the Christian era *sawah* cultivation, its irrigation techniques and communal organization, had become part of Javanese folk culture; rice production on flooded fields appears to have been one of the many techniques brought by the forebears of contemporary Indonesians from Southeast Asia mainland during the Neolithicum.[5] Other areas of Indonesia appear to have been unfamiliar with it for a long time, indeed, in East Indonesia the Europeans were responsible for the introduction of rice. Perhaps the most important aspect of *sawah* cultivation is the compact, almost rigid ecological structure that is associated with it. Where *sawah* produc- duction prevails the fields usually "lie like a wreath around the in- habited compound" area of the village, and the number of inhabitants of the *sawah* village is very closely related to the area under cultiva- tion. [6] Since traditionally every family in the subsistence sphere ob- tains only as much land as it can work adequately (2 to 5 acres) to supply its primary food requirements, and since it does not maximize production in order to make a profit, the population density, i.e., the local relationship between a given number of people and a limited area of land required to meet their subsistence needs, will always be high. In contrast the *ladang* community, with its shifting technique requires a much larger area of land per family and per cultivator, new land must be sought and the old must lie fallow for one or more seasons until its is suitable again. The society based on *ladang* agri- culture seems therefore more "open" in its appearance than the close cluster of houses surrounded by the small plots of irrigated fields in the *sawah* environment. [7]

The question has long been moot whether historic chance, popula- tion density, differences in the fertility of soil or an abundance of wat- er in a particular locale, causes *ladang* or *sawah* cultivation to prevail, or is responsible for a change from the former to the latter. Possibly the failure of one major stream of Neolithic migrants from Southeast Asia to touch on the East Indonesian islands in their wanderings re- sulted in the postponement of the introduction of *sawah* culture in this area. It also seems likely that in regions with an abundance of accessible water a form of haphazard intensive flooded field agricul- ture emerged, to become more intensive as the population increased, [8] but in the islands beyond Java this must have been rather infrequent. As one authority has remarked of the outer islands: [9] "The greater part of the country is covered with forests; even in Sumatra these ex- tend over 62 per cent of the land; the soil is on the whole less fertile, the rainfall less favorable, partly because the contrast furnished else- where by the monsoon is lacking; the available water is, as a rule, in- accessible for irrigation purposes. For all these reasons extensive agriculture is the only form of agriculture, and vast tracts of country are doomed to be left untilled."

The communal controls over land, water supply and cultivation techniques in the *sawah* milieu tended in time to be reflected in the highly formalized pattern of inter-village social relations that has characterized Javanese rural society since the dawn of history, and which in time interacted with the developing traditions of Hinduized

royal and aristocratic patrimony and control over the countryside.
The Javanese village society became a world unto itself, with a highly
developed sense of communal solidarity, sensitive to *adat* (custom)
and suffused with a magico-religious cosmology that stressed the unity
of land, people and the food they cultivated.[10]   The compactness and
relative rigidity that strikes the foreign observer of Javanese village
society today is then the product of a long evolution, the chief contours of which must have been visible long before the colonial era.
One consequence of this communal rigidity that further points up the
difference in the social structures of Java and the other Indonesian
islands, namely the increasing pressure of population, needs to be considered separately.

It seems certain that in the Javanese *sawah* village, population
density has long been high. Even when the entire population of the
island could not have exceeded 4 million inhabitants (roughly around
the beginning of the nineteenth century) this localized "over population" appears to have existed. As early as 1802 one Dutch observer
held that "Java is overcrowded with useless unemployed" and in 1816
another Dutch colonial official pointed out that in some parts of Java
the rice fields were being divided and cultivated on rotation by the
Javanese villagers because "on Java the population far exceeds the
cultivation."[11]   At a very early date the Javanese village appears to
have been familiar to those who held no land of their own and made
a living by some form of sharecropping, agricultural labor or local
trade. This phenomenon, it is well to stress, occurred at a time in
history when the area of uncultivated land on Java that could conceivably be used for cultivation by the expanding population was still
relatively abundant; nor can it be doubted that some of the expanding
population moved onto this reserve area. But the point to be made
here is that this process was in the long run not as important by far
as the, what might be called, "absorptive" capacity of the Javanese
village, i.e. its tendency to make room within, in some way or another, for a landless semi-unemployed group.[12]   This tendency, it
would seem, is a reflection of the highly developed sense of communal
solidarity and loyalty that permeates the members of the village
group, which make them loath to leave their home environment, even
though greater material rewards are to be reaped elsewhere. A telling illustration of this sense of communal unity is provided by the experience of the Indonesian transmigration service in recent years. To
alleviate Java's inexorable population pressure both the colonial and
the present national governments have long encountered migration
of villagers from densely populated Javanese villages to other less

crowded islands.   It has been found that in the more isolated villages, where the traditional pattern of communal cohesion remains strongest, the population was least inclined to migrate, even though poor and having but inferior land to work on. [13]

In the whole modern development of the Javanese economy this absorbing tendency expresses itself. Moreover, there can be no question that the effect of the Dutch colonial system was such as to confirm it. [14]   For Java was the island that was initially brought under definite Dutch dominion, the region where the Pax Neerlandica also brought with it an unprecedented rise in population: from about 4 to 44 million people in the period of less than a century and a half between 1800 and 1940. [15]   In Java dynastic war and rivalry ended first, here too, Dutch imposed order went hand in hand earliest with medical and hygienic service.   In the other islands, however, Dutch influence tended at all times to be far less direct: the searching inquiries of Resink have emphasized the extent to which Dutch colonial administration maintained the form of international legal relations with the power structures on the islands beyond Java, keeping direct interference in local affairs to a minimum, so that in many of these areas the first manifestations of Dutch control fall even now within the memory of the oldest living inhabitants. [16]   One explanation of the markedly slower rate of increase in population and the low degree of population density in all other islands beyond Java today surely is to be found in this variable intensity in direct Dutch control over Indonesia, and the greater freedom it accorded to standard Malthusian checks on population growth in the island societies of Sumatra, Kalimantan and Eastern Indonesia.

Dutch economic policy in Java tended in large measure to preserve the communal and feudal rigidity of the traditional production structure.   Initially, in the days of the Dutch East India Company, during the seventeenth and eighteenth centuries, the Dutch relied on payments of tribute, forced deliveries of produce and taxes in kind levied via headmen and aristocracy.   An increased burden was hereby placed on the village economy but its structure and organization were not basically affected; it was not until the nineteenth century that Western administrative and economic influences became incisive.   By 1800 the system of commercial monopoly under which the East India Company had operated had lost favor among Dutch colonial experts. There was growing conviction that under the old feudally based production system of the Company increases in exports would be impossible, while at the same time it was believed that such increases could be realized in other ways. [17]   In the first half of the nineteenth century we find, therefore, a series of agrarian policy experiments, all of which, despite their variations, had one thing in common: they were designed to make the land and labor of Java directly contributary to the growing international market in commercial crops and thus stressed an economic structure in which the Javanese producer would become, in one way or another, wholly involved in the self-regulating mechanics of this market.[18] This process, it is well to note, had its ramifications also in the agrarian systems of Europe at about the same time and marked the advent of the historic Liberal economic creed and its globe-encircling exchange ancillaries, so brilliantly analyzed by Polanyi.[19] In Java it also expressed itself as a "defeudalization" process, which would draw the peasant producer away from his traditional communal-feudal supports and make him a pawn in the international market economy. But the Javanese peasant rebelled against this process, and the Dutch government returned to traditional feudalism, both in the development of its public administration and in the organization of agrarian production.[20]

The aristocracy was confirmed in its authority, communal land rights—the underpinnings of traditional village solidarity—were recognized, "indirect rule," via the customary headmen became the corner stone of civil administration, while in the islands beyond Java a "policy of non interference" was decided upon under which "Dutch officials must stay away as far as possible from internal difficulties and are not permitted to take action against despotic willfulness for its own sake."[21] As private Western estate enterprise, initially on uncultivated lands in Java, began to spread, it is clear that by maintaining as far as possible the hallowed patterns of village communalism and aristocratic politico-cultural influence in indigenous life, Dutch policy perpetuated an economic structure that saw merit in warding off the process of individual and social disorganization brought by the direct new developmental impulses of the world market, but at the cost of so hardening the cake of custom that dynamic economic growth was stifled. It is well to realize that this policy was deliberate and caused at least in part by the unhappy experiences, early in the nineteenth century with "defeudalization" in the organization of the agrarian economy.[22]

Whatever its merits, the expansion of Western estate enterprise under a colonial policy that remained rivetted to the preservation of the traditional communal-feudal economic structure could not but lead in time to a further rigidification of that structure and to a kind of "involution" in which a growing rural population was accommodated by a "balloon like distension" of the village economy in its old form. [23] Geertz, in an interesting case study of the impact of Western sugar estate enterprise on the surrounding Javanese rural population has shown how Dutch policy of "segregating the Javanese social structure from the effects of Western enterprise" had not only the effect of confirming the traditional position of communal chiefs, but also reinforced the traditional ecological setting of the *sawah* village society, which ultimately provided for its growing population by slicing the subsistence pie ever thinner, while at the same time Dutch policy hampered the growth of a class of independent peasant producers of sugar and preferential treatment of some villagers led to dissimilar benefits from the whole sugar industry. [24] No lasting and meaningful impulse to development coming from a well capitalized world market oriented industry in its vicinity was possible for the Javanese rural economy under such conditions: the peasant who, persuaded by his chiefs, leased his land to the estates, became as often as not an unproductive parasite, making a marginal living from the rent earned, or from overly fragmented holdings. [25]

To accommodate an expanding population the Javanese producer found himself in time playing a variety of economic roles, each of which by itself would not provide him with a minimum subsistence income, but which together would do so. As the growth of numbers made village land fragmentation common through the length and breadth of Java, [26] the peasant began to be owner-cultivator, tenant-sharecropper and wage laborer all in one, and also to combine agrarian production with coolie work on nearby estates, with petty trade or intermittent employment in cottage and small scale industry. From whatever possible source he had to make his income, sinking into what can perhaps best be called a "scavenger economy." The case study of Tjibodas village in West Java indicates how the majority of the villagers, including those who hold an insufficient amount of land to live on, make their living by sharecropping land owned by others, by performing agricultural labor, and by engaging in petty trade, usually on a commission basis. [27] Another case analysis, that of Djabrès village in Central Java, where only a quarter of the population owns a plot of land and 92% of these landholders have plots not larger than 1.2 acres, refers to the difficulties in computing accurate occupational statistics for the population, because: [28] "Peasants working on their own lands are at the same time also wage earners on lands owned by other persons. This is also the case with persons engaged in the rooftile industry. Many people in this village have their own small tile plants, but in addition to their activities in their own plants they are also laborers in the bigger plants. In addition,

many people who have their own small plants and produce rooftiles
with the assistance of family workers consider themselves as laborers,
since they only produce half finished products which need further
processing by bigger plants, and also due to their credit relations
with the middlemen-entrepreneurs of these bigger plants who are
the only buyers of these half-finished products."

Initially, the absorption of more people in the peasant economy
did lead to an increase in production, but soon enough the phase of
diminishing returns on further application of labor is reached: "in
Javanese rice cultivation labor intensivity is already past its optimum
and the family is obliged to take all sorts of side employment in order
to keep its head above water." [29]   Under such conditions labor in the
entire rural economy takes on an increasingly less productive character;" . . . in a situation of increasing labor supply and constant output workers will characteristically be willing to restrict their own
efforts to let a new man into the line" but there is an unwillingness
to increase effort if the additional man is removed, so that there results "a kind of downward ratchet effect in which a productive process becomes addicted to labor: the more it uses the more it needs." [30]
What has struck recent observers of the Javanese economy is its labor
absorbing elasticity, which makes the application of labor saving devices both dangerous and unremunerative. [31]   For the point is that
the Javanese economy, based on a relative low productivity but, it
would seem, increasingly labor intensive, permits the existence of a
bare margin of survival to the individual while national income as
a whole declines. [32]

The enormous energy and labor expended on behalf of what is at
best a marginal return is conspicuous also in the entire network of
trade and exchange in the rural economy. Van der Kolff has given
telling examples: the woman who walks five hours to sell 15 guilders-
cents worth of groundnuts, another who goes 25 kilometres to market
and for 32 cents buys some cassava and cubeb hoping to sell these
at home for 35 cents. [33] Many hands are involved in the rural market
and exchange transactions, a seemingly endless chain of middlemen,
buyers, creditors, sellers and resellers stretches between original producer and ultimate consumer. The same tends to be true for the
commercial and industrial sectors within or dependent on the cities
insofar as these are not financed and largely controlled by non-In-
donesians. But while it may be argued that this multilithic and labor
absorbing character of Javanese trade and industry, was, as in Javanese agriculture, in part the consequence of colonial economic policy,
it must also be noted that in essence it antedates the coming of the

Dutch. We know a good deal now about the structure of the old
Indonesian trade, and there can be little question that the travelling
peddler, or itinerant retailer and middleman-creditor was its back-
bone, then and now. The pre-colonial Indonesian trade, as it flourished in the harbor principalities of the Indonesian archipelago appears to have involved a limited quantity of goods (much of it luxury items), diffused by means of much labor (one thinks of van Leur's
description of the journeying packmen doing business in all the major
markets from "Canton to Melinde") over a wide area, requiring a
lengthy chain of distributors. [34] As colonial control expanded, Javanese participation in this trade tended to diminish, the influx of
Chinese forced it more and more into insignificance. [35] But despite
this, Javanese trade, however localized, never vanished entirely, and
with the inexorable increases in population and changing social patterns of the later colonial era it came to accommodate growing numbers once again. By this time, however, Chinese competition in virtually all branches of small scale industry and retail trade required
the Javanese petty trader to be content with the crumbs of the table
and made him as often as not completely dependent on his Chinese
creditor or supplier. Lacking capital, business acumen and organizational expertise the Javanese trader remained caught in the web of
colonial economy. Yet, as in agriculture, a marginal contribution to
minimum subsistence needs was made possible through trade, provided its labor absorbing character persisted, and the principle of
what Boeke has called "minutely dispersed supply and minutely dispersed demand" [36] was retained.

Like the Javanese agricultural economy, Javanese trade appeared
to become less and less productive, accommodating growing numbers whose contribution to production was small or nil. This process
interacted closely with an economic mentality which had its origins
in the traditional communal-feudalistic sphere and which was molded
by a subsistence orientation. The tendency to confine production to
subsistence requirements, the preponderant role of social solidarity
and fulfillment of communal obligations as opposed to individualistic
advancement, attachment to land, jewelry and ornamentation as
economic objectives of primary value (an attachment governed at
least in part by traditional magico-religious motivations),—these are
conspicuous also in the Javanese trader and small industrialist. Elsewhere the typical characteristics of their business operations have
been noted, the tendency to see their enterprise only as a means of
obtaining in a desultory manner a certain amount of income sufficient
unto the needs of the day and their relative disinclination to take the

necessary steps to rationalize operations in terms of cost price, capital and labor. [37] The state of mind that one encounters in this entrepreneurial context is one which views business dealings primarily in "exploitative" terms, i.e. as means to obtain in one way or another and without much regard for the stability or future of the enterprise a necessary minimum income; it does not look upon enterprise as "productive," as requiring consistent application of the means of maximization and of efficient control. By Western standards one prefers less efficiency and a more leisured pace, and this is true not just for the untutored petty trader-entrepreneurial group, but also for the Western educated younger generation. Educated younger Indonesians appear to decline offers of Western corporations to come to work for them for high remuneration in favor of work at a lower salary level, and which appears to lie below their capacities, so long as they can work in their own style and tempo. [38]

It is here that we begin to touch on the national significance of this parasitic aspect of the "involuted" Javanese economy. When Indonesia attained her freedom from the Dutch toward the close of 1949, one nationalist ambition of long standing seemed nearer implementation at last: to transform Indonesia's economy from a colonial to a national one, i.e. limit the operations of non-indigenous (e.g. Dutch and Chinese) capital and entrepreneurial interests, and develop, among other objectives, a strong native Indonesian middle class of traders, entrepreneurs and professional men. Realizing the weaknesses of the embryo Indonesian entrepreneurial group the new Indonesian Republic sought refuge in legislation, creating especially in the fields of import, export and industry a vast body of protective laws designed to give the autochthonous Indonesian citizen (*warga negara asli*) preferred treatment over citizens of Chinese, European or other extraction (*warga negara bukan asli*). This discriminatory treatment not only heightened tensions among the 2.3 million Chinese minority in Indonesia, whose members have for centuries now held a commanding place in the retail, distributing, credit and small industry sectors of the Indonesian economy, but it also opened the door to collusion, bribery and graft between Indonesian businessmen, particularly Javanese with connections in the capital, and political figures and bureaucrats who were responsible for this legislation of preferment and its day to day implementation. Moreover, the lack of capital, business skills and rationalized efficiency among "autochthonous" Indonesian entrepreneurs and traders either adversely affected the entire carefully built network of existing commercial relationships with foreign businessmen, [39] or else led to the practice of reselling the preferred licenses to established Chinese and some European businessmen, with the Indonesian entrepreneur merely lending his name to the enterprise and becoming a "front man" for the old system of enterprise. [40]

It is evident that the special loans and credits to which the budding autochthonous Indonesian group has had access has meant little in the way of generating economic development, that, to quote the ex-governor of the Bank Indonesia, it has been "so much waste of public funds, that is the money of the people." [41] This charge does not apply of course, to the entire body of autochthonous Indonesian entrepreneurs; it is, however, characteristic of a group predominantly Javanese with strong ties to such political organizations as the Partai Nasional Indonesia (National Indonesian Party-PNI) whose influence in parliamentary circles and in the executive levels of the government bureaus in Djakarta has been a decisive factor in the extent of the corruption in the two PNI led cabinets of Ali Sastroamijojo (1953-1955, 1956-1957), [42] and which in turn has come to point up the dangers of what one Indonesian politician has delicately referred to as "the Djakarta problem."

The unproductive, "parasitic" character of this group of entrepreneurs in league with party politicians and civil servants, protected by all manner of special legislation, and focussed on the glitter of the capital city, has been analyzed elsewhere and need not be repeated here. [43] In summary one might perhaps suggest a close similarity between the parasitic labor absorbing structure of the Javanese rural economy, including its petty trade, and the operations of some Javanese entrepreneurs in the urban sector. Both are unable or unwilling to make protective expansion possible, both are content to obtain a slice of the available subsistence pie without making much effort to produce a bigger pie, both view their enterprise in "exploitative" terms as an organizational entity of haphazard means by which to make a living. Both are quite consumption conscious, i.e., a sudden windfall of high returns will be quickly translated into purchasing of "conspicuous" luxury items, but a consistent maximization and rationalization of the enterprise to make such high returns consistently possible, that is another matter. In the Westernized cultural sphere of the cities in Indonesia, and even in the more remote rural regions, one can not escape the impression that the Javanese producer has begun to broaden his range of consumer wants. But the new consumer goods are not "necessities" of life (as yet?) and incentives to maximization seem to be of but secondary importance.

Wholly in line with this tendency is the "parasitic" orientation of the younger generation of Indonesian students from which the future professional class draws its recruits. Despite their nationalism and their interest in the rapid advancement of their country it is noteworthy that an academic diploma among them often seems to be sought more for the prestige and enjoyment it can bring to the owner than as an "instrument of production" opening opportunities to labor on behalf of land and people. Former Vice-President Hatta exposed the heart of the matter when he declared that it was very undesirable that so many Indonesian students at the end of their academic training preferred higher paid positions in private and business life than employment in lower paid but essential government services. Hatta noted that foreign experts "who are used in their country to a life of luxury are willing to work in small villages in Indonesia, while we ourselves are unwilling to do so;" [44] this remark referred particularly to Indonesian graduates of medical schools. The "hunger for education" in Indonesia that has so impressed foreign observers has, it would seem, a less attractive side; the plethora of degree mills and the alarming traffic in false academic diplomas demonstrate that learning is sought more for the emoluments that its brings than for its contribution to national development. [45]

The above remark of Hatta, while undoubtedly correct in its application to those with advanced academic and professional training, requires modification in one respect: the national civil service has become a haven for growing numbers with lesser education; indeed, the latter press inexorably on the bureaucratic structure to make room for them. The enormous growth of the national bureaucracy, must, as I have pointed out elsewhere, [56] be seen in the context of two factors, (1) the traditional prestige—in aristocratic terms—of those affiliated with government service, and (2) the "parasitic" enjoyment of this prestige and the emoluments it brings today to those who hold office. Like Java's rural economy, the national bureaucratic structure is by virtue of its labor absorbing character long since past its point of optimum efficiency, so that "the bureaucracy and the educational system (also enormously expanded) are locked in a self perpetuating circle of distension in which the second produces more and more diplomaed graduates which the latter is forced to absorb." [47] Given the overly centralized character of the Indonesian government, the concentration of policy making decisions in national agencies in Djakarta, the comparative administrative helplessness of the outer regions of the country, and the alleged preponderance of Javanese in the national government's services, especially at the higher levels, [48] it becomes understandable why the national government has come

to be identified with Java and why it is viewed as a leech on their resources by inhabitants of the outer islands.[49] The expanding parasi-
tism of the Javanese socio-economy, shored up by an over centralized
and Java oriented national government and bureaucracy, has come
to be regarded as a threat not only to non-Javanese regional social
economies, but to the entire future course of economic development
of the Indonesian Republic.

II

It would be erroneous to see the Javanese socio-economy as wholly
parasitic in nature and thus ignore the evolutionary impulses visible
among some peasant cooperatives, groups of traders and petty industrialists on the island.   Modern Reform Islam in particular, has, as
was indicated elsewhere, been an important dynamic in liberating the
entrepreneurial group from traditional and "parasitic" inclinations.[50]
By the same token it would be dangerous to overlook the presence of
"involutionary" and extreme labor absorbing tendencies in the economies of Java.[51] Yet, by and large the antithesis between the social
structures and economies of Java on the one hand and the island regions beyond it is valid, lighting up the contours of the regional conflict in Indonesia today.

The basic difference in the structure of the rural socio-economy in
Java and in the other Indonesian islands, is, as we have seen, the
prevalence of *sawah* cultivation in the former and *ladang* production
in the latter.   With this difference the degree of population density
is closely connected; inaccessibility of water and poor soil quality
make extensive cultivation almost mandatory in many areas, leaving
considerable tracts untouched.   Crucial to our understanding of the
complex problems of economic development of the islands beyond
Java is precisely the relative abundance of land, even though of poorer
quality, which in many regions permitted the cultivation of commercial crops in addition to food crops.   Moreover, it may be surmised
that in some coastal regions beyond Java, where Dutch colonial authority was of more recent origin and remained less influential, the
structure of indigenous Indonesian trade, with connections both in
other Indonesian and Southeast Asian ports, was relatively less im-
paired by colonial monopoly and Chinese dominance in retail and
distributing operations than in Java.   One thinks here for example
of such ethnic groups as the Achinese, the Minangkabau, the Butonese,
the Bugis, and the Makassarese, all or most of them with lengthy traditions of maritime and overland trade on an inter-insular basis.   In
the course of the last half century the penetration of a money economy, under the haphazard and relatively indirect aegis of colonial con-

trol combined with a more positive attitude toward professional trading than usually encountered in Java,[52] led to a marked quickening
of economic life, as many peasant societies turned to the cultivation
of export crops, and as the trade, transport and communication connected with this cultivation took a greater flight.

An authoritative report on the economic changes and the attendant
socio-political disturbances in the Minangkabau area of West Sumatra
in the nineteen-twenties shows how in countless districts the peasantry turned with energy and foresight to the cultivation of such crops
as coffee, rubber and kapok. About one district we read that "Good
land is in abundant supply. Everywhere the inhabitants can be seen
clearing the woods in order to lay out coffee gardens;" of another
region we are informed that "the inhabitants are too busily occupied
cultivating coffee . . . to have time left over for rice growing" so
that rice must be imported; in yet another district, once a "poverty
stricken area," the "cultivation of rubber . . . has brought a tremendous change in the welfare of the inhabitants" and the building
of houses "Medan or Singapore style" is proceeding at a "furious"
pace. [53] There are other developmental dynamics to be noted: the
spontaneous creation of many small banks, the growth of small processing plants, the construction of roads and the "remarkable" expansion of free wage labor. The growth of production also brought
new social values, a widening range in consumption, political consciousness and a clash with tradition and the preservers of custom.
But in all this churning the evidence of a vital economic developmental process is unmistakable.

The reasons why the process set in are not all clear. The introduction of a valuable commercial crop such as rubber may have led
to a marked quickening of the entrepreneurial spirit. In some areas
the population undertook cultivation of export crops because of the
presence of Western estates in their vicinity. Elsewhere a farsighted
headman may well have urged his villagers to take cash crop production in hand, or again simply emulation of the success of one village by another may have been responsible. [54] In some areas of
Sumatra the Christian missions undoubtedly played a developmental
role. A case in point is the society of the Bataks in North-Central
Sumatra. This society, long familiar with a dynamic entreprenurial
element of its own in the figure of the group of village founders, came
under the influence of Christian missions by about the middle of the
nineteenth century, and in a few short decades the apparent combination of indigenous entrepreneurial tradition and the implications
of the new religious ideology led to a rapid change in Batak society.

Scores of Batak migrated to coastal areas to take up new monetized employment, others threw themselves into small scale industry and trade, yet others took extensive commercial agricultural cultivation in hand. The key word in Batak society, and in its regional "development association," became *hamadjuon* (advance), and the missionaries began to note with dismay that a new aggressive materialism and pecuniary orientation had gotten hold of the Batak. [55] Today both the Minangkabau and the Batak display not only impulses of continued growth, but they have grown increasingly restive that, for a variety of reasons, such growth cannot take place more rapidly. Regional and ethnic pride and an evolutionary entrepreneurial spirit are conspicuous in both regions.

Other ethnic groups outside Java show the same. Another illustration is the copra cultivation in the Minehassa region of northern Sulawesi (Celebes). Well before the Second World War the cultivation of copra, the dessicated coconut meat, had become the chief support of the East Indonesian export economy. In fact copra even then was typically a small holders product and throughout Indonesia it provided incomes to hordes of producers, transporters, processors, middlemen and creditors. In the Minehassa copra cultivation became in fact so important that it weaned the population away from the production of subsistence crops and rice had to be imported. [56] High copra prices had a strictly economic effect: the smallholders intensified their production. Because of the obvious importance of copra cultivation for the inhabitants of Sulawesi, to protect them from usurious exploitation by middlemen and to stabilize price and supply on the world market, the colonial government established careful controls through a central purchasing agency. After the Second World War and the Revolution this agency continued to function in Djakarta. The story of its mismanagement and the growing unrest among Sulawesi copra producers has already been described elsewhere. [57] Suffice it to point out that the copra producers, backed by local civil servants and army commanders, broke the hold of the national agency and in fact forced it into oblivion, while receipts of the copra trade and industry are now retained for use in the area, particularly for the implementation of long desired local development projects. The Sulawesi "copra revolt" caused a political crisis, which in broad layers of the Indonesian public was understood as a conflict between the parasitic national government "run by Javanese", and the interests of entrepreneurs in the outer islands.

It is clear that the successful stand of the Sulawesi copra producers had an important effect on entrepreneurial groups in other regions of Indonesia, especially Sumatra, where, to speak with the leader of the Central Sumatran junta that revolted against Djakarta in December, 1956, the conviction had grown that the system of government "centralization needs to be abolished, since this system leads only to unsound bureaucracy, corruption, stagnation of reconstruction in the outer areas and loss of initiative and control." [58]

It is necessary to emphasize how these and similar phenomena can be observed throughout the island regions beyond Java. The isolated subsistence economy is breaking down under the impact of a growing monetization, a broadening of wants, and a general revolution in social and cultural values. The Toradja of Central Sulawesi, for example, used to be among the most self-contained ethnic groups in Indonesia. With the coming of more or less regular Western contacts a new "conspicuous consumption" mentality took hold among the Toradja, the export of copra, rotan and other forest products has taken a great flight, and an entrepreneurial spirit has evidenced itself. [59] Areas once proverbially described as among the most isolated, such as the up-river Daya communities of Kalimantan (Borneo) today, show a marked economic vitality. The important thing to note here is that the success of the Indonesian revolution against the Dutch has not only strengthened national political consciousness, but has above all awakened regional pride based on ancient ethnic particularisms. Since the lion's share of the national government's income is obtained from a few agricultural and mineral exports and since the islands beyond Java are chiefly responsible for the production of these, it becomes clear that the productive force on the islands beyond Java has become increasingly dissatisfied with the small returns for local development alloted them by the Djakarta authorities. The revolt of the outlying provinces against the national government during the early months of 1957 is to be seen as a coming of age of Indonesia's most dynamic developmental groups, anxious to press on with their own and their region's advancement against a national government and bureaucracy that appears as parasitic and unproductive as the island economy that gave it birth. The aversion to a further spread of "Javanese imperialism" is but the fear that, what Professor J. H. Boeke once termed "static expansion," [60] will spread from Java to other areas of Indonesia and there choke the vital developmental impulses in the same way as in the "involuted" labor absorbing Javanese economy.

III

The clash of regional economic interests in Indonesia has its ideological aspects also, one of which at least deserves analysis since it places the economic conflict in a broader context. There runs through the whole of Indonesian national life today, and particularly in its politics, a basic antithesis between two schools of thought, one which is "economics minded," the other "history minded." [61] The former appears most hospitable to a highly rationalized development process along Western lines, placing a premium on business-like efficiency, maximization and training. The latter, if one may so put it, seems more mystical in its concepts of the future Indonesia, it is ultra-nationalistic and even nativistic in its outlook, glorifying what are believed to be specifically Indonesian values; it is zenophobic, stressing the need to retain the national character of the country, even (and in particular) if this would seem to make the nation less advanced by Western standards. Each of these schools of thought is suffused by Marxist, nationalist, and religious (especially Islamic) influences in different degrees and in different combinations, but for purposes of argument it seems safe to say that the "economics minded" division has its strongest supporters among the Masjumi party, and the "history minded" group among the PNI. With some qualifications the economic clash between Java and the other islands corresponds to a conflict between the PNI and the Masjumi.

The PNI, the old standard bearer of nationalism, draws the bulk of its support from Java, from the two populous provinces of Central and East Java in particular. These two provinces comprise the ancient hearth of Javanese tradition and historic glory, the region where the PNI had great success with its program combining Javanese ethnic pride and values and ultra nationalism. Masjumi on the other hand is in many ways the font of Islamic Reform in Indonesian political life; it is far and away the strongest party in the islands beyond Java taken as a whole, and in recent months has come to be identified in particular with the interests of those islands. For Masjumi's Reform Islamic ideologies appeal particularly to the rising entrepreneurial groups beyond Java, and its stress on Western style efficiency in planning and development, combined with administrative decentralization, finds a sounding board in regional pride and desire for local advancement. [62]

The longstanding political conflicts between the PNI and the Masjumi can with some justification be regarded as a struggle between the new nativistic mystique of Javanism blended with nationalism, [63] and a Westernized rationalism under Reform Islam aegis. It is interesting to see that PNI ideologies have in recent times attempted to interpret the entire course of Indonesian history in Javacentric terms, by stressing the traditional glory of Javanese "empires" which, even before the coming of the Dutch and the unifying process of the colonial era, are made out to have covered most of Indonesia. The implication is clear: the new Indonesia is the culmination of the Javanese historic process, and Indonesia is one nation because of Java's influence. Representative of this trend is the former cabinet minister and present professor of Indonesian and Southeast Asian history in Bandung, Muhammad Yamin. Yamin's concept of Indonesian history appears to involve three "realms", Seriwidjawa, Madjapahit and the present Republic of Indonesia. Madjapahit, which flourished from 1300 to 1525, for Yamin, "was an Indonesian unitary state based on the then existing Indonesian world view" [64] and in other analyses Yamin advances a new mystique of Javacentric historiography which in every respect runs counter to modern published research on the size, and historic significance of Madjapahit. [65] But, Yamin, as the propagandist of an historic Javanism, has not escaped vociferous criticism in his own country. For one Indonesian literary critic and historian "there is in Yamin no clear boundary between truth and historic fact on the one hand, and fantasy plus 'wishful thinking' on the other" and again "the illusionary greatness of Madjapahit cannot form a strong bond of unity for our people at this time. On the contrary, it even harms national unity, for people from other regions will feel that the greatness of their own regional history is being denigrated." [66] Just so, and the significance of Yamin's views and his Javacentric concept of Indonesian historical development lies in its function as a rationale of the entire complex of modern Javanism, the peculiarity of its socio-economic development sketched in the preceding pages, blended with modern nationalism in the overly centralized form of government of a new "Indonesian unitary state".

IV

Analyses of possible solutions to the regional economic conflict in Indonesia fall outside the scope of this paper, but it would seem that both the organization of the Indonesian economy and the spirit with which it is permeated, especially in Java, requires far-reaching change. For Burger an improvement in the organizational structure of the economy is the heart of the Indonesian development problem. [67] In Java, in particular, the rigidity with which available resources like land, labor and capital "are locked into a fixed stereotyped pattern of employment" [68] must be broken. This, as Indonesian publicists are well aware, requires, among other things, a turning away from the parasitic mentality in agriculture, trade and industry, necessitating "an incisive alteration in the total complex of our habits, social organization and insights. It involves a different attitude toward trade, money, saving, time, toward social hierarchy, class and rank, toward manual labor and the machine, the ability to think quantitatively, and thinking and acting within an organizational framework which transcends the familial and which is based on business-like considerations." [69]

Mere application of Western technology and methods are not enough, because "what really is involved is an essential change in our traditions, customs, world views, social organizations, labor ethos, values and motives". [70]   But, one may venture to point out, such changes are well underway in many parts of Indonesia. And it is here that the broader implication of regional differences in national economic development spring into view. Countless underdeveloped countries in the world today, particularly those in Africa and South and Southeast Asia, owe their contours as independent or future independent states to a public administrative unity imposed by colonial fiat, which lumped together the most diverse ethnic and racial groups, each at their own level of development, each with their own social structural differences and potentials of development. The case of Indonesia seems to suggest the wisdom of "regionalism" for the underdeveloped countries economically no less than politically, even though in the heat of anti-colonial nationalism the "unitary state" becomes a mystic symbol and overriding political objective. The problem of striking a balance between the centrifugal and centripetal elements in national development that has haunted all the modern industrialized nations in our time, now also is beginning to confront the underdeveloped segments of the world. [71]

1. On the background and course of the regional revolts see Justus M. van der Kroef, "Instability in Indonesia", *Far Eastern Survey*, April, 1957.
2. No census has been held since 1930, but reliable estimates of the population distribution assign Java a density of 410.6 persons per square kilometre and the other islands as a whole a density of 15.9 per square kilometre. Cf. "The Population of Indonesia", *Ekonomi dan Keuangan Indonesia* (Djakarta), vol. 9 (1956), p. 90.
3. John E. Metcalf, *The Agricultural Economy of Indonesia* (U. S. Department of Agriculture, Monograph 15, Washington, D. C., July, 1952), pp. 17-18.
4. On varieties of *sawah* and *ladang* agriculture, and their respective cultivation techniques see G. J. Vink, *De Grondslagen van het Indonesische Landbouwbedrijf* (Dissertation, Wageningen, 1941) and K. van der Veer, *De Rijstcultuur in Indonesië* (The Hague, 1949), pp. 31-50.

5. N. J. Krom, *Hindoe-Javaansche Geschiedenis* (2nd. ed., Haarlem, 1931), pp. 35, 45-48, 54; H. J. de Graaf, *Geschiedenis van Indonesië* (The Hague, Bandung, 1949), p. 14; F. H. van Naerssen, "De Oudste Cultuurstroomen", pp. 27, 29, in C. Wormser, ed., *Wat Indië Ontving en Schonk* (Amsterdam, 1946).

6. J. H. Boeke, *Ontwikkelingsgang en Toekomst van Bevolkings-en Ondernemingslandbouw in Nederlandsch-Indië* (Leyden, 1948), pp. 5-6.

7. *Ibid.*, pp. 16-17. See also Justus M. van der Kroef, *Indonesia in the Modern World* (Bandung, Indonesia, 1954-1956), vol. 2, pp. 67-68.

8. Cf. G. J. Vink, "Bedrijfseconomie van den Bevolkingslandbouw", pp. 281-282 in C. J. J. van Hall and C. van de Koppel, eds., *De Landbouw in den Indischen Archipel* (The Hague, 1946), vol. 1.

9. J. H. Boeke, *Economics and Economic Policy of Dual Societies as Exemplified by Indonesia* (New York, 1953), p. 163.

10. On the structure and socio-economic life of the Javanese village see C. van Vollenhoven, *Het Adatrecht van Nederlandsch-Indië I* (2nd. ed., Leyden, 1925); Soekanto, *Het Gewas in Indonesië, religieus-adatrechtelijk beschouwd* (Dissertation, Leyden, 1953); J. H. Boeke, *Dorp en Desa* (Leyden, 1934; W. P. van Dam, *Inlandsche Gemeente en Indonesisch Dorp* (Dissertation, Leyden, 1935); R. van Dijk, *Samenleving en Adatrechtsvorming* (Dissertation, The Hague, 1948).

11. Cited Boeke, *Ontwikkelingsgang*, pp. 6-7.

12. Clifford Geertz, *The Development of the Javanese Economy: A Socio-Cultural Approach* (Center for International Studies, Massachusetts Institute of Technology, Cambridge, Mass., April, 1956), passim (mimeo) and the same author's *The Social Context of Economic Change: An Indonesian Case Study* (Center for International Studies, Massachusetts Institute of Technology, Cambridge, Mass., July, 1956), esp. pp. 27-73. I have relied heavily on Geertz' analysis of the labor-absorbing, "involuted" character of the Javanese economy in the following paragraphs.

13. C. B. van der Leeden, *Het Aspect van Landbouwkolonisatie in het Bevolkingsprobleem van Java* (Dissertation, The Hague, 1952), p. 23.

14. See generally Geertz, *The Development of the Javanese Economy: A Socio-Cultural Approach*, passim.

15. J. H. Boeke, "Van Vier tot Vierenveertig Millioen Zielen op Java", pp. 346-356 in W. H. van Helsdingen and H. Hoogenberk, eds., *Daar Werd Wat Groots Verricht. Nederlandsch-Indië in de XXste Eeuw* (Amsterdam, 1941).

16. By G. J. Resink; "Veronachtzaamde Uitspraken", *Indonesië*, vol. 8 (1955), pp. 1-26; "Onafhankelijke Rijken en Landen in Indonesië tussen 1850 en 1910", *Indonesië*, vol. 9 (1956), pp. 265-296 and "Uit het Stof van een Beeldenstorm", *Indonesië*, vol. 9 (1956), pp. 443-448.

17. D. H. Burger, "Structuurveranderingen in de Javaanse Samenleving", *Indonesië*, vol. 2 (1949), p. 382.

18. Some historic and psychological consequences of this process I have described in my "The Colonial Deviation in Indonesian History", *East and West* (Rome), vol. 7 (1956), pp. 251-161.

19. Cf. Karl Polanyi, *The Great Transformation* (New York, 1944).

20. Burger, "Structuurveranderingen", p. 383.

21. *Ibid.* See also D. H. Burger, *De Ontsluiting van Java's Binnenland voor het Wereldverkeer* (Wageningen, 1939).

22. On this whole question see also Justus M. van der Kroef, "Colonial Indonesia: Conservatism Reconsidered", *The University of Manila Journal of East Asiatic Studies* (forthcoming)

23. Geertz, *The Development of the Javanese Economy: A Socio-Cultural Approach*, pp. 19-37 and passim.

24. Clifford Geertz, "Capital Intensive Agriculture in Peasant Society: A Case Study", *Social Research* vol. 23 (1956), pp. 433-449.

25. See in this connection also G. H. van der Kolff, "An Economic Case Study: Sugar and Welfare in Java" pp. 188-206 in Ph. Ruopp, ed., *Approaches to Community Development* (The Hague, Bandung, 1953) and W. F. Wertheim, *Indonesian Society in Transition. A Study of Social Change* (The Hague, Bandung, 1956), p. 241.

26. On land fragmentation and its resulting problems see E. de Vries, *Problemen van de Javanase Landbouwer* (Wageningen, 1947) and Justus M. van der Kroef, *Indonesia in the Modern World*, vol. 2, chapter 3 ("Java's Agriculture and its Problems").

27. H. ten Dam, "Coopereren vanuit het Gezichtspunt der Desastructuur in Desa Tjibodas", *Indonesië*, vol. 9 (1956), pp. 89-116 and the same author's *Desa Tjibodas* (Lembaga Penjelidikan Masjarakat Desa dan Usaha Tani, Bogor, 1951).

28. Lembaga Penjelidikan Ekonomi dan Masjarakat, "Beberapa bahan keterangan mengenai penduduk Djabres: suatu desa di Djawa Tengah", *Ekonomi dan Keuangan Indonesia*, vol. 9 (1956), p. 747, np. 1.

29. D. H. Burger, "Over de Economische Structuur van Indonesië", *Indonesië*, vol. 7 (1953), p. 7.

30. Geertz, *The Development of the Javanese Economy: A Socio-Cultural Approach*, p. 22.

31. *Ibid.*, passim. This labor elasticity may no longer be typical of the Javanese economy either. Edgar McVoy, "Some Aspects of Labour and Economic Development in Indonesia", *Ekonomi dan Keuangan Indonesia*, vol. 7 (1954), p. 803 remarks: "In a certain construction project observed recently by the author of Sulawesi it was noted that excavation on a hillside for a power project was being done by hand methods. About 15 young men were standing in a row down the hillside across a small bamboo bridge. They were passing rocks one to the other, one rock at a time; the last man dropped these rocks into a pile on the road at the bottom. Then other men loaded these rocks into a small cart and wheeled them about 100 yards away to a dump. There was not enough time to measure the output per man hour in transporting rocks, but obviously it was very low."

32. Benjamin Higgins, "Indonesia's Development Plans and Problems", *Pacific Affairs*, vol. 29 (1956), p. 110: "Judging from available statistics per capita national income is below the 1939 level, is probably below the 1929 level, and may even be below the level of 1919".

33. G. H. van der Kolff, *The Historical Development of the Labour Relationships in a Remote Corner of Java as They Apply to the Cultivation of Rice* (Batavia, 1937), cited in Boeke, *Economics and Economic Policy of Dual Societies as exemplified by Indonesia*, p. 104.

34. On the old Indonesian trade see J. C. van Leur, *Enige Beschouwingen betreffende den Ouden Aziatisch en Handel* (Dissertation, Middleburg, 1934), pp. 53-127.

35. On the evolution of the trading class see Justus M. van der Kroef, "Entrepreneur and Middle Class in Indonesia", *Economic Development and Cultural Change,* vol. 2 (1954), pp. 297-325.

36. Boeke, *Economics and Economic Policy of Dual Societies as Exemplified by Indonesia,* p. 85. See also Geertz, *The Development of the Javanese Economy: A Socio-Cultural Approach,* pp. 73-74.

37. Van der Kroef, "Entrepreneur and Middle Class", pp. 308-313 and A. H. Ballendux, *Bijdrage tot de Kennis van de Credietverlening aan de "Indonesische Middenstand* (Dissertation, The Hague, 1951), pp. 79-88. The "parasitic" tendencies of the rural petty trader group are probably less overt than in the urban commercial groups that have allied themselves with partisan political interests. Yet the petty traders continue to adhere to a traditional rural subsistence mentality, failing to maximize their opportunities in most cases, unless they find themselves (as e.g. in parts of Sumatra) in a different and more dynamic cultural atmosphere. In that unproductive sense of the word the petty trader group, with its strong ties to village communalism and Javanese culture, is equally "parasitic".

38. Albert Besnard in *Algemeen Handelsblad* (Amsterdam), September 3, 1955 (Reprinted as *Documentatiestuk* no. 255, p. 14 of the *Stichting voor Culturele Samenwerking,* Amsterdam, 1955).

39. Compare the summary of the 1954 report of the *Gabungan Perindustrian de Indonesia* (Indonesian Industrial Association) in *Ekonomi dan Keuangan Indonesia,* vol. 9 (1956), pp. 251-256. See also A. M. de Neuman, "On the Promotion of Indigenous Indonesian Industries", *Ekonomi dan Keuangan Indonesia,* vol. 9 (1956), pp. 683-728.

40. For details see Justus M. van der Kroef, "Indonesia's Economic Difficulties", *Far Eastern Survey,* February, 1955, pp. 17-24.

41. *Java Bode,* (Djakarta), December 29, 1956.

42. The corruption of the second Ali Sastroamijojo cabinet which resigned in March 1957, can hardly be questioned. Compare the views of Burton Raffel, "Indonesia". *The Yale Review,* Spring, 1957, p. 383.

43. Justus M. van der Kroef, "Economic Development in Indonesia: Some Social and Cultural Impediments", *Economic Development and Cultural Change,* vol. 4 (1956), pp. 116-133.

44. *Java Bode,* June 9, 1956.

45. On this aspect of educational development see Justus M. van der Kroef, "Indonesia: the Continuing Revolution", *Journal of Human Relations,* Winter, 1957, p. 46.

46. Cf. my "Economic Development in Indonesia: Some Social and Cultural Impediments", pp. 129-131. In his budget address to parliament in December, 1956, the then Minister of Finance, Jusuf Wibisono, pointed out that 38.5 percent of the total national budget is spent on salaries of government officials (*Java Bode,* December 8, 1956). In February, 1955, Wibisono declared that at that time the number of government officials fluctuated between 900,000 and a million, as compared to 140,000 in the colonial period. (*Java Bode,* February 4, 1955).

47. Geertz, *The Development of the Javanese Economy: A Socio-Cultural Approach,* p. 72.

48. Whether a relative majority of government officials is in fact Javanese is a moot point, but there can be no question that throughout the islands be-

yond Java it is felt that the Javanese dominate the government too much to the disadvantage of the outer regions. Djamaludin Malik, a leader of the *Nahdatul Ulama* (Muslim Schoolmen) Party, stated in December, 1956 that too many important government functions were held by Javanese and followers of the "Java centered" National Indonesion Party (PNI). According to Malik no person coming from the outer islands held the office of premier, head of the Central Accounting Office, chairman of the Constituent Assembly, chairman of Parliament, president of the High Council, or for that matter the Presidency of the Republic. (*Java Bode*, December 6, 1956). In his statement of explanation regarding the dissatisfaction in the outlying territories the then premier, Ali Sastroamijojo, admitted that after the dissolution of the federal Indonesian Republic in the course of 1950, the leaders of the federal states were replaced by "representative revolutionary figures" (i.e. almost entirely Javanese), especially in the leading functions (*Java Bode*, December 15, 1956).

49. The élite structure of the Indonesian republic still awaits analysis. As yet no study has been made of the extent of the following of the PNI among the Javanese business élite, particularly its relationship to the upper bureaucracy in the various government agencies and executive offices, although it is clear that collusion between these groups has been considerable. On this basis alone the view of Djakarta as a parasitic "tyrannopolis" (see my *Indonesia in the Modern World*, vol. 1, p. 160) seems not without some justification.

60. Justus M. van der Kroef, "Social Structure and Economic Development in Indonesia", *Social Research*, Winter, 1956, pp. 394-418. The psychological and cultural consequences of the acceptance of Islam for the Indonesian seem to fall into a certain pattern. There is often a certain grim asceticism and intense drive among Muslim traders in Indonesia that sets them apart, and that seems attributable to the effect of the Islamic faith (for example, both Raymond Kennedy, *Field Notes on Indonesia. South Celebes*, 1949-50 (New Haven, 1953), p. 175 and R. A. Kern, *De Islam in Indonesië* (The Hague, 1947), p. 112, refer to Islam's effect in terms of "grimness" and "dourness"). I have sought to explain the psychological mechanism involved in the acceptance of modern Islam in Indonesia as an "identification with the aggressor", with which these particular characterological traits may well be related. See my "The Colonial Deviation in Indonesian History", pp. 257-258.

51. An example of labor absorbing involution on the outer islands, making increasingly for what Geertz has termed "shared poverty", is the *ladang* economy of Timor where population growth was accommodated by a rigid expansion of the same old slash and burn technique with resulting erosion and alarming depletion of natural resources. See F. J. Ormeling, *The Timor Problem. A Geographical Interpretation of an Underdeveloped Island* (The Hague, Djakarta, 1956).

52. W. F. Wertheim, *Indonesian Society in Transition* (The Hague, Bandung, 1956), pp. 140-141.

53. *Indonesian Sociological Studies. Selected Writings of B. Schrieke. Part One* (The Hague, Bandung, 1956), pp. 100-105.

54. *Ibid.*, p. 105.

55. For the evolution of the Batak see A. H. van Zanen, *Voorwaarden voor*

Maatschappelijke Ontwikkeling in het Centrale Batakland (Dissertation, Leyden, 1934), chapter 3, passim.

56. L. A. de Waal, *Volkscredietverschaffing in den Indischen Archipel. Eerste Deel. Credietverschawng door bijzondere Personen* (Baarn, n.d.), p. 197.

57. See my "Social Structure and Economic Development in Indonesia", pp. 409-414.

58. *Java Bode*, December 22, 1956.

59. N. Adriani and A. C. Kruyt, *De Bare's Sprekende Toradjas van Midden Celebes* (Amsterdam, 1951), vol. 3, pp. 344-348.

60. Boeke, *Economics and Economic Policy of Dual Societies as Exemplified by Indonesia*, p. 174.

61. Benjamin Higgins, "Indonesia's Development Plans and Problems", p. 119.

62. On the ideological background and social supports of these and other political parties in Indonesia see Justus M. van der Kroef, "Indonesia's First National Election: A Sociological Analysis", *American Journal of Economics and Sociology*, April, June, 1957.

63. The term Javanism refers first of all to the unique mixture of autochthonous cultural traditions and Hindu-Indian traits that is called *kedjawèn* in Indonesia, and which comprises a more or less integrated cosmology, system of ritual, code of ethics and pattern of approved custom. In the second place Javanism has come to mean the revival of *kedjawèn* in connection with local Javanese nationalistic aspirations.

64. See Yamin's interview in *Elsevier's Weekblad* (Amsterdam, Sept. 1, 1956).

65. See the analysis of Yamin's views in G. J. Resink, "Uit het Stof van een Beeldenstorm", pp. 441, 449-452. Yamin's concept of the historic role of Madjapahit, which closely follows older and generally invalidated views of Dutch colonial historians, has been worked out in his dissertation *Hukum duta Indonesia dalam zaman Madjapahit 1293-5125*, as yet only published in magazine form. On the new view of Madjapahit, which completely contradicts Yamin, see C. C. Berg, "De Geschiedenis van pril Madjapahit", *Indonesië*, vol. 4 (1951), pp. 481-520, vol. 5 (1951), pp. 193-223 and the same author's "De Sadeng oorlog en de mythe van Groot Majapahit", *Indonesië*, vol. 5 (1951), pp. 385-422.

66. Bujung Saleh in *Siasat*, vol. 10 (May 30, 1956), no. 468, pp. 25-26 reprinted in and cited here from Resink, "Uit het Stof van een Beeldenstorm", p. 451.

67. Burger, "Over de Economische Structuur van Indonesië", p. 21.

68. Geertz, *The Development of the Javanese Economy: A Socio-Cultural Approach*, p. 105.

69. Sudjaymoko, "De Crisis in de Indonesische Cultuur", *De Nieuwe Stem*, vol. 10 (1955), p. 327.

70. Bambang Utomo in *Cultureel Nieuws Indonesië*, 1955, no. 43-44, p. 237. See also Suparman Soemohamidjojo, "Perangkat Pabean Indonesia", *Ekonomi dan Keuangan Indonesia*, vol. 9 (1956), pp. 444-459.

71. Considerations of space do not admit a detailed analysis of the policy implications of "regionalism" in the implementation of aid programs in Indonesia. The interested reader is referred to my "Social Structure and Economic Development in Indonesia", *Social Research*, Winter, 1956, pp. 394-418 and my "The Philippines, Indonesia and United States Aid", *Current History*, August, 1957, pp. 80-88.

13: *China: A Case Study of Aid that Failed*

DAVID NELSON ROWE

It will be impossible in this brief paper to study in detail the entire experience with the foreign aid programs in China, even with the analysis restricted to political implications and effects. Our attention will therefore be focussed on some of the chief features of that aid and on the general relationship of U. S. aid to China's internal politics and external alignment.

Even without much study it seems clear that our wartime and immediate post-war aid to China did not have great effect upon internal Chinese politics. It did not strongly influence the political nature or practices of the government with which we maintained relations during and since the war. Nor could it, seemingly, have much to do with preventing the takeover of almost all the territory of China by a regime hostile to the United States and unwaveringly aligned with our chief opponent in world affairs, the Soviet Union.

Are things any different today? The current U. S. aid program for Taiwan (Formosa) differs in numerous ways from the wartime and immediate post-war programs. Is it succeeding any better than earlier programs did in supporting the national interests of the United States in regard to China? Just what are we doing now in this respect?

First we should sketch in the background of our wartime aid to China. We do not need to detail the long history of mutually friendly relations between the United States and China before World War II. We should note, however, that like all friendships, it had had its ups and downs. Wartime aid to China was begun in a very small way before Pearl Harbor, prior to which, indeed, the United States had been sending material of war to Japan through normal channels of trade. With Japan's push southward to take over Indo-China and threaten the holdings of the other western colonial powers in South Asia, the United States found new support for its policy of opposition to Japan which had been rooted in the Stimson doctrine of non-recognition of the Manchurian aggression of 1931 and after. The result was an allied embargo on war materials to Japan, the freezing of Japanese credits in the United States, and the initiation of a policy of help to the Republic of China in the summer of 1941. China was blockaded by the Japanese Army and Navy, so that right up to December, 1941, little help reached China except for a few added official American personnel, whose contribution was largely limited to the offering of advice to the Chinese government.

That U. S. "aid" at this time took the form of advice perhaps helped to set the pattern that later prevailed so much of the time, under which aid of all kinds was tied in with U. S. attempts to influence the internal and international politics of China.

Soon after Pearl Harbor the United States provided a credit of five hundred million dollars to China. There was at that time little or nothing else the United States could do for China. After long years of war with Japan, the government was holed up in China's far west. The Japanese had by then effectively isolated China by land and sea from any possible major material assistance. In addition, the United States just after Pearl Harbor had little or no war material she could have sent China even if the Japanese blockade had not been present.

The credit of five hundred million dollars was designed to have a practical impact on China's monetary position. But its chief effect was political. It was an act of political warfare. The American people, stunned by the force of Japanese armed might at Pearl Harbor, thus gave expression of their support for the National Government of China which had resisted Japan for most of the ten years since Japan's army began its aggression by taking over Manchuria. By this supply of funds they are saying in effect that China should hold on until U. S. aid in military terms could be brought to bear on the defeat of the common enemy.

The credit was provided to the National Government of China. This was the only government in China recognized by the U.S. There were at the time nearly a half-dozen other regimes on Chinese soil. The Japanese had sponsored at least three major puppet "states" in China. There was the USSR's own puppet government in Outer Mongolia. And then there were the Chinese Communists. To all these regimes, the U. S. credit of five hundred million dollars in February 1941, could mean only that the United States was committing herself for the future to the National Government, both for the purpose of winning the war against Japan and for the post-war period.

If this were so, the United States seemed to commit itself publicly to the idea the National Government of China would play an important and weighty role in the defeat of Japan. It was possible to provide such financial assistance without making any commitment on the major military question (then bypassed completely) as to how the U. S. and China could best collaborate in the winning of the war. Apart from agreeing to the vague idea that China must be kept in the war against Japan in order to tie down Japanese forces, it was difficult or impossible to do much planning about joint strategy. The U. S. was too much occupied with its own mobilization after Pearl Harbor to be able to give attention to military strategy for the ultimate offensive in the Far East.

In this way it was possible for both the United States and Chinese governments to accept rather uncritically some basic assumptions about their future relations with each other, assumptions which were to become major problems later on when they had to be tried in the hard environment of strategic planning. The U.S. credit in February 1941 symbolized our own rather naive belief that China could contribute greatly and positively to the defeat of Japan. The belief survived long, and died hard, even in the minds of those who should have been best informed. Attempts to correct this unbalanced view in 1942 were met both in official Washington and among the supposedly best-informed intellectual circles with pointed allegations that the informant was "trying to tear down Chiang Kai-shek" or that he had disloyal "pro-Japanese" tendencies.

It was equally difficult to correct the misapprehensions created in China by the then seemingly generous financial gift of the U. S. government. The Chinese government and people for the most part simply did not comprehend the inadequacy and weaknesses of American military power. Unofficial American propagandists in China before Pearl Harbor had asserted that once the U.S. came into the war with Japan it would be all over within six months. (With a U.S. victory, of course.) Perhaps the Chinese should have lost some of their rosier expectations when the first substantial aid they received took the form of gold bars instead of guns, ammunition or soldiers. But instead it took many long months of waiting before the Chinese could face up to it. By this time, the National Government, already bled thin by years of war with Japan, faced growing political demoralization at home because of failure of its American alliance to bear fruit in a more discernably rapid defeat of Japan.

In turn, official Americans in China, some of whom had already for years been unsympathetic with the National Government, became increasingly incompatible with it. In the flood of new personnel going to China at this time were also a number who apparently brought with them predispositions of hostility toward the National Government of China and everything it stood for.

Thus by the time large deliveries of military equipment to China appeared possible for the future, operational relations between the U. S. diplomatic and military representatives in China and the Chinese government were at their worst. It was in this atmosphere that General Stilwell, with the backing of the American Ambassador and official Washington, proposed the abandonment of the precedent that all aid to China should go to the National Government. He urged that U. S. arms be distributed to the Chinese communists, on the ground that this would lead to an earlier victory over Japan. Never had any military proposal carried heavier political implications. We were proposing nothing less than the arming of a minority rebellious faction dedicated to the overthrow of a government to the support of which we were openly pledged. It was well known by this time that the earlier working relation between the National Government and the communists under the so-called "United Front" had long since collapsed. In its place was substituted a scarcely-concealed renewal of civil war, limited chiefly by the realization on both sides that the ultimate struggle for power in China would have to await the ending of the Pacific War. By 1944, then, the civil war between the communists and the government in China was seventeen years old. It could hardly have escaped the notice of even the most narrowly militarily-minded Americans. Gen. Stilwell was not such. A former Army Chinese language student and Military Attache to the American Embassy, he had lived a number of years in China, and knew much about Chinese politics.

President Chiang Kai-shek's summary refusal to consider any policy of arming the Chinese communists was the only possible action for him under the circumstances. For his government it was a matter of life or death not to allow power to flow into the hands of any of the rival claimants for control inside China, whether Japanese or Chinese. But the depth of the opposition to him among American officials kept the issue alive. The American Ambassador to Chungking eventually resigned in protest over the recall of General Stilwell. Foreign Service officers attached to the American military in the China-Burma-India area and those in staff positions in China were quite ready to enter into cooperation with the Chinese communists at that time if they could not "reform" and "revitalize" the National Government along lines satisfactory to them. President Roosevelt had therefore urged Chiang Kai-shek to appoint Gen. Stilwell commander of all Chinese and American forces in China "including the Communist forces." In order to force this policy on Chiang Kai-shek President Roosevelt sent him an ultimatum through Gen. Stilwell. He threatened that unless Stilwell's proposals were accepted, U. S. aid to China would be withdrawn.[1] President Chiang rejected this threat, whereupon President Roosevelt backed down, and recalled Gen. Stilwell from China.

In his final report to the War Department on these matters Gen. Stilwell made the following statement: "Nowhere does Clausewitz's dictum that war is only the continuation of politics by other methods apply with more force than it did in CBI (China-Burma-India Theater)."[2] The American government's attempts through Stilwell to intervene in the internal politics of China in favor of the Chinese communists were such as to place the entire relationship between the Chinese government and the U. S. government under a permanent cloud of suspicion. Particularly suspect to the Chinese Government was Gen. George Marshall, who was known to have backed Stilwell in his policies. On the American side the military and civilian authorities were bitter with the rancor of defeat of this proposed policy for the war in China, and there can be no doubt that the entire future of U.S.-Chinese relations was thus gravely affected by mutual mistrust.

Why must we give so much emphasis to wartime aid policies of the United States toward China? Precisely because all our post-war aid policies, whether supposedly "economic" in character, or supposedly directly military in nature, share most of the characteristics of our wartime policies of aid to our allies. Although the post-World-War-II aid policies were evolved in a time of ostensible "peace," they were and are in reality caused by and justified by the so-called "cold war." It is indeed true that overt military hostilities, economic warfare and political warfare are sometimes separated by only the thinnest possible lines. In actuality they are often most difficult to distinguish, one from the other. The failure to recognize that all U.S. aid is, either directly or indirectly, part of a struggle for power in the world leads to many of the errors and failures of aid policy.

The statement is attributed to wartime German military leaders that Americans know nothing of military strategy, that they win wars simply through mastery of production and transportation of massive war supplies. This may or may not be true. In analogy, however, it does seem true that we have often failed to understand the politically strategic aspects of both wartime and "peace" time aid. And it is not surprising that our greatest failures have occurred in our re-

lations with just those countries about whose native cultures we are
generally the most ignorant. As a case in point, in these countries we
are the most deficient in the ability to distinguish the difference between "war" and "peace." China, for example, has been in a constant state of revolution, chaos and upheaval for a century or so. In
light of such things as the critical lack of systematic academic study
of China in our country, is it any wonder that when we finally became
entangled in the Sino-Japanese war we utterly failed to understand
China's internal politics? It thus turned out that we were capable
on our own of contributing to the defeat of China's external enemy,
Japan, but were totally unprepared and unable to protect our ally,
the National Government of China, against internal takeover by the
communists, who have now turned out to be a dangerous and active
enemy of the United States.

Of course the wartime policy of arming the Chinese communists
was abandoned after Stilwell's recall. By virtue of our mastery of
production, supply and transportation, and by great efforts, we eventually brought enough arms to China so that by the end of the war we
had trained and equipped thirty divisions of the Chinese Army. It
should be noted, however, that this effort was small by comparison to
what we had exerted in Europe and the Pacific. Moreover, none of
our aid to China's armed forces had any immediate or direct bearing on the defeat of Japan which, and predictably, was largely a matter of sea, air and amphibious attack in the Pacific Ocean area. Thus
the chief impact of our wartime military aid policy in China was
political disturbance, not military success.

In this respect the world-wide political evaluation of our wartime aid
to China was proved ultimately to be wrong. Thus Russians at Yalta
seemed to assume, for instance, that military aid to the National
Government by the U.S. would be strongly continued after Japanese
surrender. The nature of their interest in Manchuria, Mongolia and
Sinkiang, Chinese border territories, shows this clearly. For example,
their takeover in Manchuria developed there a safe haven for the
Chinese communists, where the Red Armies were re-formed and
equipped to become the first field armies the communists ever had.
By contrast, the thirty newly-armed Chinese government divisions,
victorious in all initial engagements with the communists, were inhibited from attacking them in Manchuria by a Russian blockade
which the U. S. refused to challenge. And eventually, no doubt to
the intense surprise of the Russians, Gen. Marshall set up an arms
embargo in his efforts to bring about collaboration and a coalition of

the communists and National Government. He thus starved out the government forces.

For, indeed, U. S. aid to China was the prime blackmail weapon in General Marshall's ill-fated attempt to bring the two Chinese factions together into one government after the war. Here Marshall seemed to take off again from where General Stilwell had failed. The predictions of disaster to the joint war effort against Japan which had been used to show that the Chinese communists should be armed in 1944 had been proven wrong. Now there were fresh predictions of the total downfall of the National Government unless the civil war were ended by a coalition government including the communists. But there was a great difference between 1946 and 1944: in 1946 the threat (first given in 1944) to withhold military aid was actually made good. It was "peace" then, not war, so that the supposedly joint war effort was no longer involved. All that was involved was victory in the Chinese civil war and the future of China's internal politics!

Marshall's solution for the civil war was classically simple. These two "parties" should join together and bury their differences for the common good. This was nothing less than an attempt to make over Chinese politics on the American two-party model, and do it fast! It should be remembered, however, that even American political history contained one long and bitter civil war fought over political irreconcilabilities. And it had been preceded by a revolutionary war in which political differences had also been submitted to the final arbitration of force, and not without foreign intervention on behalf of the rebels.

General Marshall could not force the communists into an agreement; he could apply no sanctions against them. But against the National Government he could apply the sanction of withholding military aid. Since the Russians were supplying the communists with everything they needed, Marshall's arms embargo against the Chinese government could have only one effect: to cause them to lose the war against the communists. Without gasoline and ammunition the machines and arms the Nationalists had secured from the U. S. during the war were useless, and most of them were subsequently captured by the communists when the government forces collapsed.

Generalissimo Chiang's basic error at the time lay in his seeming inability to believe that the United States would really abandon him to his fate. He kept on expending his supplies in futile efforts to hold key cities in Manchuria which were under blockade by the communists and which he had to supply by air. Meanwhile, the arms embargo, in which Britain and other arms-producing countries participated with the U. S., lasted from August 1946 to the end of May 1947. Its openly avowed purpose was to bring about a coalition government, with the communists admitted into the government of China. But when Chiang Kai-shek in November 1946 agreed to this (the communists then refused to join) the embargo was not lifted! This clearly was designed to convince all doubters in China that the United States had abandoned the National Government in favor of the communists and helped accentuate the already rapid fall in morale among pro-American elements. After the embargo was lifted in May 1947 only a very small amount of munitions was delivered during the rest of that year, for reasons not easy to determine.

After the war ended in 1945, and up to the takeover of the China mainland by the communists in 1949, only negligible amounts of military aid were sent to China. China received during that time only about one-third as much military aid as was sent to Greece, a small country with an army of less than 200,000 men, where the government was also engaged in a civil war with communists. Much is said of the non-military aid that went to China after V-J Day, but in proportion to the need and the size of the problem of relief, let alone economic reconstruction, the amounts were negligible. Over the four years after the end of the war the total came only to about two cents per person in China per week. [3]

Finally, after the military situation in China had deteriorated so far that it was practically irremediable, the United States enacted the China Aid Act of 1948 and sent under its terms a total of some $115,-000,000 worth of military equipment to China. By the time this material was received and distributed the military situation was so bad that most of it was captured by the communists in their final victories over the by-now demoralized Government forces. Much of the material sent was not what was needed, namely ammunition. There was no over-all plan, seemingly, by which needs were to be analyzed and supplies sent accordingly.

How can one account for all this? Probably only in terms of the growing acceptance in official circles in the American government of anti-Nationalist and pro-Chinese-communist political orientation. Thus aid of all kinds was, as always, tied to politics, and with such a pattern of orthodox politics in the U. S. government, what happened in the field of aid to China was a natural result. It is difficult, if not impossible, to account for this in any other way.

Thus foreign aid policies of the U. S. government had a very material part in the fall of the National Government of China and the takeover of China by the Chinese communists, at the same time that the Russians *were* giving all possible aid to the Chinese communists. Their aid took the form of captured Japanese military material sufficient to arm the communists for five years of all-out warfare. Without this the communists could not possibly have won against the Government. They transformed their forces from sketchily equipped guerilla groups into strongly armed regular armies, trained with Russian assistance. Without this help their greater operational flexibility as contrasted with that of the Government could not have won the day. This was clearly indicated by the initial victories which Government forces won over them immediately after Japan's surrender.

After the fall of the China mainland to the communists, the National Government retreated to Taiwan (Formosa) with some half-million troops, largely lacking in supplies. About 1,500,000 civilians also made their way to the island. In spite of the early official American view that the communists would take the island by invasion, this did not happen. And in the summer and fall of 1950 the Korean war and the eventual entry of the Chinese communists into it changed the entire situation. Beginning with an interdiction against communist invasion of Taiwan, backed up by American naval power, the United States gradually went over to a policy of military aid to Taiwan. At the same time the ECA program, which had barely gotten started on the mainland, was renewed and diversified.

It is important to take note here of the sequence just stated. Direct intervention by U. S. armed forces in the Chinese civil war took place when President Truman unilaterally announced that the Navy would be used if necessary to prevent communist invasion of Taiwan. Evidently our repugnance to involvement in "fratricidal strife" in China had somewhat lessened under the impact of hostilities in Korea. And this occurred at the very start of the Korean war when there was no general American belief that the Chinese communists would enter that war. Lacking any real naval power, the communists could hardly challenge the American military protection of Taiwan. Thus Taiwan had genuine military security against external attack. This has proved the primacy of military considerations in the revolutionary environment of China. For behind this shield, and with continuing military aid, it has been possible for the first time to initiate a program of U. S. aid in the economic and social fields which has achieved much. Internally, Taiwan has enjoyed high levels of domestic security. Here is at least one part of China, and one time in China, when American desire to practice "uplifting politics" could be indulged without jeopardizing, and in the effort to strengthen, the basic elements of law, order and security

Accordingly, and increasingly, the military defenses of Free China have been strengthened by a planned program of supply and training. Most of this effort has gone into the Army and Air Force, logical in view of American naval predominance in the western Pacific. But the Chinese Navy has not been entirely neglected by any means.

Under the Chinese-American treaty of mutual defense the U. S. is committed to help protect Taiwan and its immediately surrounding islands against any attack. In return, the U. S. general defense in the western Pacific gains from the availability of this position to us and its denial to the communists, and from the availability on Taiwan, close to the Chinese mainland, of well-trained and equipped armed forces of some 600,000 men. These are backed up by a pool of available reserve military manpower numbering at least 1,250,000, rather quickly usable in time of emergency. We do not need to know the exact size of U. S. military aid to Free China, to realize that the cost to us of these resources is negligible by comparison to the costs of maintaining anywhere in the area a comparably effective American force in being.

To the Chinese Government the chief costs of this military alliance and the support extended under it to its military forces lie in the strategic controls which accompany it. The avoidance of any further war with communist China stands high in the group of policy objectives of our government. The National Government of China, on the other hand, lives only for the day when it plans and hopes to return to the Chinese mainland. All its political, economic and military programs on Taiwan are aimed at this objective. The assumption is that the communist regime is bound to lose ground steadily in China, and that since its international objectives include the spread of communism everywhere, it is eventually bound to come into major conflict with the Free World. It is believed generally in Free China that at that time, or earlier, communism on the mainland will go down to destruction and the National Government will be restored to power with the support of the Chinese people.

The American military and economic support, the aid program, on Taiwan is from our own point of view strictly defensive, and is aimed at merely holding the line against further communist expansion in the Far East. But the National Government's aims are positive, not negative, and they conflict directly with ours. How long can such contradictory aims be ignored or merely kept beneath the surface without emerging into open disagreement? Here again, as during the last war, the United States is in flat disagreement with its ally on major aims of the alliance. The ally, vitally dependent upon our support, accepts the aid in spite of holding to an utterly divergent ultimate purpose. Fortunately for both allies, perhaps, their area of cooperation is sufficiently broad and covers so many directly significant mutual concerns that they can be heavily absorbed in working together and for the time being do not feel the disturbing effects of the basic underlying contradiction in their ultimate aims.

Under current world conditions, however, it may be forecast that this fundamental disagreement on basic aims cannot be permanently bypassed. Sooner or later it is likely to endanger the cooperation between China and the United States. Thus, even today, with communist China clearly identified as a mutual threat, the United States and the Republic of China are in fundamental disagreement as to how to deal with it. This begins to sound a little too much like the days of 1942 and 1943 when the U. S. and China began to draw apart, at that time on the issue of priority between the defeat of Germany and the defeat of Japan, and only later on the question of arming the Chinese communists.

The concentration of the National Government on its aim of ultimately returning to the mainland does not mean, however, that it considers unimportant what it does on Taiwan. Quite the contrary, the Government since 1949 has been determined to do everything possible to correct past errors and omissions and to build a record of achievement in Free China that will justify its claim to a return to power. Also, it wants in Taiwan a strong local base of its own power, not only in the military, but also in the economic and social fields. Accordingly it has embarked on a broad program in Taiwan, the results of which have already been remarkable in many ways.

In this program U. S. foreign aid has played an important part. One of the most successful enterprises supported by American funds has been the Joint Commission on Rural Reconstruction (JCRR). This organization, aimed at general agrarian improvement, was begun on the mainland before the communist takeover. It, in turn, was based on the experience of the Chinese government in sponsoring agrarian reform in China before 1937. Due to the limited extent of government control of the countryside between 1945 and 1949, JCRR had only a limited impact. During that time, however, at least two basic features of JCRR were established. First, its activities in the countryside were firmly based on the previous experience of Chinese and American workers experienced in Chinese conditions and who had worked in this field before, and in China. Here again we must stress that agrarian reform in China was originally begun before the Sino-Japanese War, and was in no sense the result merely of American initiative or American suggestions. Second, the activity was a joint Sino-American enterprise, and not merely a matter of U. S. aid, conceived in U. S. terms, and delivered over to Chinese use without too much consideration of its applicability in the Chinese environment.

Thus on Taiwan the JCRR has had much to do with the success of agrarian reform, including land redistribution, the adjustment of rents and taxes to the advantage of the farmers, the improvement of production, and the improvement of rural health and education, to mention only a part of its work. Land reform in Taiwan is the only case of the sort in Asia which includes all the following characteristics:

1. The reform was voluntary. It was not imposed on the Government from the outside as was the land reform in Japan under the occupation. It would have been done with or without U. S. aid or participation.

2. The reform was bloodless; it required no war and was not achieved by violent revolutionary methods.

3. Land redistribution in Taiwan was non-confiscatory. Landlords were compensated, and adequately, for the land given to the peasants.

4. Compensation to the landlords took the form of bonds issued against capital property owned by the government as a result of its takeover from the Japanese. Subsequently the government turned over much of this property to the shareholders. Their holdings in these properties constituted an adequate hedge against inflation.

5. Thus land reform has incidentally helped to create a new class of industrial shareholders, i.e., small capitalists.

The redistribution of land and the reduction of rents and taxes have given the farmers of Taiwan the best standard of living in Asia with the possible exception of the Japanese. Its effects have been greatly strengthened by simultaneous technical improvements in production and by raising the level of rural health and education. All this can be readily seen in the Taiwan countryside and is particularly noticeable to anyone whose standard of comparison is based upon knowledge of mainland China and the other chief areas of Eastern Asia.

However, the question still must be answered, namely, what gain to the national interest of the United States can be claimed as a result of U. S. aid funds spent in this way? The prevailing tendency seems to be to claim fundamental political outcomes from such socio-economic enterprises. It is said that with a "decent standard of living" the Asian peasant is less susceptible to communist utopianism. It is, in fact, always somewhat surprising to see how many Americans seem to have succumbed to these notions of economic determinism in politics. Perhaps there has been an intrusion of this school of thought into the variegated multiplicity that is American culture. Perhaps it is also typically American today that a concept of this kind is considered generally valid outside the West, as well as within western culture.

This is all a very risky business, to say the least. Socio-economic changes of the kind being established in Taiwan may easily have quite unpredictable results. In modern Japan, for instance, the great increase of production caused by some degree of industralization, far from stabilizing the country, helped lead it into a disastrously over-extended course of imperial expansion.

Will Taiwan's rural revolution lead, for example, to such a catastrophic population increase as to nullify and overwhelm the gains in production in all fields? If so, what effect will consequent deprivation have on a population which has previously experienced even relatively small amounts of improvement in standards of living? What can be done to prevent such effects? These are only a few of the unanswered questions flowing from what is doubtless one of the most admirable enterprises that the U. S. government has ever been connected with in Asia.

Much of the political impact of this joint Sino-American enterprise is so fundamental and so overlaid by more immediate practicalities as to be largely invisible to the casual observer. The sophisticated student may understand part of what is going on, provided his sophistication is at least partly Chinese, that is, provided he does not look at rural Taiwan from a strictly western point of view. Up to date it appears that no real study has been made of the impacts of rural reform in Taiwan upon the political attitudes, practices or objectives of individuals or small groups. Such a study could best be made cooperatively, including western students of Chinese society, culture and politics, and Chinese students of western society, culture and politics. Experience shows the rewarding nature of this type of teamwork in the study of problems of this kind. But the immediate point here is that American aid in this field does not rest upon much of an idea as to eventual political outcomes.

The only thing that now appears definite is that the political outcomes of current rural reform in Taiwan will take a long time to develop. This is not likely to displease Americans, who often seem to assume the inherent validity of anything to which they can attribute a "grass roots" character. They often fail to understand how disintegration can permeate a political order at the grass roots level while remaining for the most part hidden from view. For example, the "informal" nature of much traditional Chinese social control, the personal government at the top level in traditional China, and the habitual recourse to conspiratorial politics in old China, all tended to inhibit the spontaneous exhibition of political change. Thus political disintegration was allowed to conceal itself, and was for the most part forced to stay hidden until it was beyond remedy. If these patterns of the past elude our attention, we then may be surprised when sometimes current political changes eventuate in chaos, however temporary. To make disintegration merely temporary and partial and to lead the development into constructive channels requires the discovery and mobilization of all the knowledge we can possibly get. In this particular case such study seems long overdue.

The importance of considerations of this kind lies partly at least in their relation to American public opinion and policy formation. The usual American demand for quick results must be tempered strongly in this case. Real changes in political institutions, habits and practices will come slowly even under the optimum conditions now prevalent in Taiwan. If contrary expectations are aroused among Americans and their policy-makers, only to be unfulfilled in the short run, disastrous implications for our current policy of supporting Free China against communist China may be involved. Probably a realistic attitude on these matters can only result from a great deal more and better American public education on China than now exists.

The government-to-government relations typical of U. S. foreign aid programs elsewhere are also typical in the Taiwan program. The Nationalist Party has always stood for a strong measure of governmental involvement in and control of the Chinese economy. This attitude has been strengthened by long years of continuous war mobilization. Now that its rule is limited to Taiwan, the Chinese government controls all major aspects of the economy even more tightly than has ever before been possible. It cannot possibly support from its own internal resources the degree of mobilization enforced by defense and preparation for an eventual return to the mainland. But it bends every effort to progress toward increasing self-sufficiency in manufactures and the development of production (mostly agricultural) for export.

All this is actively supported by the U. S. aid program, and this continues to strengthen both in principle and practice the domination of government in the economy. This domination does not have to contend with the same hostile predispositions set up by a long history of relatively free enterprise such as characterizes the western countries. Modern economic activities are sufficiently new in China, and are sufficiently conditioned by the revolutionary disorders of recent Chinese history so that business and government have always perforce been tied closely together. In addition, there is the long history of bureaucracy in imperial China and of its relation to economic enterprises.

The national government's role in business has grown stronger, with American aid, not only relative to the private businessman. It also tends in this respect, particularly within the constricted territorial limits of Taiwan, to overshadow the provincial and local governmental units. This decreases the significance of the local, as against the national, government. Americans may talk individualism, private rights and liberties, but their economic aid policy in China is related to the growth of centralization of politico-economic power in Free China today.

Without commenting at all on the features of our own governmental bureaucracy at home along these lines, it seems clear that the American administrators of foreign aid in Taiwan, as elsewhere, do not fight against this trend as much as they might. Their job as they see it too often, after all, is to dispose of American funds. The most direct way in which to do this is to work with their opposite numbers in the bureaucracy of a foreign government. It is to the interest of both sides in this activity, for example, to spend these funds in comparatively large sums allocated to relatively few projects. For this reduces the total amount of paper work per dollar involved in planning, budgeting, getting approval by both governments, and accounting for the resultant expenditures and outcomes. Since in Taiwan today most business in the larger units is of the government or closely related to it or controlled by it, the tendency is to channel aid government-wards instead of toward the development of multiple-unit independent business, whether large-scale or small-scale.

In view of the practical situation of governmental involvement in the economy in Taiwan, perhaps the best available means of diminishing this influence of U. S. aid and increasing its influence in the opposite direction is by using U. S. influence to foster relations between U. S. private business and its opposite numbers in Taiwan. It is believed that much more can be done along this line than has been done in the past.

The increase of private American economic involvement in Free China would uphold free enterprise in both countries as a logical

consequence of our announced policy of support, military and political, for the Republic of China. Most of all, there is no better way
than this to provide for the businessmen of both countries practical
experience of each other's problems. The undiscriminating export
to Far Eastern countries of American techniques of production and
distribution is manifestly impractical. Mutual adjustments are needed in every case. Americans are too wont to assume the existence
everywhere of environments uniformly hospitable to their own tried
and true methods. At the same time, many Asians tend to attribute
magical omnipotence to every American instrumentality. These areas
of ignorance in both countries should be decreased in the interest of
greater realism of general policy of the countries and peoples toward
each other.

There is one final feature of U. S. aid operations in Taiwan that
should be mentioned. This is the tendency toward over-staffing on
the American side. It is particularly strong among those involved
with military aid. It is currently estimated that there are about 10,-
000 Americans, men, women and children, in Taiwan. Most of these
are military personnel and their dependents. In a total population
of some ten million, this does not seem a large number. But these
people are largely concentrated in the area of Taipei, the capital
city. Taipei has also received the largest number of those Chinese
who came from the mainland after 1949, so that it suffers from chronic
strain on its facilities.

Americans are known everywhere for trying to take overseas with
them their own standards of living. In Taiwan this produces a considerable strain on facilities and services. This, in turn, results in
tensions and frictions between the Americans and the Chinese. It is
not that the Americans try for levels of facilities so far above what
they would have at home. It is merely that even such a level is so
conspicuously above the usual local level that for the Americans to
achieve it gives them a disproportionate share of what is available.
For example, when nearly every American home has a telephone, it
is more than a little irksome to a Chinese businessman to have to
wait a matter of years before the very limited quota derived from
controlled imports of instruments and central facilities gets around
to include his wants.

It must be understood further that very few of these Americans
receive any systematic indoctrination on China, the Chinese people
or Chinese culture. They are sent out for two-year terms and to
perform specific jobs. Many of them suffer from ingrained racial attitudes acquired in the United States and which seem ineradicable.

Even so, a minimum of careful instruction, done by Americans who are qualified, has been proven useful in helping them to adjust to the cultural and social environment and to adopt the most productive and efficient ways of dealing with their Chinese associates in the training and equipment of the Chinese armed forces. The need for this sort of thing has been recognized by the highest American diplomatic and military authorities in Taiwan, and some sporadic efforts have been made to provide it. These efforts have been warmly approved by the Chinese. But nothing less than a systematic approach with the best possible personnel will do the job.

The need for this type of thing can easily be seen when the least thought is given to the highly unfortunate riots which took place against official American personnel and facilities at Taipei, 1957. These riots struck a severe blow at the stability of Chinese-American friendship. They can be attributed in part at least to the inadequate preparation of most American personnel for life in Taiwan and to conspicuous failure of such personnel to understand and adjust to the problems of their host country. The Chinese, on their side, have been too reluctant to deal immediately with numerous small grievances and on a "going" basis. Such grievances are too often left to accumulate and set off larger troubles.

Over-staffing of Americans abroad is bad enough when it is considered only as an excessive charge in the resources of the American taxpayer. But when personnel is not only quantitatively but qualitatively out of line in foreign countries, trouble is bound to occur. Unnecessary and avoidable troubles of this kind must be dealt with summarily in order that we may concentrate on the more fundamental political problems of relations with our allies. We should not have to deal with the problem of popular alienation of friendship when it is caused by factors of this kind. This gives too much aid and comfort, unnecessarily, to our communist enemies.

With U. S. aid going out to different countries all over the world it is impossible to conceal the relations of dependency upon the United States that are being set up. Such dependency will always be unpalatable. All we can do is to make it as little so as possible. This is a task of particular urgency in all Far Eastern countries. These nations are keenly interested in partnership but find particularly repugnant anything that can be related to the unequal status to which many of them were relegated under colonialism. China never was entirely a colonial possession of any one power, but was subjected to multiple derogations from her national sovereignty and administrative and territorial integrity. She is thus, and understandably, highly sensitive to the persistence, as applied to American military personnel on Taiwan, of what amounts to judical extraterritoriality.

Practical equality of nations is so clearly unattainable that the legal, formal, and, in many cases, ceremonial symbols of equality become vitally meaningful to those who are striving to elevate themselves and achieve a full measure of internal and external respect.

It has naturally been impossible in this brief paper to make an all-inclusive study or analysis of U. S. foreign aid policy toward China, even in its political aspects and implications. We have, however, perhaps made a sufficient analysis of the matter to justify some conclusions, however tentative. In brief form they are as follows:

1. Military security and stability are primary concerns in the revolutionary environment of modern China. The first requisite to adequate support of any political order in China, in directly political matters, is internal security, and the principal means for gaining this are military. Thus, military aid, with or without military intervention by the U. S., must take precedence over economic aid.

2. International political affiliation is likely to proceed from the facts of the external and internal political environment of Far Eastern countries. It comes first, and foreign aid may come thereafter and flow from it. It is not sound to count on any economic aid program as the producer or chief guarantor of international political affiliation. Security dependency is more reliable.

3. Economic aid brings on political change very slowly at best. Assumptions have yet to be adequately tested as to the relation between economic aid and political stability or the "improvement" of the political environment.

4. When in the interest of "blackmail," to secure by this means a particular line of policy, removal of aid is threatened, it is already too late to secure said policy.

5. Government-to-government aid, the normal thing, probably has a net effect of increasing the power of government over individuals, both in China and the United States simultaneously.

6. There is much room for increasing the part played by private enterprise in both the United States and China through and in connection with foreign aid programs.

7. Particularly in military aid programs, but to a lesser extent in all aid programs, the American tendency to overstaffing of U. S. personnel is dangerous and leads to pernicious political effects.

8. Adequate public relations policy in relation to foreign aid must include environment research and the systematic orientation of all U. S. personnel on the cultures of the countries in which they serve.

9. The dependency relations set up by foreign aid are inescapable. All we can do, and we must do this, is to play them down and make them as little distasteful as possible.

[1] As far as can be seen, this ultimatum is not mentioned in the State Department's White Paper on China policy, 1949.

[2] *United States Relations with China*, Department of State, 1949, p. 70.

[3] S. T. Possony, *A Century of Conflict*, 1953, p. 344.

PART VI

14: *Overview*

JAMES W. WIGGINS

The symposium for which the papers in this volume were prepared did not lead to complete agreement among the members of the group, nor was this the purpose of the meeting. Hardly a proposition was advanced which did not elicit a critical response from one or several of the scholars present. Attitudes toward foreign aid of various sorts ranged from support over shoulder-shrugging acceptance of inevitability to complete rejection of the goals of foreign aid programs as well as the means by which the ends were being sought. It is obviously impossible, in view of these facts, to expect a monolithic conclusion from the several days of discussions. As stressed in the preface each author's contribution is his own, as are his conclusions from the symposium deliberations.

We might also point out that the social and behavioral scientists represented here claim no special competence in deciding whether foreign aid is good or bad by virtue of their professional training and experience. Each may justifiably claim competence in the analysis of certain assumptions concerning development, the probable effectiveness of specific means for achieving specified ends, and the unintended results of the use of these means. Decisions about governmental benevolence to foreign governments can only be realistic, however, when such analyses of consequences are fairly faced. He who buys a rose also buys the thorns, and the wise buyer takes the thorns into account in his decision—but at least this buyer can be reasonably sure of the rose.

While some enthusiastic proponents of gifts by the United States government to other governments are not always concerned to make the distinction, it is important to separate direct military aid from economic and technical aid. If there were any historic cases in which nations had, for pay, fought against their own national interests there would be stronger bases for the effort to make mercenaries of the troops of nations now receiving military aid. If, on the other hand, history reports that nations tend to defend their own best interests—regardless of payments by other nations—the position for aid is clearly weakened. It is not really strange that the nation now considered the greatest, and only serious threat, to the United States was, during World War II, the recipient of countless millions in aid. It is certainly not clear that the United States purchased friendship with the U.S.S.R. by her generosity.

But, assuming, in the face of the evidence, that military aid makes friends of foes, a further and more serious question arises in connection with economic and technical aid. Gifts distributed under this rubric are said to be designed to facilitate "development" of the recipient countries. For several obvious reasons the word development is used in preference to Westernization. In the first place, the euphemism, "development," is not so offensive to the nations which are urged to ask for, or to accept economic and technical aid. In the second place, conspicuously practiced aggressive cultural domination is distasteful to the people of the United States and conflicts with the nation's anti-imperialistic tradition.

It is inevitable, however, that the economic and technical development of any nation, based on United States aid, must be Westernization. The United States cannot export anything but its own way of life, since that is all it has. A plea for development, therefore, is a plea for the imposition of Western life-ways on the asking society. The process may begin with the "gift" of medical technology, the export of physicians educated in the United States who may take with them medically approved United States diets for American patients, and end by insisting that the people of India drink two glasses of milk per day.

With exports of capital, especially, development must mean Westernization. To accept machines and tools from any industrial power must involve acceptance of the products of those machines and tools, as well as the mentality required to operate them, else they cease to be capital. But there is even another element in government-to-government gratuities. The typical scheme of social organization provided or proffered by the donor government is nationally-centralized bureaucratic organization. This may be the most alien pattern for many undeveloped countries. Competent students of economic development have even suggested that undeveloped countries, by accepting capital from alien governments or international bodies, invite a social organization of "compulsory non-development."

It is possible, of course, that United States government aid to undeveloped countries may *not* be accompanied by the aggrandizement of its institutional patterns if the agents of change are themselves alienated from the values and economic structure of the society which supports them and their experiments. But the imposition or support of alien orientations is even further from the intent of the donor nation.

There can be no question, of course, that the nationals of undeveloped countries who seek development aid from abroad are themselves alienated from their own society's values. They not only represent their people as paupers and incompetents, but also go further. They denigrate their own nations by pleading for foreign technicians to come into their lands to re-make them in the images of the technicians. It is not surprising, therefore, that many of the governments which employ pleaders for aid are both totalitarian and unscrupulous in the use of naked force in the maintenance of power. There is overwhelming evidence that most people, in developed as well as undeveloped lands, want most to be let alone.

But again, it may be assumed, in spite of better evidence, that undeveloped peoples want to be Westernized and industrialized. They are encouraged to imitate the United States, since the United States is now industrialized. Unfortunately the explanation of industrial development is complex, obscure, and equivocal. Neither economists nor other professional groups agree on the causes for industrial development, and some of the chapters in this volume show this disagreement.

If any nation is to help another develop economically, it must first understand its own development. The causes for the industrial development of the United States cannot be found through the examination of the contemporary industrial economy, but rather in the study of the whole social, cultural, geographic, and international context within which it has developed. This requires extensive knowledge of the nineteenth century and the early twentieth century, as well as more recent events. Such a study could lead to the avoidance of many of the so-called prerequisites of industrialization which are now found in developed countries, but which did not appear even there until industrialization was already well under way.

The importance of distinguishing between requirements for development on the one hand and more or less accidental consequences of industrialization on the other, may be emphasized by two illustrations. Two "essentials" for development, and two of the preliminary forms of technical aid often furnished undeveloped lands are medical aid and literacy training. Both of these essentials are only now coming to full flower in the United States, long after the nation has reached the charmed circle of the developed. Not until World War I did medical education in the United States establish enforceable standards of professional competence, and competent critics suggest that the level of genuine literacy has declined in the nation almost in proportion to the increasingly favorable statistics.

It is in nonliterate undeveloped areas, of course, that the unthinking use of literacy training as the solution for backwardness becomes most remarkable. While much of value may have been learned by the professionals engaged in this work, the permanent value for the newly literate is dubious. If it is necessary to create a written language where none exists, there is no literary civilization available to the readers. Their literacy may fade as fast as that of the college student in the United States who studies French or German for a year, and never looks at his language again. The alternative to the production of new written languages may be the teaching of English— or another Western language—with the importation of the written civilization the language reflects.

The problems produced by the acceleration of life expectancy in undeveloped lands are described by Warren S. Thompson. His plea for the export of birth control techniques by the United States is a necessary consequence of reduced death rates with a fixed food supply. This suggestion conflicts, however, with the religious convictions of substantial and influential segments of the taxpayers who are asked to underwrite the project.

By whatever means forced Westernization and industrialization are attempted, there are certain consequences which may be expected, intended or not. George A. Theodorson has identified a number of these consequences, with particular emphasis on the modification of the social patterns of non-Western peoples who become industrialized.[1] It is really unnecessary to labor the point, for UNESCO has already begun to organize a world-wide fight on delinquency—which, surprisingly, has developed in some undeveloped areas even faster than industry. If the accuracy of United States statistics can be accepted, there is reason to expect in undeveloped areas rising crime rates, rising incidence of insanity, and kindred social and personal disorders with the destruction of the old, nonindustrial order, brought about by Westernization.

It is difficult indeed to believe that this is the way to make such societies immune to the communist appeal.

Since economic and technical aid have been offered for more than a dozen years, an evaluation of results might be possible. At the level of local government in the United States the evaluation of governmental activity is in the hands of the independent grand jury. At the intergovernmental level, however, all evaluations are made by interested parties. The donor government is dependent on the self-evaluation of its employees, and the activities are so far removed from the observation of the electors that the very human desires of the employed to remain so cannot be checked by the taxpayer. The administration of the donor government must, however reluctantly, admit success in order to remain in power.

The recipient government may be unable to evaluate development efforts correctly for several reasons. Its leaders wish to retain power as do the donors. There is no precedent available for measuring "forced-draft" development, so it may be difficult to be certain that the experiment is either succeeding or failing. And finally, the recipient government may frequently be entirely at the mercy of the foreign technician. If the government, or the country, had competent technicians the outsiders would not be present. So again the "intruder's" evaluation must be accepted—and his future depends on reporting success.

There is an alternative. The expert in the undeveloped country may be convinced that, although the program is not entirely successful, more aid would guarantee it. This approach is used in other problem areas and has an honorable history. Robin Hood's terminal illness was not improved by letting a little blood, so his physician, it is reported, let more and more until he died.

When the donor nation is convinced that limited success is a result of limited aid, and moves toward unlimited aid, it not only evidences little ingenuity, but may be trapped. Anthropologists report that Eskimo hunters fix a sharp knife in the snow, and put a drop of blood on it. Their prey, the wolf, observes, tastes the blood. Then there is more blood, for the wolf cuts his tongue, and as he licks he bleeds . . . to death.

Regardless of the results of subsidized efforts to Westernize undeveloped countries, the subsidies themselves become significant components in the total economies of the countries involved. Increasing dependence on the subsidies is not merely likely, but rather has been characteristic of many of the countries most favored by the aid programs. Like the drug addict, who needs larger and larger doses as the addiction continues, the economies of some undeveloped nations seem to require more and more aid, merely to keep in operation.

Donor nations must either continue their benevolence forever, as in fact some proponents enthusiastically suggest, or they must at some time withdraw their support of government-directed development. If withdrawal occurs, the shock to the addict may produce convulsions, among nations as among individuals. The longer the artificial support continues, the more the total institutional structure of the undeveloped country adjusts to it, and the greater is the shock of withdrawal.

No unusual insight is required to decide that the donor will be blamed for the withdrawal of his benevolence.

The social scientist cannot claim special magic for deciding between the good and the bad. He may have some special basis for discussing the probabilities in alternative courses of action, and he bears the responsibility to the society which supports him to point out unintended as well as intended consequences of choices made by his society. This symposium has emphasized some of the less publicized consequences of the choices which are constantly being made about foreign economic and technical aid.

There is apparently reason to doubt that economic development of undeveloped lands is so simple, so free of undesirable effects, and so certain in techniques as it has been described elsewhere. There is considerable reason to doubt that the continuation of government-to-government aid will achieve in any significant degree the objectives for which it is designed. There is, finally, considerable evidence to support the probability that the outcomes may well be the opposite of those intended.

[1] "Acceptance of Industrialization and its Attendant Consequences for the Social Patterns of Non-Western Societies," *American Sociological Review*, XVIII, 5, (October 1953) pp. 447-484.

Index